THE MYTH OF ABSOLUTISM

The Myth of Absolutism

Change and Continuity in Early Modern European Monarchy

Nicholas Henshall

Longman
London and New York

Longman Group UK Limited,
Longman House, Burnt Mill,
Harlow, Essex CM20 2JE, England
and Associated Companies throughout the world.

*Published in the United States of America
by Longman Publishing, New York*

© Longman Group UK Limited 1992

First published 1992

ISBN 0582 05618 7 CSD
ISBN 0582 05617 9 PPR

British Library Cataloguing in Publication Data

A catalogue record for this book is available from the British Library.

Library of Congress Cataloging in Publication Data

Henshall, Nicholas, 1944–
    The myth of absolutism/Nicholas Henshall.
        p.   cm.
    Includes bibliographical references and index.
    ISBN 0–582–05618–7 – ISBN 0–582–05617–9 (pbk.)
    1. Despotism – History.   2. Monarchy – France – History.
3. Monarchy – Great Britain – History.   I. Title.
JC375.H46   1992
321′.6′0940903–dc20   91–44483
                                                                        CIP

Set by 9 in Bembo
Produced by Longman Singapore Publishers (Pte) Ltd.
Printed in Singapore

Contents

Acknowledgements

I am indebted to the sixth-formers of Stockport Grammar School. Their inability to understand 'absolutism' made me realise I did not understand it myself. The staff of the Cambridge University and British Libraries have been endlessly helpful and efficient. Many scholars have helped me by modifying some of my more startling proposals; the responsibility for those with which I have persisted is my own. I owe much to conversations with David Armitage, Colin Armstrong, Derek Beales, John Crook, Richard Rex, Donald Roberts, Joe Shennan and Robert Tombs. John Derry, David Parker, Francis Scott and Tim Thornton gave their time to comment on earlier drafts of the book. The work of Jeremy Black has stimulated much of its argument; his interest and advice have been constant. I am grateful for the generosity of the Governors of Stockport Grammar School, who gave me leave of absence, and for the encouragement of the Chairman, Alan Kershaw, and the Headmaster, David Bird. The Master and Fellows of St John's College, Cambridge, elected me to a Schoolmaster Fellowship and offered a haven for writing and research. My greatest debt is to David Starkey, whose guidance has been indispensable and whose influence will be obvious throughout the book. But for him it would not have been written.

The publishers would like to thank the following for permission to reproduce copyright material: Oxford University Press for Appendices I and II which were adapted from *Patrons, Brokers, and Clients in Seventeenth-Century France* by Sharon Kettering. Copyright © 1986 by Oxford University Press, Inc. Reprinted by permission.

Preface

Historians who wander from their specialism expect to be savaged. This keeps them close to home, like senior citizens afraid of being mugged. Yet an uneasy feeling of vulnerability cannot be allowed to silence speculation on the contours of early modern government. The rapid discoveries of recent historical scholarship have not been assembled into a coherent pattern. As specialisation increases, the portions of the past studied by historians become narrower and they sometimes miss the wider consequences of their own perceptions. The uniqueness of developments in one country or period is often exaggerated when a sideways or backward glance would correct the distortion. Historians also tend to address the academic community. Yet whether the state's role was expanding or liberty diminishing are significant questions for all who want informed perspectives on the present. Their presumed availability is the greatest justification for attending to history at all.

For this reason I have written partly with general readers in mind. For them I have avoided too much reference to foreign sources and made the proceedings as entertaining as possible – as the frequently delightful subject matter deserves. I also address students and scholars. The book is not merely another textbook summary, too reverential towards established clichés to offer a fresh synthesis. It makes recent research more accessible and suggests a new pattern which makes sense of it.

There are obvious dangers in trying to appeal to three kinds of reader, but the chance of success outweighs them. Academic findings strike an immediate chord in academic circles: outside them a fifteen-year echo seems to operate. A coherent synthesis requires decades. Experts must be tolerant when these rarified acoustics are coarsened by an impatient voice.

TO MY PARENTS, IN GRATITUDE

Introduction

> In the early seventeenth century many Englishmen believed that there
> was a design to convert England into an absolute monarchy.
>> (J Miller 1987 *Bourbon and Stuart*. George Philip, p. 32)

> From James I to Sir Edward Coke to John Pym . . . all agree that
> England is an absolute monarchy.
>> JH Hexter 1982 *Parliamentary History*, vol. 1. Sutton, p. 208)

Clearly we have a problem. Possibly the historical consensus is nailing
its colours firmly to the fence. Or 'absolute' is a catch-all word which
historians use as they please – of any monarch, it has been suggested,
who had more power than twentieth-century scholars deem appropriate. A comparative approach confuses the situation further. Compared with contemporary English monarchs, one historian tells us,
Francis I is an 'absolutist' king. Another hails Louis XIV as the first
true embodiment of 'absolutism'. But no, a recent work assures us:
the *really* 'absolutist' rulers were the Enlightened Despots of the late
eighteenth century. Only they displayed the contempt for traditional
rights and privileges which is the hallmark of the concept.

This permanently receding vista reflects the difficulty of deciding
what historians mean by 'absolute' and 'absolutism'. It becomes
apparent that they are not synchronising their definitions. In fact, the
origins of the two words are very different and it is vital not to
conflate them. 'Absolute' was common during the early modern
period, 'absolutism' not until the 1820s. Our quarry is the latter, but
it is impossible to pin it down without also cornering the former.
Four themes seem to encapsulate 'absolutism' as normally used.

First, 'absolutism' is intrinsically despotic. It encroaches on subjects'
rights and privileges and overrides bodies empowered to defend
them. It is the enemy of liberty.

1

Second, 'absolutism' is autocratic. Consultation is shunned, dialogue discouraged and decision-making centralised. Rulers marginalise Estates and corporate bodies formerly used for powwows with power groups. Power is monopolised by the monarch and those to whom he delegates it.

Third, 'absolutism' is bureaucratic. It operates independently of corporate bodies with power and interests of their own. By employing agencies dependent solely on the crown, whether bureaucrats or 'new men' independent of the nobility, absolute rulers decouple themselves from society and its ability to sabotage their commands.

Fourth, 'absolutism' is not English. Whig historians selected 1689 as a handy date for the final divergence between Continental 'absolutism' and English limited monarchy. England is henceforth the standard-bearer of liberty and government by consent.

What follows is scarcely an insurrection against orthodoxy. Recent scholarship has exposed all these propositions as misleading descriptions of what early modern European monarchs actually did – or tried to do. The edifice of 'absolutism' is cracking and the old cliché is repeated without conviction. The inverted commas placed round it nowadays indicate the proprietors' loss of nerve, though the punctuation of some historians is defiantly unrepentant. The building still stands, but no one seems to have noticed that it is hanging in mid air. The relevant research and articles have to be pursued in many corners of the discipline and no one has yet assembled the materials for demolition. But neither has a recent case been made for a preservation order.

One can argue endlessly about how many of the features above are necessary to produce 'absolutism'. It is more profitable to enquire how many 'non-absolutist' features can be accommodated before the label is discarded. Some will say this is a quibble about terminology: as long as historical phenomena are accurately described, the labels we attach make little difference. Historical experience teaches the contrary. Terminology has a power of its own and its associations can generate heat, though not necessarily light. More seriously, Marc Bloch once wrote about wrong labels which eventually deceive us about the contents. What is in a name? Quite a lot if it distorts realities.

This book challenges two ancient stereotypes. Historical interpretation is still shaped by national pride and a Whig desire to be on the side with a future. England has always stressed the modernity of its *ancien régime* and France that of its Revolution. Both have mistakenly subscribed to a contrast between French 'absolute' monarchs who monopolised power and English 'limited' monarchs who shared it.

Most monarchs were both. They were absolute when they wielded their sweeping prerogatives and limited when they negotiated over their subjects' rights. Consultation and consent were as prominent in 'absolutist' Europe as in freedom-loving England; but in their presence historians have been stricken with selective myopia. The past has proved an inexhaustible quarry on which to grind their axes. Behind both official histories lurks the satisfying conviction that, in their very different ways, England and France got it right. Self-congratulation is a dangerous basis for historical enquiry: it is too easy for the wish to become father to the thought. Propaganda is a genre historians should study but not write.

'Absolutism' has been built into historiography in four main ways. Monarchs undoubtedly attempted to establish control over their patchwork of territories and institutions, to concentrate decision-making in themselves and to ensure their decisions were acted on. What provided the impetus?

Marxists stretch 'absolutism' enough to wrap round an entire socio-economic system. To them it was a mechanism whereby the landed nobility repressed the peasantry. In Eastern Europe they were allowed to rivet serfdom on their labour force in return for serving the crown in army and bureaucracy. In Western Europe serfdom was dead. Landowners replaced feudal coercion of the peasantry with 'absolutist' coercion by the crown, nobles being integrated into the state machine by the purchase of office. Unfortunately for the theory, the nobility were often the chief opponents of the 'absolutist' state and in Sweden they were its conspicuous victim. The main purchasers of office were non-noble members of the bourgeoisie. While most early modern monarchies ran a gravy-train on which nobles had the best seats, they were not the only ones in the booking hall.[1]

An opposite view depicts 'absolutism' as the deliberate implementation of a theory, rather than the product of impersonal forces. Early modern lawyers, philosophers and bishops invented it as a modernised version of monarchy which was efficient, streamlined and rational. But while theory was constantly deployed as justification for what monarchs wanted to do, it is unlikely to have motivated it. Richelieu demonstrably commissioned theory to justify his actions. It is more likely that monarchs innovated in response to specific practical problems rather than a grand design.[2]

The two most widely accepted accounts of 'absolutism' consequently locate its impetus in the empirical need for domestic transformation. One version focuses on war and the 'military revolution'. The French army was typical in its growth from 50,000 men in the sixteenth century to 400,000 in 1700. This necessitated the growth of a fiscal–military state geared to war and survival in a ruthlessly competitive world. Taxes had to be imposed and collected, if necessary without the co-operation of obstructive Estates. To increase taxable wealth, economic growth had to be promoted: trade and industry were clamped into a strait-jacket of government regulation. These imperatives in turn required the creation of a bureaucracy unaffected by the delaying tactics of existing power groups. An alternative version stresses the attempts of early modern governments to improve the spiritual and material welfare of their subjects. Memories of Frederick II's cracks about cannon fodder make it hard to keep a straight face. Yet the concept of the 'well-ordered police state' has to be taken seriously, if only because it was seen as inseparable from the ruler's power. 'Poor peasant, poor king' was the crisp comment of a member of Louis XV's think-tank.[3]

Yet neither of these dynamics required 'absolutism'. The well-ordered society was implemented through existing Estates, gilds and town corporations. The new element was central regulation of what had previously been left to local initiative or mere chance. The establishment of a fiscal–military state was attempted without recourse to the mechanisms associated with 'absolutism'. Brewer has recently shown that one was created in England. The implication is that it was easier to achieve in the context of a parliamentary than of an 'absolutist' state. It is possible that this is the wrong conclusion to draw. France arguably did *not* attempt to create a fiscal–military state by 'absolutist' methods. It tried to use the same methods as England – consent and co-operation, which were the only realistic options available. Mainly because it lacked a national representative body to bind the realm, it was simply less successful.[4]

If strong monarchy was created by consensus and co-operation rather than the need for and provision of military might, then its basis is to be found in skilful management of ruling élites rather than armed force. Large armies were its symptom rather than its cause. More vital to its explanation is the recovery of ideological cohesion among nobilities, as the religious diversity inherited from the sixteenth-century Reformation was eliminated or marginalised.[5] A recent authority has argued that an acceptable model of 'absolutism' can be reconstructed from these elements – a suggestion which is open to the objection that consensus between monarchs and ruling élites was the essential basis of all medieval and early modern regimes.[6] Ideological consensus prevailed between monarch and aristocracy in Poland but can scarcely be said to have produced 'absolutism'.

What follows is an attempt to decouple early modern developments from 'absolutist' associations . It entails restoring government to its social context, not in the Marxist sense of its relationship to exploitative social classes, but in the subtler sense of the kind of regime which contemporary social needs and assumptions made possible. A word like 'bureaucracy' instantly evokes nineteenth- and twentieth-century expectations. We must evoke early modern ones.

It also involves much scrutiny of phenomena which not so long ago were deemed old-fashioned – kings and ministers, nobles and courtiers. Though they are now becoming fashionable, their newsworthiness may be short-lived. Brewer's influential study has swung the spotlight back from the royal court to the parliament house and the excise office. In many quarters, especially French university cities, history 'from the bottom up' is still preferred – cat massacres by Parisian apprentices or contraceptive practices among the peasants of Provence. Rebels and poachers remain bigger business than the protagonists of authority.

The first three chapters give a roughly chronological account of the French monarchy in the sixteenth, seventeenth and eighteenth centuries: if the concept of 'absolutism' cannot be sustained there, it can be sustained nowhere. Chapters 4, 5 and 6 survey the contours revealed and propose similar configurations for England. Chapters 7 and 8 retain the broad canvas but use a narrower brush: they tackle the relationship between royal powers and subjects' rights. Chapter 9 attempts to locate the origin of the myth.

REFERENCES

1   Miller J 1990 *Absolutism in Seventeenth Century Europe*. Macmillan, pp. 6–13; Anderson P 1979 *Lineages of the Absolutist State*. Verso
2   Miller J 1990, pp. 7–8; Parker D 1983 *The Making of French Absolutism*. Arnold, p. 90
3   Miller J 1990, pp. 7–8; Raeff M 1983 *The Well-Ordered Police State*. Yale University; Gagliardo J 1991 *Germany under the Old Regime*. Longman, pp. 107–13
4   Raeff M 1983, pp. 152–4; Brewer J 1989 *The Sinews of Power*. Unwin Hyman
5   Evans RJW 1979 *The Making of the Hapsburg Monarchies 1550–1700*, Oxford University Press
6   Black J 1991 *A Military Revolution? Military Change and European Society 1550–1800*. Macmillan, pp. 67–77

CHAPTER ONE
Valois and Early Bourbons

MEDIEVAL INHERITANCES

Early modern France began with an operation known in modern estate agency as exchanging contracts. Until the late fifteenth century great provinces like Brittany and Burgundy were feudal fiefs, more or less independent of the French crown. Their dukes and counts had sovereign legislative and judicial powers over their provinces, which were defined by a common set of customs consisting of rights and liberties *vis-à-vis* their ruler. The monarch was merely the greatest feudal noble – one whose ancestor happened to have been elected king in the tenth century. He focused his efforts on the royal domain, a wisp of territory around Paris which was smaller than several of the fiefs. Patiently he absorbed the others, but a roll-call of dates emphasises how late it was before anything resembling the geography of present France emerged. Languedoc was annexed in 1271, Dauphiné in 1348, Normandy in 1358, Guyenne in 1451, Burgundy in 1477, Anjou, Maine and Provence in 1481, Orleans in 1499, Angoulême in 1515, Auvergne and Bourbon in 1527 and Brittany in 1532.

From the king's viewpoint the operation was messy. Abolition of provincial rights was seen only as a penalty, legitimately imposed after military defeat or rebellion. As a fief of the Holy Roman Empire Dauphiné could not be integrated into the king's lands, lest he find himself a vassal of the Emperor. Instead it was given to his heir (hence the dauphin). When annexing a province, the king solemnly swore to observe its rights and privileges, and signed a charter or contract to prove it. His new subjects then swore allegiance to him. The deal was based on mutual obligation, the king promising to respect the good old customs and the province pledging its loyalty as long as he did. The implication was that it could renounce it if he did not.

The vital difference between early modern France and its modern counterpart is still frequently overlooked. Until the Revolution 'France' remained a geographical expression.[1] Like most European monarchs, the French king did not rule a nation-state, nor was national feeling a significant force in it. A 'nation' in the political, racial or linguistic sense was too nebulous to command loyalty – a key determinant in this period. Men were loyal to their family, their lord, their town, their province, their class, their religion or their king. Rarely were they loyal to their country. Kings naturally attempted to ally themselves with some conception of the national interest, especially when facing foreign attack or internal rebellion, but their subjects interpreted even this parochially. Militias could be relied on to arm themselves against approaching danger. They could rarely be persuaded to demonstrate practical concern outside their own region.

Without the bonding agent of significant national feeling, administrative and legal unity was absent. In each province representative institutions focused local loyalties and defended local rights. By the sixteenth century there were more than twenty provincial assemblies of Estates, so-called from the estates or orders of society which they represented – usually clergy, nobles and town-dwellers. When provinces were integrated into the royal domain, the sovereign powers of their counts and dukes were terminated. This was a crucial development. Henceforth French monarchs insisted on a monopoly of sovereignty and ultimate rights of justice, legislation and taxation were vested in the crown. But that in no way invalidated the contract: provincial rights and customs were robustly waved in the face of central authority by Estates eager to guard their inheritance. They ensured that French law was a patchwork quilt, especially in the north where custom was unaccompanied by the Roman law prominent in the south. Only in the fifteenth and sixteenth centuries were legal customs written down, and even then there was no attempt at uniformity. In the eighteenth century Voltaire remarked that a traveller changed laws as often as horses.

DECENTRALISED CORPORATIONS

It is often assumed that the demise of local feudal autonomy was followed by the erection of centralised monarchical authority. There was no such development. Francis I was the first monarch to benefit from the annexation of all the great fiefs. He bound the provinces to the centre, but not by substituting for the guardians of local pride and self-government agents dependent on himself. Instead he bought their support. Representing the full majesty of the monarch in each province was a governor, usually the greatest noble landowner in the area. He was entitled to parade under a royal canopy like the king, that the elements might not impair the dignity of himself or, by association, his master. His function was that of a mediator who represented the interests of king to province and of province to king. The duke of Montmorency, governor of Languedoc, collected lavish gifts from the notoriously tight-fisted Estates for ensuring that their affairs received favourable attention from the royal council. His presence at court enabled him to massage provincial egos as patron-age-broker. Royal favours to which he had access were distributed in Languedoc: titles, offices, jobs and perks were employed to assemble a gang of local followers (clients) who would guarantee an enthusiastic response to royal requests. By this amiable device the local élite was nudged into dependence on the crown.[2] That at least was the ideal. He could use his personal following within the province to undermine the crown's authority, or he might be so obnoxious to his charges that no application of lubricant could secure co-operation. Everything depended on the tact and loyalty of the governor, and on his rapport with corporate power groups.

Definition of these is vital to an understanding of the *ancien régime*. Corporate power groups were the characteristic social and political organisation before 1789. They reflected the society of orders or estates into which France was divided.[3] By this device individuals sharing the same interest were constituted as a collective legal personality, with corresponding rights in law – hence their title of 'corporate' or 'constituted' bodies. They were endowed with organs for expressing their collective will, discharging their functions and defending their powers and privileges. Specimens are *parlements*, provincial Estates, town councils, village assemblies, noble assemblies and assemblies of the clergy. As the institutional embodiment of the interest groups into which France was divided, they did not exist primarily for the convenience of the government. Nor did they owe their power to it. The crown nevertheless used them as administrative and consultative agencies; so they must be sharply distinguished from other royal mechanisms like the council of state and the intendants, created by the crown and deriving their authority solely from it. Some historians argue that early modern monarchs in France tolerated corporate bodies out of fear and inertia. They compromised with the rusty mechanisms of the past while constructing their own up-to-date machinery, which should one day have replaced them but never did. Their attitude was negative: corporate bodies were an inconvenient relic of medievalism which at worst had to be pandered to and at best ignored. The real centre of gravity was elsewhere.

An alternative view is that the crown's relationship with the corporate bodies was fundamental as means and end. The word 'centralisation' is too simple for the subtle process involved. So is 'decentralisation' but it is more accurate than the opposite. The king hijacked the influence of corporate power groups for royal purposes, in return for kingly favours. Appreciation of their nature is crucial to an understanding of how French monarchs operated. They strengthened their authority by delegating it to sources of independent power in the localities. The paradox is not hard. When the human and material resources of central government were slender, it was sound policy to recruit local power groups where royal agents were inadequate or non-existent. Local government was still not seen as part of the state. It consisted of a number of sources of independent power, with which it was possible for the state to form relationships.

One of the requirements of 'absolutism' is that the ruler should cut himself off from roots in the community and rely on his own agencies, imposed on it from outside. The institutions which have sprung organically from the community are suspect: its natural rulers and élites wield power for which they are not beholden to the monarch and can afford to be less deferential. All are contaminated with wills and purposes of their own. Thus his instruments are sterilised against social and political pressures and lie inert in the royal hand: there is no chance of their developing sturdy wills of their own and no need for the king to listen to the opinions of any but his chosen councillors. This is precisely what the Valois kings did not do. Though the rapid growth of the printing press and the annexation of the fiefs enlarged the scope of central government and brought it into direct contact with more of its subjects than ever before, the mechanisms stayed the same. A more expansive kingly role required a larger rather than a smaller supporting cast – local communities, corporate bodies, representative assemblies and aristocratic factions featured prominently in the royal script.

Viewed from this perspective the Estates were constructive rather than obstructive. Though not dependent on the king for their power, deft handling could harness them for royal purposes. To Major we owe the perception that Valois monarchs and Estates were not adversaries, both eager to make inroads on the power of the other so that as one waxed the other waned. Consultative Estates were not the victim of strong monarchy, as 'absolutist' historians assume. They were its creation.[4] Estates were a useful mechanism for sampling the sentiments of the community and procuring its consent. As repositories of regional loyalties and experts on local conditions, their assessment of a problem was more finely tuned than any government agent's. The crown had everything to lose and nothing to gain by smashing them. Estates in turn regarded a strong crown as a safeguard against oppression by local robber barons: kings were seen less as enemies of rights and liberties than as their defenders. This explains why in most provinces they consolidated their power as the monarchy established its own: central monarchical government and local self-government grew together. State-building and Estate-building were reciprocal actions.

It is otherwise hard to account for the policy of fifteenth- and sixteenth-century monarchs, who encouraged local participation even as they tightened monarchical control. Louis XI increased the administrative duties of the towns and enlarged their powers and privileges; in the sixteenth century important urban centres such as Rennes, Nantes and Saumur received charters confirming autonomous rights. They claimed to negotiate their tax contribution with the government. The citizens of Rouen began to refer to themselves as a 'republic'. Duties undertaken by municipal authorities embraced law and order, health and welfare, social and economic regulation, defence and supervision of primary and secondary schools. At the same time, country villages began to elect syndics or permanent officials to administer their justice and finance. Similar officials were established by provincial Estates to run their corporate affairs, collect taxes and oversee their interests between sessions (usually a few days a year) – sometimes at the request of the crown. They also established clerks and archives, well before England's parliament.

Nor did monarchs perceive noble power as a threat, providing they could exploit it for their own purposes. On the assumption that no early modern kings were skilful enough to manage this, an older school of historians argued that they relied instead on a new class of bourgeois administrators. When these subsequently received titles, they became a new class of service nobility, replacing the 'old' nobility which was conveniently undergoing economic decline. This is wrong on most counts. Administrators drawn from the bourgeoisie and lesser nobility were not new but medieval. The nobility had always been a service nobility, constantly renewed through royal office. Textbooks stress the distinction between robe nobles (*noblesse de robe*) who derived their titles from office, and sword nobles (*noblesse d'épée*) who inherited them. This was increasingly academic, since robe nobles usually abandoned their offices within a generation.[5] The robe constantly intermarried with the sword and aped their life-style. And the older noble families were not declining, nor were they encouraged to. The crown wanted obedient nobles, not weak ones.

Justice was also decentralised. Instead of one *parlement* or sovereign court of appeal in Paris, more were inherited from the feudal rulers of Languedoc, Guyenne, Dauphiné, Normandy, Provence and Burgundy. This spared litigious Frenchmen an expedition to Paris every time they lodged a judicial appeal. It was also a recognition of local interests, rights and customs – of which the provincial *parlements* were resolute defenders. Henceforth the sovereign courts aped the provincial Estates in the role of representatives of the king's subjects. They also participated in the king's legislative and administrative authority. Royal decrees which affected the rights of his subjects were vetted by the *parlements*. If they were found to relate satisfactorily to existing law, they were accepted, registered and promulgated. If not, an objection or remonstrance was sent to the king, who modified his proposals or issued a *lettre de jussion*, ordering registration regardless. Even then the king might have to preside personally over the *parlement* in a *lit de justice* in order to force it to give way.

To these formidable powers was added the *parlement*'s right of making laws, subject to the veto of the royal council. Known as *arrêts*, they covered most areas of government activity. Social and economic regulations extended to the repair and lighting of highways, the supply and price of food, wages and working conditions, prostitution and vagrancy, poor relief and apprenticeship, prisons and hospitals. Cultural and ideological activities also attracted the *parlement*'s attention. The regulation of colleges and universities was taken from the church during the fifteenth century: henceforth the courts supervised everything from the content of courses to the eradication of cheating in examinations. They also oversaw festivals, public spectacles and theatres, in which their interest extended to the price of tickets. Most crucially of all, they censored books. In 1526 Francis I ordered that no religious work could be printed without the *parlement*'s permission, and by the eighteenth century they were fighting to keep at bay a flood of fashionable political subversion. In all this the *parlements* acted independently of the crown. Though ultimately subject to its sanction, they boasted a constituted authority and a pronounced will of their own. Nor was this the judges' private fantasy. In 1588 the Paris *parlement* closed down a troupe of Italian actors whom the king had invited to perform. Two centuries later it banned an imposing array of Enlightened titles by Voltaire, Rousseau and Diderot.[6] Many of them were favourite reading at the court of Versailles.

The most striking example of decentralisation was the early demise of the Estates-General. Early modern France was like a jigsaw assembled by an impatient child: several pieces fitted more approximately than others. The resulting institutional variation rendered impossible the development of anything resembling a national parliament on the English model. In the fourteenth century the Estates-General was first convened as a forum for counsel and consent on matters of public interest, and on taxation in particular. It consisted of representatives of the first estate, the clergy, the second estate, the nobility, and the third, mainly the bourgeoisie of the towns. But it was not a truly national institution and therefore failed to override the forces of provincialism. Distant areas frequently declined to send delegates, and taxes approved by the Estates-General had to be renegotiated with local communities. From the beginning it was summoned only in times of crisis, such as during the war with Edward III and the civil wars of the fifteenth century. It also displayed an unwelcome tendency to stray from issues of legitimate concern to matters of state, such as foreign policy, which were the king's undoubted prerogative. Consolidation of royal power would have been enhanced by a single representative body to bind the whole realm. As it was, French kings quickly learned to see the Estates-General as at best a liability and at worst a threat. For 500 years their attitude was consistent: it was denied regular meetings and control over significant aspects of government. It did not, as usually supposed, lose its power in the sixteenth and seventeenth centuries owing to the rise of 'absolutism'. It never had any.

There was a rough distinction between *pays d'état* like Burgundy and Languedoc, where taxes were negotiated with and collected by the Estates, and *pays d'élection* where they were levied directly by the crown's own officials, the *élus*. But this over-repeated generalisation conceals interesting features at grass-roots level. Even where royal *élus* collected taxes assorted Estates continued to meet, regularly or irregularly, at local or provincial level. From Major's research we now know something about these previously obscure institutions, of which the best example is the Estates in the *généralités* and *sénéchaussées* of Guyenne. Meeting in the subdivisions of the province, these Estates have been overlooked because nationally minded historians keep their eyes glued on the larger units. Because of repeated territorial changes in Guyenne, the provincial Estates ceased to meet. In their place the crown encouraged the development of Estates in the smaller unit of the *généralité*, established shortly before for tax purposes. After 1561 it allowed them to choose what form of tax they would pay, to levy sums for their own purposes, to appoint a clerk for their record and an official to receive the taxes. It also guaranteed that the money raised would be used to pay royal debts and for nothing else. The area was not an especially remote one, but the government evidently believed funds would be readily extracted from it with the help of these Estates rather than without it. The *sénéchaussées* were smaller areas of local government. In the early sixteenth century they teemed with representative forms of life. Some displayed continuity with earlier institutions but others were previously primitive: they seem to have needed the hand of strong monarchy to give them a backbone. Only then did the Estates of Commingues begin to meet several times a year and dominate local administration. Nor were these small Estates a rubber stamp. They often rejected new taxes and negotiated reductions in old ones. All had syndics and officials, and most had standing committees to act for them when not in session.[7]

Financial uniformity was impossible in the face of this multiplicity of local interests and traditions. The main direct tax was the *taille*. In the north it was levied according to individual status and nobles were exempted (*taille personnelle*); in the south it was determined by the status of the land (*taille réelle*) and nobles paid on any land which was technically non-noble. Burgundy paid no *taille* at all. Nor did many of the towns. Dauphiné paid *taille réelle* in the mountains and *taille personnelle* at sea-level. The *aides*, indirect taxes on the sale of commodities, entailed even more baroque variations. The older provinces paid at different rates. Poitou, Auvergne, Artois and Languedoc compounded with alternative payments. Burgundy, Brittany and Provence paid nothing. Goods carried into areas of non-payment were taxed at the provincial frontier: an internal tariff wall isolated the southern third of France. The third main tax was the *gabelle*. In the north and centre the government claimed a monopoly of the sale of salt and commanded a minimum purchase. In the west the *gabelle* was a flat-rate tax, while Brittany paid none at all. Hundreds of additional tolls and tariffs consummated the confusion. There were said to be 120 on the Loire alone. Rational eighteenth-century administrators knew they were witnessing the triumph of unreason, while nineteenth-century historians tried in vain to unravel the complexities and gave up.

Financial administration displayed similar eccentricities. The distinction between ordinary and extraordinary revenues (those to which the king was entitled in his own right and those which he was granted in emergencies) was outdated by the beginning of Francis' reign. The *taille* was collected each year without formal grant and was thereby converted into ordinary revenue. Yet only at the end were the two separate systems of administration fused under the *trésorier de l'Epargne*. Collection of indirect taxes was privatised. They were farmed to substantial money-lenders or simply the highest bidder: tax-farmers (*traitants*) were private contractors who advanced to the crown the potential yield of a province, thereby purchasing the right to collect rather more for themselves from the taxpayers. Local tax collectors thus enriched themselves at royal expense and increased their independence. They were fiscal amphibians – partly government officials and partly private financiers. Since public office merged into private property, 'bureaucracy' is an inappropriate word. Entrepreneurial monarchs were also responsible for more sophisticated ways of raising loans. Francis was the first to issue interest-bearing bonds guaranteed by the municipal authority of Paris. Financiers who lent money to the crown were usually tax collectors themselves: the hope of repayment of the former gave them a vested interest in efficient performance as the latter. He also abandoned attempts to collect all revenues in a single central treasury. As before, royal revenues were retained and payments made locally, thus avoiding the risk and delay of trundling bags of cash along primitive, ill-policed roads. Not only was this the antithesis of centralisation, but in the provincial *bureaux des finances* a corporate vested interest was created – one destined to play havoc with government reformers for the next two and a half centuries.[8]

Regional and corporate autonomy was reinforced by the sale of office. In 1515 Francis commanded 5,000 *officiers* or office-holders – a tenth of the officials available to Louis XIV to rule a marginally larger population. He seems to have been the first king to create unnecessary posts solely for profit. Twice he created *élus* in Guyenne: on both occasions he instantly abolished them, once the alarmed Estates had compensated the purchasers. His motive was evidently cash flow rather than centralisation. By 1560 thousands more had been created, mainly for auction. When the number of judicial offices outran the amount of work available, Henry II launched a shift system whereby officials worked for six months a year. He also created an additional tier of jurisdiction above the *sénéchaussée*, which an older school of historians solemnly discussed in terms of administrative sophistication. Henry's main objective was probably 500 new offices for a quick sale. A further payment transmitted all posts to children. All offices conferred status and exemption from taxation; the more important conferred titles of nobility. They were eagerly snapped up by upwardly-mobile bourgeois. Again 'bureaucracy' is the wrong word. By the end of the sixteenth century another powerful interest group was entrenched in the provinces, increasingly irremovable and quivering with corporate ambition.

AGENTS OF CENTRALISATION

Such were the power groups and corporate bodies which did not owe their power directly to the ruler. But an account which stressed only the elements of decentralisation would be one-sided. At the centre were powerful centripetal agencies, though historians dispute their effectiveness in the early sixteenth century.

The authority inherent in the king himself derived from his role as supreme judge. The chancellor, the king's chief judicial officer, had the key role: for most of the early modern period the judicial, political, legislative and administrative functions of government were not separated. The king judged affairs of state, including relations with foreign states, as his absolute prerogative, in which he was obliged to share his power with no one – though he was expected to seek counsel and advice and in practice had to work in co-operation with powerful groups. But theoretically his decisions were final and his commands irresistible: there was no higher authority to which appeal might be made. 'Absolute' power had this specific connotation, now generally forgotten. It asserted that royal authority could be thwarted by no appeal to foreign popes or emperors and shared with no feudal noblemen. Disobedience, opposition and rebellion could never be legitimate: they were treason or *lèse-majesté*. Since the demise of the great noble fiefs the king had a monopoly of supreme or sovereign power: it was wielded by him in person or by others in his name. In one sense government was becoming more complex and *less* personal: the monarch was unable to authorise everything himself. Yet whatever initiatives were taken by officials their powers were derived solely from the king, and in that sense monarchical power remained absolute. This insistence was requisite precisely because many denied the royal right to the last word, whereas we tend to assume that obedience to the crown was a deeply ingrained habit.

The rise of absolute monarchy in France was principally about making it so.

In the provinces and localities the king harnessed power groups for purposes of mutual interest. The key to this was royal patronage and its focus was the king's court. The court was the only central institution of government and therefore the vital link between centre and localities. It had several functions. It was the royal household, which provided for the physical needs of the ruler and his family. It was the centre of government, where policy was decided. But precisely because the king lacked a high-powered bureaucratic machine for railroading the country along prescribed lines, the court was essential in two other capacities. It was the centre of display, where royal splendour, festivals and rituals supplied the sales talk for marketing monarchy. Above all it was the centre of patronage, where the ambitions of the social and political élite were gratified or frustrated – and thus where the crown won or lost their support. Consequently it was also the centre of faction, where competing aristocratic gangs fought to promote themselves and discredit their rivals.

The institutions which embodied the king's will all met at court. Francis I inherited effective agencies in the *conseil d'état*, the executive body of high officials, the *conseil des affaires*, its inner ring of trusted advisers, and the *grand conseil*, its judicial offshoot. As the court meandered ceremoniously from palace to palace, from the Louvre to Chambord to Fontainebleau, the councils went with it. As Francis once put it, in another context, they had to 'trot after him'.

In 1547 secretaries of state were introduced as linkmen between king and councils. As they were never selected from grandee families (see p. 20), they have stimulated a theory about 'absolutism' rising with the bourgeoisie. This is open to several objections. Most of the secretaries were already lesser nobles when they were appointed and through office and marriage swiftly became greater ones. Furthermore, grandees were not so much excluded from these posts as unable to accept them. Though they involved close contact with the king and his patronage, they centred on the menial, professional and ungentlemanly tasks of letter-writing and accounting. Lastly, though grandees were restricted to the great household offices of seneschal, steward and chamberlain, the usual assumption that they rapidly became purely ceremonial is incorrect. The Valois and their successors continued to rely on them for the highest diplomatic and military services.

With the semi-independent institutions Francis bargained, negotiated and on occasions got tough. In the Estates' tendency to agree automatically to the crown's demands or to be coerced when they resisted Knecht detects symptoms of decline – and therefore the rise of 'absolutism'. These were probably less sensational than he believes. Automatic voting of levies, in Tudor England as much as Valois France, was a normal extension of the conviction that the king's needs must be met. And though Francis might on occasion autocratically overrule consultative institutions, he never permanently reduced their rights and privileges. Knecht identifies centralisation and uniformity as his achievement. Few of Louis XIV's biographers would claim that much for *him*.[9]

COLLAPSE AND RECOVERY

This limited consolidation of monarchy was shattered by the twin catastrophes of repeated royal minorities and murderous religious antagonisms. Minorities were not in themselves fatal to royal fortunes, but they made harder the management of the political élite. Decisions on policies and patronage made by kings were easier to accept as final than those made by their deputies. The balance of faction at court was destroyed, patronage was misdirected and the crown found itself with too little local influence to give a lead. Factional discontent thus engendered was ignited by religious antagonism, as Protestant and Catholic gang bosses clashed in the localities. Fanatical religious division destroyed the possibility of consensus and compromise between crown and ruling élites. With ideological cohesion eroded, co-operation and mutual obligation between king and nobles were eclipsed. The support of confessional organisations buttressed the reappearance of independent aristocratic power bases in the provinces. As royal power receded, provincial nobles and elected assemblies quietly appropriated the crown's financial and judicial rights, while aristocratic faction proceeded to rip the country apart.

Theories of resistance proliferated: obedience was not owed to heretic kings and tyrannicide was agreeable to God. The aura of the absolute monarch, resistance to whom was *lèse-majesté*, was tarnished; local power groups and corporate bodies ceased to be recruited for royal purposes and the king's sovereign rights slipped back into the hands of his leading subjects. From 1588 to 1591 a Committee of Sixteen ruled Paris and drove the king from his capital. The Sorbonne released France from its allegiance to a tyrannical king, and seven months later Henry III was assassinated. This was the legacy of civil war and anarchy addressed by Henry IV and Cardinal Richelieu. It is scarcely surprising that they decided the theory and practice of monarchy required renovation.

Parker reminds us that Henry is celebrated as a maker of war, love and epigrams. Less cinematically, his grasp of competent kingship enabled him to resurrect the ailing monarchy. Antidotes for religious venom were found in his adroit conversion to the Catholic faith and his guarantee of freedom of Protestant worship by the Edict of Nantes in 1598. Above all, he renegotiated deals with élites. Even irreconcilable members of the Catholic League, such as the duke of Mayenne, were finally pacified. Sully, his finance minister, was alone in early seventeenth-century Europe in increasing the resources of a major government. He considered that some Estates, *parlements* and town councils were exploiting their privileges and practising abuses at the fiscal expense of others. He was also anxious to restore the balance between royal and other power groups prevailing before the civil wars. Where personal considerations made it possible and political factors desirable, as in Guyenne, government *élus* were introduced; elsewhere the old arrangements continued. Where elected town councils had revolted, such as Limoges in 1602, municipal self-government was restricted; elsewhere, as in Rouen, nothing was changed.[10] There was no systematic attack on representative institutions as such. The issue was loyalty and the target unreliable agencies, representative or otherwise. Office-holders were placated by the introduction in 1604 of the *paulette*, an annual tax which henceforth they might pay in order to bequeath their offices. This created a hereditary office-holding nobility, the *noblesse de robe*, and forged their alliance with the monarchy. For the next two centuries this was the elevator on which successful bourgeois entered the ranks of the nobility.

Henry's success was the result of the reoccupation of the throne by a skilled political operator. Political consensus was established and the prestige of the monarchy restored. He benefited from widespread disillusionment with the chaos and oppression issuing from the dominance of noble faction. Expertly balancing and playing off the power groups arrayed against him, he exploited their divisions and broke up alliances of local nobles and princes of the blood. Judicious distribution of patronage centrally and locally reassembled a network of royal clients he could trust. His methods were traditional. He rarely resorted to physical force, since it was a scarce commodity. The loyalty of troops was conditional: it soon ran out if they were required to attack fellow Frenchmen. He relied on co-operation and persuasion, on bargaining and compromise. Above all he relied on patronage, on the resources, offices and titles in the king's gift. Like Francis I, he won support by buying it. When in 1610 the twenty-fourth attempt on the life of the heretical usurper succeeded, he bequeathed to his heir an authority which was both strong and stable. Henry's regime was tested by the royal minority after his death, and it held, but its success was based on no fundamental reforms nor on the extension of his absolute authority.

There had, nevertheless, been disquieting features. In the 1590s, with the Spanish poised to invade, the *parlement* persistently thwarted Henry's financial needs. In 1597 it urged that the king's choice of councillors, an undoubted royal prerogative, should be made from its own nominees. Its claims escalated in 1616, when it convened on its own authority a meeting of the full Court of Peers (the Paris *parlement* reinforced with high nobles and princes of the blood). The topic of debate was the good of the realm – like other subjects from which the *parlement* had been repeatedly excluded, a matter of state. Louis XIII never forgave it for this insult during his minority. Another problem was the office-holders. The *paulette* created a formidable vested interest. Offices were now items of personal property and would be deployed in the best interests of the owner rather than the public service which was their ostensible justification. Similarly their loyalty was not to the emerging idea of an impersonal state: they were united by a personal bond to the monarch who guaranteed their property.[11] Office holders were also rendered immune from dismissal as well as permanently and unsurprisingly hostile to the growing demand for a reduction of offices.

The gravest single threat to the ruling house was always the great nobles and the princes of the blood. The former were usually present or former rulers of territories beyond the frontiers of France: the Montmorency clan held extensive lands in the Netherlands and Germany. The princes of the blood were descendants of earlier Bourbon or Valois monarchs. Since both groups were known in France as *les grands*, 'grandees' is a useful equivalent. Grandees possessed unique social cachet. To emphasise their superiority to mere nobles, both groups married into ruling families of other countries and thus had a personal interest in international affairs. It was therefore vital for them to participate in the formulation of foreign policy.[12] Consequently they never relinquished their ambition of dominating the central councils where matters of state were discussed, or, in the case of Louis XIII's brother, of acquiring the crown itself. They also claimed hereditary provincial governorships with sovereign powers.

In other words they wished to return to the feudal France which had vanished a century before: sovereignty was to be divided up and a monarchical state transformed into an aristocratic one. The demand for strong, absolute monarchy derived from the conviction that it alone prevented grandees from bullying their weaker brethren.[13] They were one of the few identifiable groups which sought to arrest its progress. Since their capacity for infighting at court was as formidable as their power base in the country, their potential for trouble was impressive. They had found local independence harder to achieve since the fifteenth century, and aspired instead to gatecrash at the highest levels of central government. And because monarchs had for several centuries appointed ministers from the lesser nobility or gentry, who relied on the ruler for their power rather than depending on their own, a renewed princely presence in the councils of the king represented a serious threat to the traditional system. Most sinister of all was the danger of princes and *parlements* launching a joint attack on the crown's prerogatives.

The early decades of the seventeenth century revealed support for strong monarchy. In 1614 the princes of the blood revolted against the regency of Marie de' Medici. They exploited their links with foreign powers and threatened to plunge France into civil and international conflict. To mobilise support against them the regent summoned the Estates-General. Its pronouncements furnish illuminating evidence of contemporary preoccupations. First there was a sharper accent on the divine right of kings: the crown was held directly from God, not from God via the people. No power on earth could deprive kings of their right to rule, or absolve their subjects from their duty of allegiance, for any cause whatsoever. Nor did the assembly disappoint the regent's hopes of a united front against the princes, and a further revolt by their forces was acclaimed with deafening silence. The overwhelming majority of the second estate were lesser nobles, about 200,000 of them, who entertained no hopes of dominating the king's councils. Their *cahiers* (lists of requests drawn up for the asssembly) made clear their contempt for the selfish ambitions of the grandees, who, though they were few in number, exercised a disproportionate influence.

A prince like Conti with a revenue of 400,000 *livres* a year moved in court circles and loitered expectantly in the corridors of power. A *seigneur* on 400 *livres* a year was essentially a local figure, prominent in the lowered eyes of his tenants but unknown at court and reliant on a well-connected broker for royal favours. Between grandees and lesser nobles were about 500 politically prominent families (such as the Richelieus) which did not expect high office as a matter of course but frequently got it. Understanding has not been advanced by historians who treat all nobles as equally dangerous to the crown – and therefore as equally in need of emasculation. The politically significant segment of the ruling class was small. But a stone lobbed into this diminutive pond caused major waves.

The consensus against the princes was gratifying to the government, but other grievances were less musical to its ears. The clerical, noble and third estates were of course not united, but there was broad agreement in condemning the venality or sale of office, the number of officials and the excessive burden of taxation. The closest approach to unity was achieved in the fervour with which financiers and tax-farmers were attacked. Both were denounced as leeches and parasites who profited from the king's necessities and helped to maintain an exorbitant level of taxation. But there was less in these attacks than meets the eye. Periodically the government had to bow to the clamour and set up a *chambre de justice* to investigate charges of corruption. This was always a charade: nineteenth-century standards of bureaucratic probity should not be expected in the seventeenth-century. Since the crown needed loans and advances as urgently as their suppliers needed the crown, reform was announced, token sentences were imposed and nothing was done. In a trade-off typical of the 'absolutist' state, the financial agents made a show of repentance and continued their activities. An inquiry of 1607 started asking questions about one of Sully's own clients and was abruptly terminated to avoid embarrassment.[14] Furthermore, many of the *officiers* who demanded sacrificial financiers in the Estates-General of 1614 were duplicitous, since they would have been among them. Their intention was to have their rivals investigated and so reduce the competition.[15]

The same themes were rehearsed in the Assembly of Notables which was summoned in 1626. This time Marie de' Medici and her younger son, Gaston d'Orléans, brother and heir to the childless Louis XIII, led a dissident faction against Cardinal Richelieu, who gradually became chief minister after 1624. France was involved in the Thirty Years War and the regime was about to launch an attack on the Huguenots, who were Protestant heretics with the bad habit of calling on foreign powers or rebel princes to protect them against Bourbon Catholic initiatives. Before engaging more deeply in such undertakings, Richelieu sought a more permanent solution to the financial crisis in the shape of a commercial and colonial initiative. The Assembly was summoned to endorse the cardinal's plans for trading companies and other mercantilist mechanisms by which to regiment France's forthcoming economic expansion. There were initial squabbles over whether those present should vote individually (the greater number of judges would defeat the clergy and nobles) or as corporate estates (the first and second would defeat the *officiers*); and the influential clergy, nobles and judges who composed it gave a swift thumbs down to his proposals. In other respects their performance disappointed him less. A consensus emerged against high taxation and supernumerary office-holders, currently targets of his reforming zeal. The Notables roundly condemned the princes and Huguenots for raising private armies and erecting fortifications, dominating high offices of state, negotiating with foreign powers and levying unauthorised taxes. These prerogatives were deemed to lie with the king and the ministers of his choice. In such matters of state the high nobility were judged less likely to be the people's protectors than their oppressors.[16]

RICHELIEU

The demands of these two assemblies were the basis of Richelieu's domestic policies for the next fifteen years.[17] Clearly what has been regarded as his 'absolutist' initiative had strong support from below. Equally clearly it was a traditional programme aiming to restore royal authority after a period when it had been constantly challenged. This he proceeded to implement with unparalleled ruthlessness. His *Political Testament* referred to the situation he inherited: '. . . the Huguenots shared the state with Your Majesty, the grandees acted as though they were not your subjects and the provincial governors as though they were sovereign powers'. His target was the overmighty subjects who were again wielding royal sovereign powers. Richelieu was undoubtedly a creator of the absolute power of the crown. Sovereignty had formerly been shared with, and latterly usurped by, the nobles, corporate bodies and provincial power groups of the feudal regime. Richelieu finally and irrevocably monopolised it for the central government – a concentration so basic for the modern state that we take his achievement for granted.

In 1627 Montmorency-Bouteville was beheaded for duelling under the cardinal's window in the Palais Royal. By making a sensational and merciless example of the youth, Richelieu demonstrated two things – that the crown claimed a monopoly of violence and that royal edicts had relevance even for honour-obsessed nobles. In 1628 the political and military powers of the Huguenots were destroyed when Richelieu blasted his way into their headquarters of La Rochelle. This achieved two objectives. Protestant nobles began to convert to Catholicism, and thus heralded the restoration of ideological unity between crown and élites symbolised by Louis XIV's Revocation of the Edict of Nantes in 1685. Even more crucially, royal authority was imposed. For two years a Protestant assembly had wielded supreme authority over financial and military administration – a blatant case of encroaching on royal prerogatives. Louis XIII dubbed it illegal and better suited to a republic.

The crown's increasingly effective monopoly of what it considered its prerogative was underpinned by its heavier accent on the divine right of kings. Divine right implied divine insights. Enshrined at the heart of French government was 'the mystery of the monarchy' which enabled its incumbent to determine matters of high policy with a competence approaching infallibility.[18] An edict of 1641 forbade the *parlements* to interfere in matters of state unless invited to give an opinion. *Lits de justice* were defined as the forum for such matters and remonstrance was allowed after and not before registration. Grandees were firmly barred from the king's councils. Their attempts to replace the man behind their exclusion compelled Richelieu incessantly to renew his grip on the royal mind. His repeated escapes from the clutches of overwhelming court coalitions put him in the Houdini class.

Nor did other modes of opposition suffer neglect. Richelieu was determined to eradicate the feudal notion that loyalty to the crown was subject to customer satisfaction. This did not invalidate the contractual obligations of the crown: but henceforth there was to be nothing subjects could do if it broke them. They must obey just the same. Again, we tend to take for granted the obedience inspired by government fiat: seventeenth-century Frenchmen did not. Grandees, especially those with international connections, liked to remind their monarchs that the bond of obligation was mutual by periodically exchanging masters. Condé's aggrieved desertion to Spain during the Fronde is merely the most spectacular example. At a lower level, many nobles saw little reason why the king should have the last word if they happened to disagree with him. Scraps of Roman law, familiar since the fourteenth century, had simultaneously reintroduced the idea of an ultimate power residing in the people and sharpened royal demands for obedience that was absolute and unconditional. Richelieu was arguably the first to give them a real cutting edge and his methods were unsavoury.

His weapon was the law of treason or *lèse-majesté*. Previously only England deployed the law rigorously against grandees such as the Howards. Condé, who led a Spanish army against his own monarch in the Fronde, was pardoned and restored to his estates.[19] The treason for which Montmorency was beheaded in 1632 was similar to Bourbon's in 1523: both believed they were the victim of injustice. But Bourbon's ability to exploit old conceptions of honour and obligation permitted him to create international havoc for Francis I and survive. Not any longer. By stretching the law to comprehend verbal attacks and insubordination, Richelieu beheaded a minister like Marillac and a propagandist like de Morgues merely for criticising his regime. The justification was *raison d'état*, another old idea which argued that state necessity impelled governments into actions which might repel a fastidious individual. (As Pooh Bah wailed: 'It revolts me but I do it.') The conduct of the icy cardinal himself, the rigged trials of 'enemies of the state', the nocturnal executions of the *chambre de l'arsenal*, the special commissions for crimes of *lèse-majesté* and the sentences without any trial at all, combine to make his regime one of the most sinister in French history[20] – even after allowances have been made for the theatrical villain immortalised by stage and screen. This melodramatic interference with due process of law has little to do with absolute monarchy: Louis XIV managed comfortably without it. Richelieu is more accurately seen as a despotic interlude in an otherwise lawful Bourbon regime. His despotic methods erected warning signs round the awesome area of royal authority in the only way that could be effective in troubled times – through fear. The means were temporary. The end, deification of royal prerogative, was permanent.

The supposed instruments of 'absolutism', the army and the intendants, were not among Richelieu's significant innovations – though this is to question ancient legend. Far more prophetic for the future was his unprecedented reliance on his own clients or creatures to control the realm. All in royal favour attracted supporters, but Richelieu's following was unprecedented because his power base extended far beyond the court. Bergin has demonstrated how he amassed governorships of towns and provinces for himself and his family: Saint-Simon called him 'the best relative the world has ever seen'. He also snapped up available land with the avidity of a property developer. His political and territorial foothold in Brittany, Anjou, Poitou, Aunis and Saintonge gave him direct personal authority throughout western France and enlarged his sphere of patronage.[21] His special relationship with the king additionally allowed him to appropriate huge blocks of royal patronage.

Richelieu thus constructed his own network of ministerial clients. The chief minister was the king's client and placed at royal disposal his own clients, but the faction through which he ruled was not the king's but his own. Unreliable provincial governors were bypassed and patronage channelled directly to local nobles and corporate bodies. The occupant of every available administrative post was tied to him by links of loyalty and gratitude, to the dismay of factions whose members were excluded. He also relied heavily on his family and was an unabashed nepotist. His network enmeshed all the secretaries of state, for whom he secured increased salaries and advantageous marriages. Victory over Marillac and Orléans in the Day of Dupes (1630) enabled him to insert his own clients instead of theirs at court and as provincial governors. He overcame opposition in Brittany by placing his own clients in key positions and lured influential Bretons into his network. He took out the unfriendly governor of Provence, the mighty duke of Guise. His hostility having attracted Richelieu's attention, he found himself surrounded and outmanoeuvred by the cardinal's creatures. They numbered the military lieutenant, the top judges of the local *parlement*, the archbishop of Aix, the city boss of Marseille and the general of the royal galleys. When Richelieu further encircled him with eight of his creatures as provincial, naval and army intendants, Guise gave up. The result was government by personal relationships. It relied on loyalty and gratitude to a benefactor, not on obedience to a superior in a bureaucratic hierarchy. The chief mechanism for securing compliance with governmental policy was a mafia with tentacles extending to the remotest parts of the realm.[22] Richelieu was the 'godfather' and the governing élite one big, happy family – in some cases literally.

The greatest concentration of force lay in the army which had by the fifteenth century been recognised as the king's. But the acquisition was little more than nominal while units were commanded by nobles who raised and equipped troops as independent entrepreneurs rather than servants of the king. War with Spain in the 1630s required rapid expansion to 80,000 and traditional control mechanisms became inadequate overnight. Yet Richelieu did not allow his commanders the freedom conceded by other governments to independent entrepreneurs. They could not sell or transfer their units without permission; they were not compensated for disbandment. Consequently officers continually faced financial ruin and felt no obligation to remain at their posts. Officer absenteeism was worse than in any other army.[23]

Abuses were minimised by the deployment of intendants as inspectors who lacked local roots and were supposed to be more reliable than provincial officials. Royal agents despatched from the centre were no novelty, but in the 1630s their visits became more frequent and by the 1640s there was at least one in each province. They were charged with the raising of extra war taxation and the control of military commanders whose unchecked power would pose a supreme threat. Richelieu's *Political Testament* (if genuine) portrays them as a remedy for defects within the existing framework, not creators of a new one. Though they became permanent, their introduction was pragmatic.[24]

Richelieu's failure to nationalise the army underlines his essentially traditional attitudes. Co-operation with established élites and powerful corporations was the backbone of his system. He made municipal authorities rather than the crown responsible for poor relief and hospitals. Funds were to be raised by taxes consented to by each locality and collected by elected officials. Brittany was always the most recalcitrant of *pays d'état*, yet he tamed it by the least innovative and aggressive of methods. By working through local constitutional and consultative mechanisms he avoided all appearance of despotism.[25] Richelieu's views on the Estates were also traditional. Members of the royal council had long held different opinions, and Major argues that the treatment of the Estates reflected which councillor was responsible for which province. Some dealt with them gently and others more firmly. Guyenne was administered by Maupeou, formerly a trusted henchman of Sully, and like his descendant a century and a half later he distrusted bodies with corporate authority of their own. In 1621 he gave the Estates of Guyenne their death blow by imposing government *élus* on the province and thereby reducing their sphere of responsibility. By contrast, Languedoc, Provence, Auvergne and Lyonnais were supervised by more lenient councillors, and when the hard-liner Marillac established *élus* in Languedoc his colleagues engineered their suppression.[26]

Similar disagreements continued after Richelieu took charge. His own preference for traditional agencies was not shared by Marillac, who seems to have forged ahead regardless with centralisation. The struggle with Spain generated unprecedented demands for taxes. Clergy, nobles, townsmen, *officiers* and peasants were subjected to relentless pressure to increase their contribution. Inevitably the government came into conflict with corporate groups, but many fiscal exactions proved short-lived. The regime was firmly based on compromise and permanent adjustments in liability could be avoided by paying up.[27] More serious was Marillac's imposition of *élus* on the great *pays d'état* in 1626–29 – Dauphiné, Burgundy, Provence and Languedoc. Richelieu recorded his hostility to the intractable Estates of Languedoc, but his memoirs fail to mention the other victims and show his support for those of Burgundy.

It seems likely that the general attack on the *pays d'état* was not of his making. In Dauphiné the government exploited the deadly rivalry between the second and third estates over their taxable status: the third estate lost interest in the provincial assembly once the second had lost its immunity. Only a rump assembly survived, dominated by the towns. But the government's careful definition of its composition in 1639 removes any suspicion that it plotted the Estates' demise.[28] By contrast, the other provinces exploded in revolt. After decapitating Montmorency, the disloyal governor of Languedoc, Richelieu withdrew the *élus* in return for 3,886,000 *livres*. He then reverted to his normal strategy of co-operation, procured by generous patronage. By the end of 1631 Burgundy and Provence had also recovered their right to grant taxation, in return for ready money. The imminence of France's open participation in the Thirty Years War made compromise more desirable than confrontation. There is no clear evidence that the policy of revoking centralising measures in return for cash payments was pre-planned. Yet Francis I's creation of *élus* expressly to abolish them at a price may be a clue.[29]

Historians of 'absolutism' have usually assumed that the apparent decline in the number and importance of representative bodies in the early seventeenth century resulted from a deliberate policy of the crown. It did not. Such a policy would have been pointless, since corporate bodies were administrative as well as consultative – and in most ways superior to agencies more directly under the crown's control. *Elus* were far from being the panacea which historians of 'absolutism' imagine them to have been. Their introduction into the administration of Rouergue (Guyenne) quadrupled the cost of collecting the taxes: their fees and salaries amounted to more than the total cost of the Estates' activities, most of which were devoted to education, public works and social welfare.[30] Their arrival also incited resentment or revolt. Consequently the preference seems to have been for corporate bodies where they were reliable. Only where Estates persistently failed to co-operate did Richelieu violate provincial privilege. In the *pays d'état*, *élus* were a fall-back remedy where local authorities failed. In the *pays d'élection*, where *élus* were already established, Estates continued to exist.

Richelieu thus relied on partnership with the corporate élites of society rather than the bureaucratic techniques of 'absolutism'. Much of the apparent decline of prominent Estates represents a shift from one mode of consultation to another – from national to provincial as the Estates-General finally ceased to meet, from provincial to local as in some areas smaller assemblies proved more robust. Consultation also occurred with alternative corporate bodies, assemblies of the Church, the law and the towns. The perceived usefulness of these various mechanisms arguably reflected shifting alignments, personal and social, *within* central and local power groups rather than an altered relationship *between* them.[31] Government planning is less satisfactory as an explanation of the fate of individual bodies than is the element of chance.

Richelieu's alleged 'absolutist' initiatives are therefore thrown into doubt by several new discoveries – the lack of unanimity about royal power in government circles, the employment of centralising devices merely as fiscal blackmail and the over-simplification of crown versus localities explanations. But he made what proved in the long run to be an irreversible contribution to the crown's absolute authority. After Richelieu, Frenchmen knew that the king was entitled to the final word.

THE FRONDE

The Fronde of 1648–53 hovers between tragedy and farce. In some ways it was a tacky remake of the English Civil War, with a poor script and a cast of tens. How, it has been asked, can one take seriously a revolt named after the catapults deployed by Parisian urchins against the coaches of the rich? Elsewhere it has been proclaimed as the most important single event in France during the seventeenth century.[32] If so, the accolade is due to its results rather than its causes, which were a fluke combination of grievances uniting groups who were normally rivals – *parlement*, robe nobles, sword nobles and grandees.

The Fronde has been interpreted in many ways. For Marxist historians it was essentially a popular revolt against the class-front presented by crown and aristocracy. 'Absolutism' was the device by which the feudal nobility prolonged its exploitation of the peasantry.[33]

From this perspective the Fronde was a continuation of the desperate peasant revolts which disgraced the 1630s and 1640s, most notably the so called *Croquants* of the south-west and the *Nu-pieds* of Normandy. Since this ignores the inconvenient fact that the leading aristocrats were in revolt *against* the government, most historians have favoured a more constitutional explanation. The popularity of strong monarchy was beyond doubt. Even criticisms of the oppressive Richelieu focused on his foreign rather than domestic policy, the essentials of which seem to have been widely accepted.[34] What was not popular was minority government, with a deputy monarch wielding power oppressively on the young Louis XIV's behalf.

All governments make enemies and Richelieu and Mazarin had made many. The cardinals viewed grandees and provincial governors as unreliable patronage-brokers, more likely to distribute patronage for selfish purposes than the crown's. They found themselves increasingly squeezed out as Richelieu and Mazarin brokered patronage through their own ministerial clients among the middling and lesser nobility. The grandees consequently thirsted to repeat the programme of Cinq-Mars in 1642 – remove the king's minister, install themselves and initiate a foreign policy of their own choosing. The *officiers* resented the crown's attacks on their rights and privileges – the reduction of their salaries, the threatened suspension of the *paulette* and the usurpation of their functions by the intendants. The judges of the *parlements* were aggrieved by the crown's habit of railroading them at the first sign of opposition and its repeated contempt for legal processes – its special commissions, its arbitrary arrests and its *lits de justice*. What was resisted was insensitive treatment of ruling élites. This prompted a backlash against those prerogatives which had mistreated them. This in turn redefined the terms of dispute, which escalated into more fundamental conflict. Study of the previous period has been distorted by the search for causes of an event which had in fact generated its own momentum. The Fronde was essentially a protest against the despotic abuse of power by Richelieu and Mazarin, not a 'constitutional' attempt to dismantle the 'absolutism' of the French crown – though that is the usual interpretation. It is good evidence for the growth of 'absolutism' if the Fronde can be presented as an attempt to arrest it.

The problem is to determine who was the aggressor – the crown with its fiscal innovations, intendants and allegedly incipient 'absolutism', or the *parlement* and princes with their demand for a greater role in government and arguably republican tendencies. The answer is both, crown first and then *parlement*. Most commentators deny that the *parlement* was the innovator. Certainly at first it intoned the traditional constitutional litanies – that the French monarchy was limited by law and that the subject's property in land, privilege or office was protected by that law.[35] The despotic innovator was the crown, driven to desperate measures by the Thirty Years War's devastation of the royal finances. By the 1640s Mazarin was boxed in. All possible financial devices had been tried and though it is easy to criticise his policies it is harder to suggest alternatives. Yet he made every possible tactical error. Having challenged the hereditary *officiers* in 1642 by ordering the intendants to preside over their *taille* assessments, in 1648 he did so again. This made them something more than inspectors and more like the local bureaucrats of legend. The edicts of January 1648 violated every concept of legitimate power, not only by their matter, which renewed the *paulette* on condition that four years' salary was relinquished, but also by their manner, a repetition of the *lit de justice* of four years before. On that occasion the *parlement*'s spokesman objected to the use of absolute power to enforce new taxation during a royal minority.

Minorities were difficult in other ways. They were a time when princes of the blood recollected whose relatives they were and traditionally expected a major role in government. It was easy to oppose the current ministers, since in no meaningful sense were they the choice of an under-age monarch. Attempts could therefore be made to topple them without appearing to oppose the king's choice. For the same reason those touting for a patron were loath to attach themselves to a man who might be an impermanent fixture once the ruler came of age and expressed personal preferences. At such times it was hard for a minister to acquire clients. Mazarin was thus doubly handicapped by serving a minor. He was also an Italian cardinal of dubious origins who spoke pigeon French and was apparently good for little but low intrigue. French xenophobia had a field day. This prince of the Church was accused, *inter alia*, of murder, sodomy and fornication with the Queen Mother. The principal aim of the princes was to substitute themselves for Mazarin. The result of these assorted grievances was an alliance of the weirdest bedfellows. Office holders who had previously been rivals now closed ranks, and grandees who had regarded all of them as interlopers welcomed them as trusted allies.

Had they merely sought to correct the crown's 'absolutist' excesses and adhere to the programme subsequently constructed for them by historians, civil war would probably not have erupted. But Mazarin was understandably jumpy after the treatment meted out to monarchs and chief ministers in contemporary England. He sniffed republican designs and lashed out savagely, notably with the arrest of the leading princes in 1650. Government aggression provoked an equal and opposite reaction from the *parlement* and princes. It had begun by demanding and securing the abolition of the intendants and declaring the government's tax decrees invalid. Its subsequent pronouncements claimed to make sovereign decisions in all matters, propose and dismiss ministers and councillors of state and, in association with the grandees, issue decrees on matters of state.[36] Short of claiming to declare war and sign treaties, a more daring raid on the royal prerogative can scarcely be envisaged. Mazarin's palpitations about republicanism, in the loose sense of subordinating the monarch to a committee, merit more sympathy than most historians have extended.

Conti, governor of Champagne, and Longueville, governor of Normandy, revolted to add weight to their claim to dominance of the royal councils and independence in the countryside. Condé was attempting to force himself on the crown as chief minister.[37] On hitting the buffers he varied his military career by fighting in Spain's armies against France. All gave proof, if Louis XIV neeeded any, that the deadliest threat to French monarchs came from within the royal court – from their own officials, courtiers and family. At various times his uncle, his heirs and his commanders were in revolt against him: in 1651 the gates of Paris were opened to the rebels and the guns of the Bastille put at their disposal by the king's cousin. On the whole historians have underplayed this menace, in happy possession of hindsight and the knowledge that revolts by a territorially based nobility were a doomed species of protest. In 1648 it was not apparent.

Traditional explanations of sixteenth- and seventeenth-century revolts omit the ingredient of faction. At one level, to be sure, disputes were ideological. Rebels equipped themselves with a rationale designed to justify rescuing a king from the clutches of evil ministers. Sixteenth-century resistance writers proved a useful source of ideas, with their emphasis on the duty of *parlements* and princes to redirect errant monarchs to paths of legality. But these were not 'constitutional' ranged against 'absolutist' ideas. Most protagonists accepted royal prerogatives as long as they were used wisely and for the good of the realm. As soon as they were not they were challenged. Royal powers were dynamic, not static, and were not acquired automatically: it had often been argued that a government during a royal minority had restricted powers and could not initiate legislation. At another level the struggle was institutional – crown versus *parlement* and crown versus grandees. Both these levels of analysis are inadequate without another. For the military opposition to the grandees' attempt to storm the royal council came from other grandees, such as Choiseul, who remained loyal to the crown. The surest contemporary sign that prerogatives were being mishandled was the exclusion of self-important members of the political nation from power and patronage. This was another compelling reason for them to advocate a reshuffle in the central councils. Institutions like the *parlement* were riddled with faction. If they revolted against the crown, it signified that the king's or minister's clients among the judges were temporarily outnumbered by those who looked to his enemies. Since the strings of most institutions in France were pulled by very few political bosses, it was ultimately a problem of balancing the different groups at court. The first duty of early modern monarchs was management of the ruling élite. That included not offending them all at the same time and thereby allowing the resulting coalition to dictate to the crown.

In one sense the government defeated the Fronde by dissolving the alliance on which it was based. The crown's prerogatives were retrieved and preserved from a committee of judges and princes. In another it had not been defeated at all. Those prerogatives were henceforth deployed with a caution bordering on neurosis. Their despotic abuse by the cardinals was terminated. And the sensibilities of grandees became a prime consideration of government. The Fronde was a lesson the young Louis XIV would not forget.[38]

REFERENCES

1   Darnton R 1979 *The Business of Enlightenment*. Harvard University, p. 295; Hampson N 1989 What was the Third Estate? In *A Tale of Two Cities*, Comag, p. 89
2   Knecht RJ 1982 *Francis I*. Cambridge University Press, pp. 345–8
3   Behrens CBA 1985 *Society, Government and the Enlightenment*. Thames and Hudson, pp. 13–23
4   Major JR 1980 *Representative Government in Early Modern France*. Yale University, pp. 177–9
5   Wood JB 1980 *The Nobility of the Election of Bayeux 1463–1666*. Princeton University, pp. 77–81
6   Shennan JH 1968 *The* Parlement *of Paris*. Eyre and Spottiswoode, pp. 86–95
7   Major JR 1980, pp. 97–122
8   Parker D 1983 *The Making of French Absolutism*. Arnold, pp. 19–21

9   Knecht RJ 1984 *French Renaissance Monarchy: Francis I and Henry II.* Longman, p. 24
10 Greengrass M 1984 *France in the Age of Henri IV.* Longman, pp. 107–11
11 Shennan JH 1986 *Liberty and Order in Early Modern Europe.* Longman, p. 23
12 Mettam R 1988 *Power and Faction in Louis XIV's France.* Basil Blackwell, p. 19
13 Mousnier R 1979 *The Institutions of France under the Absolute Monarchy 1598–1789, Volume 1: Society and the State.* Chicago University, pp. 640–2
14 Munck T 1990 *Seventeenth-Century Europe.* Macmillan, p. 40
15 Mettam R 1988, pp. 106–9
16 Mettam R 1988, pp. 122–6
17 Hayden JM 1974 *France and the Estates-General of 1614.* Cambridge University Press, pp. 215–16; Parker D 1983, p. 90
18 Mousnier R 1979, p. 656
19 Kamen H 1984 *European Society 1500–1700.* Hutchinson, p. 116
20 Elliott JH 1984 *Richelieu and Olivares.* Cambridge University Press, p. 135
21 Bergin J 1985 *Cardinal Richelieu: Power and the Pursuit of Wealth.* Yale University, pp. 80–94, 119–57
22 Kettering S 1986 *Patrons, Brokers and Clients.* Oxford University Press, pp. 141–61; Mousnier R 1984, pp. 148–51
23 Parrott D 1987 French Military Organisation in the 1630s: the Failure of Richelieu's Ministry. *Seventeenth-Century Studies,* ix, pp. 160–3
24 Mousnier R 1984 *The Institutions of France under the Absolute Monarchy 1598–1789, Volume 2: The Organs of State and Society.* Chicago University, p. 507
25 Dunkley KM Patronage and Power in Seventeenth-Century France: Richelieu's Clients and the Estates of Brittany, in *Parliaments, Estates and Representation,* June 1988; Major 1980, pp. 497–8, 599–607
26 Major JR 1980, pp. 484–6
27 Parker D 1983, p. 70
28 Major JR 1980, p. 554, 616–18; Hickey D 1986 *The Coming of French Absolutism.* Toronto University, pp. 188–90
29 Knecht RJ 1991 *Richelieu.* Longman, pp. 140–1
30 Major JR 1980, pp. 463–6
31 Parker D 1980 *La Rochelle and the French Monarchy: Conflict and Order in Seventeenth-Century France.* Royal Historical Society
32 Coveney PJ 1977 *France in Crisis 1620–1675.* Macmillan, p. 37
33 Anderson P 1979 *Lineages of the Absolutist State.* Verso, *passim*
34 Church WF 1972 *Richelieu and Reason of State.* Princeton University, pp. 38–9
35 Shennan JH 1968, pp. 265–77
36 Mousnier R 1984, p. 622
37 Bonney R 1988 *Society and Government in France under Richelieu and Mazarin 1624–61.* Macmillan, p. 156
38 Mettam R 1988, p. 173–4.

CHAPTER TWO
Louis XIV Reassessed

By common consent Louis XIV is the apogee of 'absolutism'. Henry IV, Richelieu and Mazarin are lean, sinewy pioneers and Louis XV and XVI bloated decadents. Between them shimmers the spectacle of Versailles and its chief performer, with his dazzling stage presence and split-second timing, his lines perfect and his entries unfluffed.

ROYAL AUTHORITY

'Absolutism' implies that Louis promoted a monopoly of power for himself and the decline of corporate bodies as government agencies and organs of consultation. Instead of using bodies with power in their own right he allegedly governed through an army and bureaucracy which owed power only to him, while laws were made and taxes imposed autocratically. Recent research makes this doubtful. He was probably more anxious to reassert his authority over policy areas where it had recently been challenged. Corporate bodies like the *parlements* were firmly excluded from matters traditionally subject to the royal prerogative, not from government in general. Louis was consolidating old powers rather than claiming new ones.

When Louis announced, on Mazarin's death in 1661, that he would not appoint a chief minister, the implications were profound. Not only was the king taking over the work of Richelieu and Mazarin in co-ordinating the activities of the councils, departments and secretaries, making decisions and refereeing the contests between them, but he was also publicly assuming personal responsibility for the actions of the government. Louis XIII had kept his head down and allowed his ministers to draw the flak; but his son's *Memoirs* state his demand that every government decision should have his approval and that his authority should be shared with none. When his involvement was remote, as in the mind-numbing minutiae of economic regulation, Colbert nevertheless stressed the king's personal interest in the matter. Louis' ministers rather than the king fielded much of the criticism until his fortunes seriously declined in the 1680s; but few doubted that the king was in charge. This was regarded as a return to normality after the rule of ministers and favourites for half a century. Far from being suspected as a sinister move towards 'absolutism', it was welcomed.

Louis was also determined to allow no one minister or faction to monopolise his favour. His *Memoirs* announce his intention of balancing and playing off rival gangs, whether of courtiers or ministers. Louis studiously avoided the disasters of previous decades, when patronage had periodically been allocated on the criterion of who shouted loudest. He was also loyal to the ministers he appointed. During a personal rule of fifty-five years he got through seventeen members of the Council of State, and most of those were from three families. This acted as a brake on the power struggle, since it was clear that the king was not easily swayed. His successors were more impressionable, with disastrous effect. Thus he immediately addressed the central problem of seventeenth-century France: management of the robe and sword nobility. Nor was he willing to permit the creatures and clients of political bosses to invade every artery and capillary of the body politic, as in previous regimes. Faction would continue to play a major role in establishing government power and bonding the provinces to the centre, but at the heart of these manipulative networks would be no mere ministerial following. It would be the king's.[1]

The decision-making process was inseparable from the king's majesty. Action was ordered in his name, and because he associated himself closely with policy the fiction could be believed that he was personally behind every government measure. The reality was somewhat different. Though there are no records of the Council of State's deliberations, the indications are that Louis XIV's habit was to referee a rugby scrum of conflicting advice and competition for his ear. The king encouraged fisticuffs as it furnished him with alternative courses of action and enabled him to divide and rule by playing off rivals. But if they canvassed for wider support outside the council chamber, he was quick to dismiss them. Louis once smacked down Colbert merely for continuing the argument after the king had made his decision: the public spectacle had to be one of unanimity. But if ministers collaborated beforehand to submit similar advice he was in trouble, for his expertise in specialised areas was unlikely to exceed that of departmental experts. There was then little scope left for royal choice.[2] Another way in which the monarch's personal role was reduced was for ministers to make decisions on their own, without reference to king or council, and issue orders in their own name – hence the later charge of 'ministerial despotism'. It was ministers who received petitions for royal audience or redress of grievance, ministers who had daily conversations with the king and ministers who reported to him what they considered to be important news.[3] But none of these manoeuvrings behind the scenes altered the essential fact. Whether Louis formulated policy himself or left his ministers to get on with it, it was royal authority which was invoked and could not be legitimately resisted. In that sense the king's power was absolute.

The royal prerogative embraced legislation. But no one imagined that the king's law-making power was an unrestricted right to issue diktats about anything he pleased. The Bourbons' celebrated legislative sovereignty consisted of powers which had been immemorially part of the royal prerogative. Historians' failure to recognise this has created confusion: they imagine that in jealously promoting their legislative prerogative Louis and his successors were claiming sweeping new powers to create and alter a body of law. A rather different picture emerges from the work of those who study French law rather than French history.[4] In fact law-making was part of the king's undoubted right to conduct and finance foreign and religious affairs: his edicts and ordinances embodied his activities in these specific policy areas. Law-making was intertwined with policy-making far more than in England – a fact which contemporary theorists make clear to all without 'absolutist' preconceptions.

Compared with the comprehensive body of statutes enacted by king and parliament in England, Louis XIV's legislation makes disappointing reading. Royal legislation concerned matters of state or public law, so that declarations of war were solemnly inscribed in the corpus of the ancient laws of France.[5] Private law, which guaranteed subjects' rights and relations between them, was the preserve of the *parlements*. It was seen as existing apart from, prior to and independent of the monarch. Enthusiastic propagandists hailed the king as the source of law and justice. They were in flat contradiction of the facts while France retained hundreds of local law codes, the exact geographical application of which no one could remember. Goubert made a tart note of this twenty-five years ago, but the point was not taken up.[6] Royal legislation rarely touched this legal bedrock. When it did, it was not creating or altering law: it was merely declaring what existing law was, codifying it or altering legal procedures to improve the administration of justice. The reign produced only one example of such legislation in the shape of Colbert's attempt to substitute uniform legal procedures for the exuberant variations currently in use. His new civil, criminal, maritime, colonial and commercial codes of the 1660s and 1670s look impressive on paper but were largely ignored by the *officiers* charged with implementing them. The king's absolute power was thus twice limited – once by the restricted sphere within which it could legitimately act and again by patchy enforcement on the part of his officials.

The monarch had sole right of initiating new laws. It was emphasised that though the *parlements* monitored royal legislative power they did not share it. Though the king laid many prerogative matters of state before them, they were obliged to register them without demur, unless invited to engage in discussion. But like the king with his prerogative the *parlements* were determined not to be trespassed upon. The exercise of the royal prerogative might infringe the legal rights of individuals, which were a royal no-go area equated with subjects' liberty. Magistrates therefore checked that royal legislation did not subvert existing laws and liberties. This also ensured that it was known and promulgated, and it was recognised that laws displaying the *parlements'* seal of approval had a better chance of being obeyed. The reality of Louis XIV's law-making is therefore less autocratic and comprehensive than its reputation.

THE COURT OF THE SUN KING – A CLICHÉ RE-EXAMINED

Discussion of Louis XIV's court usually focuses on the more operatic features of Versailles. In recent years historians have begun to treat its etiquette, masques, carnivals, ballets and processions, with their insistent symbolism of Apollo, as alternative forms of political discourse which marketed monarchy to visually-aware spectators. While his insistence on cultural splendour and obsequious ceremonial was shrewd policy, all this was merely stage-setting for the all-important task of kingship – management of the élite. So the élite had to be present. Louis' court therefore contained a broad spectrum of opinion: it was never restricted to those in agreement with government policy. At the end of the reign men such as Burgundy and Boulainvilliers criticised current policy from within the ruling circle of royal advisers. All available control mechanisms radiated from the court, on which descended those seeking royal favour at the highest level. Versailles has sewn an unusually rich crop of misconceptions, even by the standards of a reign not short of them. Louis XIV did *not* order the nobles to reside at Versailles where he could keep an eye on their harmless pastimes. Vauban, the king's fortifications engineer, estimated in 1707 that there were 52,000 of them, which at the rate of five or six individuals a family gives a figure of up to 300,000. As every visitor can testify, Versailles is an extensive palace and it has always been crowded. But at that rate it would have been packed like seeds in a sunflower. Recent estimates are lower. Bluche suggests a total of 200,000, of which Versailles housed approximately 5,000 by 1715. The system of seasonal quarters meant active service lasted only six months a year; so Louis had 10,000 nobles at court or 5 per cent of the whole class.[7] Lesser nobles were not up to the lifestyle, and if the king had ordered them to live at court they would have ignored him.

Nor did they need to live at court, for patronage-brokers were in business to help small-town gentlemen who resided in the provinces. Versailles was the centre of patronage for those who could afford it. It was the grandees who were drawn to court, and they entered the fray with relish. This was not entirely Louis XIV's personal miracle. In all late-medieval states there had been a tendency, still unstudied, for the great to realise their ambitions through influence at court rather than their own military might. The Sun King merely accelerated it and raised the courtly arts to heights of aristocratic obsession. Minute symptoms of the king's shifting favour were scrutinised by expert eyes: a royal greeting of two words instead of ten would occasion courtly consternation – and glee in the rival camp. Because the speech and body language of the court signalled so much more than mere courtesy, variations were highlighted against a background of behaviour which was precisely regulated according to rank and title. Princesses of the blood had their parasols carried for them in the procession of the Blessed Sacrament, while other noblewomen had to carry their own.

The court was the arena where the king observed rival factions, assessed applicants for his favour, played off potentially dangerous power groups and balanced the winners. An equilibrium of factions was always the aim: favours had to be distributed with great calculation, so as to attach the maximum number of valuable allies to the royal cause and leave no group with a monopoly. As the king was the ultimate source of power and patronage, there was feverish competition for proximity to the royal person. The celebrated rivalry for the privilege of holding the royal shirt at the *lever* was thus far from the empty pursuit of trivia to which the nobles are popularly supposed to have been reduced. There was little difference between the influence wielded by those who ministered to his personal needs and those who ministered to his state. Gentlemen of the bedchamber and secretaries of state were all royal servants attending the king personally and therefore in a position to bend his ear. Demand for household offices was so intense that Louis instituted a service rota. The duc d'Aumont was First Gentleman of the King's Chamber; but there were three other First Gentlemen who had to share the honours on a shift system.[8]

The court attracted hopefuls with many affiliations – from adherents of the current ministers to those who plotted for their instant dismissal. Some courtiers pursued high office, though grandees knew it was closed to them. Others were patronage-brokers, up from the country to replenish supplies so that they could descend like fairy godmothers on their grateful neighbours. The court was a cosmos with its own rules and standards of behaviour, many of which were seen as flouting the decencies of society as a whole. Vicious infighting made it vital for courtiers to conceal their intentions: guile, hypocrisy and dissimulation were bankable qualifications. Honesty was a courtly catastrophe. Alliances were lightly made and broken: a useless patron was dropped without compunction. One whose credit was declining could present an agonising dilemma: he might restore it and survive to reward those who had stayed faithful. Then again, he might not.

As well as a clearing-house for patronage, the court was a military parade ground. There Louis assessed, selected and rewarded his military leaders. Far from being a club for aristocratic playboys, Versailles was often the prelude to their death on the battlefield.[9]

INSTRUMENTS OF ABSOLUTISM?

A vital prop of 'absolutism' is identified as a standing army. It would be futile to deny the expansion of the army under Louis XIV, as by the early eighteenth century he could field 400,000 men. Much of the work of nationalising the private armies had been achieved by Le Tellier before 1661, but this did not eliminate the ability of nobles to terrorise remote regions with their armed bands. Nor did it end ancient problems of funding, supply and command, and the extent of royal control over these has been grossly exaggerated. Captains and colonels retained their expertise at swindling the government. Captains inflated numbers of recruits and failed to report deserters, in order to claim pay for non-existent troops: the strength of the forces on paper bore little resemblance to reality. Inspections by intendants offered a welcome foretaste of Laurel and Hardy. Men were enlisted specifically for review and then dumped. Alternatively, rapid troop movements between inspections permitted unsuspecting intendants to review the same companies twice. Unprofessional attitudes persisted. Aristocratic commanders resented direction of campaigns by lowly war secretaries such as Louvois. In 1673 a marshal in the field countermanded an order to retreat from the Netherlands, and in 1692 the king himself was obliged to reiterate his order to besiege Charleroi before Luxembourg complied. Much is heard about innovations in military technology and the revolution in tactics effected by adoption of the bayonet; but not until 1727 did the crown provide weapons. Only in the 1760s did royal agents strip captains of their recruiting role and soldiers take an oath of loyalty directly to the king.

Louis XIV's monopoly of military power was far from complete. Urban militias, commanded by municipal officials, existed till the Revolution. Attempts to seize the artillery of interior towns and redeploy it to frontier defence were firmly resisted. Prising armaments away from inland châteaux was an uphill struggle throughout the century.[10] Nor was the army as reliable a weapon for imposing royal policies on the country by force as historians of 'absolutism' imagine. Noble captains were reluctant to turn their troops on fellow nobles and deployment for the maintenance of internal order would have been interpreted by their troops as an open invitation to loot the realm. Soldiers displayed less enthusiasm for coercing taxpayers than for ambushing tax collectors. The failure of Louis XIV's army to perform its 'absolutist' role is scarcely surprising. The prototype for all subsequent professional standing armies was that of the Dutch: between 1600 and 1700 its size quintupled. A device pioneered by a republic is a dubious hallmark of 'absolutism'.[11]

Vital supporters of any monarch were his officials. Louis XIV had ten times more than Francis I to rule a marginally larger population. There was undoubted expansion in the central departments. In 1660 the entire foreign office could have been transported from Paris to Vincennes in a coach. In 1715 it would have taken twenty. But the central departments employed no more than 1000 staff and there was a police force of 2000 for the whole kingdom. Colbert employed fourteen inspectors to supplement the work of thirty intendants in imposing 200 regulatory edicts each year on a population of twenty million. Loose talk of Louis XIV's bureaucratic machine dwindles to a king and three ministers to make the decisions, thirty councillors of state, less than a hundred masters of requests to prepare the material and a few hundred scribes to record the orders.[12]

Central to all conceptions of 'absolutism' are the intendants. Bonney, Knecht and Mousnier present them as a turning point in French history. In them the crown relied for the first time on bourgeois professional bureaucrats rather than corporate bodies run by power groups of local nobles. It freed itself from their whims by severing its links with the traditional social structure.[13] This notional shift in the social basis of the state is to be distinguished from the Marxists' formula of the state as an aristocratic conspiracy. It rests on equally meagre evidence. Unlike the *officiers* the intendants did not purchase their posts: their appointment was by commission revocable by the government. They were not supposed to be posted to their native area: they supervised financial areas known as *généralités*, where they had developed no ties or vested interests and were moved on after three years before they did. Yet even these basic rules were flouted. Bouchu was Burgundy's intendant from 1656 to 1683. He was the son of the president of Burgundy's *parlement*.

Nor were local links necessarily deemed disastrous by the government. After the violent opposition to their activities expressed by the Fronde, Louis XIV and Colbert deployed intendants only as moles and ordered tactful handling of local institutions and power groups. This was part of their drive for restored relations between the crown and its *officiers*. The aliens only observed; members of the community did the actual work. The continued insistence of some historians on the royal break-through effected by the intendants is astonishing. Their restricted role as reconstituted after the Fronde was notable neither for originality nor efficiency. Medieval monarchs had established successive species of outsiders in the localities as part of their attack on over-mighty magnates. In many ways the medieval *baillis* were more thoroughly sanitised agents of the crown than the locally contaminated intendants. If natives of the north they were posted to the south. They were forbidden to acquire property or marriage partners for their children in their zones of office. Moved elsewhere after two or three years, they were subject to rigorous inspection prior to departure. Though frequently transplanted, it is true that most ultimately took root in local soil. Nor did the intendants perform so impeccably that they looked like the end of the process. At one point Colbert considered plans for creating inspectors to inspect the inspectors who were inspecting the *officiers*. But even he quailed at the prospect of inspection raised to the power of three, if not *ad infinitum*.[14]

Their performance was inadequate for several reasons. Colbert added obsessively to their data-gathering functions and by the end of his time in office their remit was endless. That necessitated assistance in the form of sub-delegates, deplored by the minister for their local partialities and serving to knit the intendants more closely into the fabric of the province. Their independence of the local community is a myth. As well as being representatives of the central government in the provinces, they also represented to the government the views *of* the provinces, many of them culled directly from the locally orientated sub-delegates.[15] By the eighteenth century they could be described more as the servants of the people than of the ministers. Colbert's correspondence with the intendants reveals the mixture of central, local and personal advantage in their administrative behaviour. It also reveals his exasperation with their incompetence. Acting on the principle that everyone cheated if allowed to, Colbert scrutinised the addresses and dates on intendants' letters and worked out how fast they were getting about their business. They could not win. If they toured their *généralités* too rapidly their statistics were denounced as impressionistic. If they loitered too long they were savaged for fatuous delays. This slave-driving approach may have kept them on their toes, but it could not solve the central dilemma: the government knew as much as the intendants wanted to tell it. Record tax returns and production graphs tending to the vertical were the route to promotion, and absurdly optimistic portraits of the French economy can be constructed from their reports. (In fact they have been.) Their most historiographically misleading trick was to announce that they had solved non-existent problems.[16]

There is a more fatal objection to the depiction of intendants as demolition men hired to undermine noble power groups and corporate bodies. They could not do without them. The intendant of Provence confessed to royal ministers that he was powerless when local élites combined against him.[17] The correct analogy is with repairers sent to mend and make good, to apply legal expertise where it had not been available before and generally smarten up the performance. An alliance with local power groups was essential if the intendants were to forge useful links between centre and localities. It strains credulity to be told that they were, in theory and practice, the antithesis of the old way of running things. Their appointment from the ranks of the *parlements* emphasises their continuity with the traditional system. Many were themselves clients of noble factions at court or were personally recommended by provincial governors whom they were allegedly designed to upstage. Robe nobles themselves, they worked closely with governors drawn from the sword nobility and exploited their patronage network as well as establishing their own.[18] Effective government was still based on the personal relationships of the clientage system, not the impersonal orders of a bureaucratic chain of command. In the last decade much of this has become widely known but the implications for 'absolutism' have received more muted coverage. Do the reassessed intendants remain an integral component of 'absolutism' or have they been relegated to the conceptual fringe? Do they represent the presence or absence of 'absolutist' methods? Answers are awaited.

Emmanuelli has provided an explanation of how this muddle arose.[19] No sooner had nineteenth-century historians embraced the concept of 'absolutism' as a description of contemporary Europe than they projected it on the past (see chapter 9). It was dyed indelibly with their own contempt for provincial perspectives and their obsession with the rise of the centralised nation-state. The intendants were eagerly seized on as the early modern equivalent of prefects and other agencies of unification employed under the Third Republic. The false impression was given that they were superimposed on structures of which the destruction or supersession was planned. This was based on an acceptance of Bourbon propaganda as reality. Historians succumbed to a potent brew composed of the picture the government created of the intendants and the image they sought to create of themselves. The sweeping powers adorning their commissions fooled scholars into believing that they superseded the traditional power groups. Unfortunately this was propaganda designed to overawe the localities.[20] It is perilous to swallow the official texts of an institution without looking beneath the surface.

If the intendants are unconvincing instruments of 'absolutism', the venal office-holders, or *officiers*, had lost none of the weaknesses displayed under Richelieu. By Louis XIV's reign there were nearly 60,000 of them. Fiscal officials occupied the lower rungs, while most of the judicial posts conferred titles of robe nobility. They stand halfway between the agencies owing their power to the king and those with independent power of their own. Though they were the monarch's officials, theoretically obliged to obey commands issued on the strength of the royal prerogative, their hereditary tenure gave them an independence not shared by those owing their power directly to the monarch. It is misleading to call them bureaucrats. All without hesitation put their private interests first if they clashed with public ones: ideals of impartial public service were non-existent. A pungent example of non-co-operation is provided by the failure of Colbert's legal codes, stymied by the inaction of the agents employed to enforce them. The government continued to pounce periodically and tribunals made select examples. But after the *officiers'* performance in the Fronde it was desperate to avoid confrontation. Rivalry with the *intendants* weakened once it was clear that the new regime envisaged a less provocative role for them, but gratitude was not manifested in obedience. Nevertheless French officials were the envy of Europe. The hereditary element bred traditions of service and fathers trained their sons for the post they would inherit. Passably efficient administration was bought cheaply by the state: salaries were small and more akin to interest payments on the loan which had been advanced in payment for the post.[21]

PATRONS, BROKERS AND CLIENTS

The basic determinant of political behaviour was clientage. It has serious implications for 'absolutism'. The formal institutions of central and regional government were merely the spheres within which clientage operated. Politics and conflict are inseparable, but it is a mistake to view early modern politics as a contest between institutions. The struggle was usually between the factions within them. All institutions inspired corporate loyalties, but cutting across them were the deeper loyalties of client and patron on which individual social and political advancement depended. Attachment to corporate or ideological positions was subordinate to the interests of aggrieved or excluded factions. Institutions were not monolithic, but behaved according to the attitudes and influence of the factions which composed them. Monarchs and ministers were quick to exploit these affiliations as control mechanisms. As the crown was assembling its own supply of armed force in the seventeenth century, it increasingly required political rather than military service from its clients. It wanted assistance in its government of the provinces.

The problem was the power structures with an independent source of authority: ministers wanted friends within them who could be relied upon to give a lead. This dimension has so far been neglected – and not surprisingly, since people covered their tracks. But the sleuthing of Kettering and her colleagues begins to uncover what has so far been hidden.[22] Diagrams of alliances (see appendices 1 and 2 pp. 227–9) reveal the minor mafias extending from palaces and châteaux to administrative bodies in obscure corners of the realm. The highest judges of the *parlements* were usually clients or creatures of royal ministers: their brief was to exploit their own following within the institution in order to swing it behind government policy. There was usually more than one faction, however, and a contentious issue could be touch and go. Thirty-nine judges in the *parlement* of Toulouse held the ten top offices in the court from 1600 to 1683. Factions accounted for twenty-six of them, fifteen in one, eight in another and three in a third. One of the gang leaders had used his clients to keep the *parlement* loyal to Mazarin during the Fronde. The converse could operate with equal effect. Colbert kept dossiers on the affiliations of the judges in all the *parlements*. Where the crown identified an enemy, patronage was deliberately withheld in order to weaken the opposition. Here a Marxist approach reveals its limitations, with its emphasis on 'absolutist' support for an aristocratic 'class front', as opposed to the crown's selective support for its friends.[23] Though at times the horizontal ties of class might seem prominent, the determinant of early modern France was the vertical link of clientage.

Manipulation of institutions by rival factions is a recognised feature of fifteenth- and sixteenth-century France, but the rise of the 'absolutist' bureaucratic state was thought to have bulldozed it. Recent work by Mousnier, Beik, Kettering and Campbell shows that it did not. Behind the scenes all was not as it seemed on the smooth institutional surface. The persistence of clientage reflects the limited development of bureaucratic authority under the Bourbons. Until the nineteenth century, official position in a formal power structure was not by itself enough to command obedience. Nor was it possible to control by this method alone the corporate institutions which possessed power in their own right. Formal office needed reinforcement by obligations of personal loyalty and informal connection.[24] The secretaries of state introduced in the mid-sixteenth century are usually described as 'bureaucratic' (so, by some authorities, are the *officiers*). And in a sense they were. They had a professional training in law or administration and a reasonably specialised function, they kept systematic records, they could not buy their offices and they were more responsive to their master than the *officiers* who could. But a few bureaucratic features do not add up to bureaucracy.

Neither the secretaries nor any other part of the Bourbon machine functioned in ways remotely resembling the bureaucracies of the nineteenth century.[25] Their records were usually regarded as their own property and deposited in their family archives – significantly selected as a more appropriate resting place than that of the state they were supposed to be serving. The function performed by an official bore little relation to what would now be called his job description. It was defined, most unbureaucratically, by his standing in an entirely different hierarchy of patrimonial relationships based on a code of social deference and loyalty alien to the nineteenth century. Our earlier study of the intendants showed that similar appearances are deceptive. The standing of the man determined the nature of the office, and not vice versa.[26] The crucial factor was influence with the king. There was consequently no clear divide between household and political service: a gentleman of the bedchamber like d'Aumont could wield as much influence over policy as a secretary of state. Surviving evidence leaves little doubt about this submerged iceberg lurking beneath the surface of events. Letters, diaries and memoirs are obsessed with patronage and government archives are crammed with requests for it. Historians have imposed nineteenth-century categories on seventeenth-century people. They would have done better to listen to them.

Bonding provincial institutions to the centre were patronage-brokers, who distributed royal favours to win support for the crown in the regions. They were chosen from the middling and lesser nobility as a counterweight to the grandees and court nobility who commanded their own clientage groupings. Provence reveals an illuminating example of the patron–broker–client system.[27] The *parlement* of Aix was split between the clients of two rival *gros bonnets* (bigwigs), Henri de Forbin-Maynier, baron d'Oppède, and Charles de Grimaldi, marquis de Régusse. At different times they were brokers who used their patronage powers as a political machine to influence *parlementaire* decision-making. Oppède was a client of Colbert, who found him an invaluable ally in the management of the Estates, *parlement* and municipal authorities of Provence. Agents like him were especially vital in attaching to the central government the peripheral provinces of the east and south.

Fifteen or more of his kinsmen and clients occupied high office in the town government of Aix. He also wielded extensive influence in the provincial Estates. In 1664 he reported to Colbert before a meeting of the assembly that as it contained many of his clients it would assuredly fulfil the minister's wishes. As the intendant of Provence was also a client of Colbert's, he could rely on Oppède's services as local fixer and troubleshooter. Selectively opening doors and securing offices for those who would be most useful, he maintained his following by a stream of material benefits. He also intervened on behalf of his clients when adroit queue-jumping was required or the usual channels proved inadequate. In 1661 he requested Chancellor Seguier to intervene in a lawsuit on behalf of his first cousin. In return for his brokering Oppède took a commission, since a portion of royal patronage was diverted to the use of his own friends and family. The process was circular. As Oppède was renowned for his friends in high places, his gang expanded faster. And the more support he won for the government in Provence, the more fuel Colbert pumped into the pipeline.

Ministers were bombarded with letters from provincial brokers, each eager to project an image of dependable influence and discredit their rivals. At a distance of 400 miles it was hard for secretaries of state to piece together an accurate local picture. Régusse lost the battle because his reputation was destroyed by d'Oppède's innuendos against him: he suffered from no longer being a broker but managed to hold his own through a network of lucrative commercial connections. Similar rivalries at court complicated local power struggles in ways which would have been unthinkable in a bureaucratic chain of command. Pierre de Bonzi, cardinal-archbishop of Narbonne, manipulated the Languedoc Estates on behalf of his patron, Colbert. He was undermined partly by his notorious adultery. His not especially narrow-minded but highly chauvinist monarch finally expelled the woman from the province. More damaging was his quarrel with an *intendant*. Had they both worked for Colbert their enmity would have been subsumed in common loyalty to their boss; but his rival's patron was Colbert's enemy, Louvois. Bonzi was beaten when Colbert's death left him without a friend at court.[28] Another complication was that relationships between brokers and their clients were fluid and patron-hopping was frequent. Behind extravagant professions of eternal devotion lay the calculating search for a master who could deliver juicier benefits. Some clients happily served two patrons without having to make a final choice. The same was true in relation to central government and, though other brokers veiled their operations behind a smokescreen of rhetoric, Oppède and Régusse were honest in their selfishness. They were in the racket for what they could get out of it: from top to bottom it was based on mutual self-interest. Clientage relied on persuasion rather than autocratic command, on personal loyalty and gratitude rather than bureaucratic hierarchies.

Oppède started as a lesser noble, but his successor as royal broker underlines Louis XIV's retreat to more resoundingly aristocratic norms. The family of François de Castellane, comte de Grignan, was descended from Charlemagne and participated in the First Crusade. His monumental château dominated the Rhône valley north of Avignon and boasted a façade with 365 windows and a staff of eighty servants. According to Madame de Sévigné, Grignan's daughter-in-law, there were rarely fewer than a hundred guests. These included the monarchs of Spain and Portugal and regular throngs of bishops, cardinals and ambassadors *en route* to and from Italy. As military lieutenant-general, he led the nobles of Provence in most of Louis XIV's wars, and in 1707 the old man halted Eugene's advance into France. He died on the road from Marseille at the age of eighty-five, coming home after representing the king at the annual meeting of the Estates. By then he was virtual viceroy of the province. Yet a contemporary noted that he had little inclination for administrative matters: his real taste was for the aristocratic pleasures of hunting, feasting and entertaining. Clearly the king was here entrusting his authority to a servant who was already a great nobleman. Nor did Grignan let him down in a spell of office spanning four decades.[29] Equally clearly, the crown's relationship with such a man could be based only on co-operation, not on command. In no sense were orders autocratically transmitted down a bureaucratic line: the trick was to persuade groups with independent power that their interest overlapped with the king's. Clientage can be made to work as part of 'absolutism' only if that concept is drained of half its content.

THE ELITE

Louis XIV was more sensitive than his predecessors to the aspirations of the grandees. An aristocrat to his fingertips, he was never happier than when immersed in military planning and the management of dogs, horses and entertainments. He was aware that the activities of military commanders, provincial governors and diplomats were essentially aristocratic: their posts should be filled resplendently with nobles of the highest status rather than with riff-raff who would have to defer socially to half the people they encountered. Though he checked on false noble titles and cracked down on corrupt seigneurial justice, it was made clear that he had no intention of appointing robe nobles to positions traditionally reserved for sword nobles. This cured aristocratic paranoia which had been building up since the sixteenth century. He discontinued the practice of replacing disloyal provincial governors with new nobles of inferior status and rarely appointed at less than ducal level. When it was expedient to deprive a family who had enjoyed hereditary tenure of a governorship, he took pains to avoid making dangerous enemies. Longueville, governor of Normandy, had been a leading *frondeur*. Louis transferred his powers to a safer man but agreed as a consolation prize to recognise him as a prince of the blood royal, in view of his descent from a Valois bastard line.

The king could hardly be unaware of the grandees' resentment of exclusion from power and patronage under the cardinals – nor of their behaviour in the Fronde. While princes of the blood held Paris for the rebels, he had been obliged to lie in bed in the Palais Royal and be inspected by a plebeian deputation who verified his non-removal by the wicked Mazarin. It was a humiliation he never forgot. Much is heard of his determination to deprive the grandees of the capacity for a reprise. His intention of conciliating them is less celebrated. For if he had noted grandees among the *frondeurs* he also spotted Montmorency-Bouteville, whose father Richelieu had beheaded for duelling. Mousnier's great work on the formal institutions of government takes little account of hidden power structures and unrecorded conversations. He finds few sword nobles advising the king because he is looking in the wrong place. But they were there. Noailles, Chevreuse, Chaulnes, Villeroy, d'Estrées and d'Aumont were among his most trusted advisers. They were married into ministerial families like Colbert, Le Tellier and Lionne; they were entrusted with the education of young members of the royal family; and they occupied top ecclesiastical, military and diplomatic posts.[30] The only sanctum which they did not penetrate was the council of state or *conseil d'en haut,* to which strong monarchs had appointed great sword nobles at no time in the previous four centuries.

Louis chose as his councillors and secretaries of state robe or lesser nobles who owed their exalted positions entirely to royal favour. This practice was traditional and not, as still frequently alleged, novel. Since the fourteenth century the benefits of excluding grandees were obvious. They were selfish and unreliable, with a tendency to serve on their own terms rather than the king's. Louis was more relaxed in his approach: he was a good judge of character with an instinct about who could be trusted. If he took advice from grandees, it was because he asked for it and not because they had a right to give it. Resentment of the king's parvenu advisers is one of those developments which are momentously located in a writer's *own* period, with implicit claims for its unique importance. Like the rise of the middle class, of whose mythology it forms a part, it was always happening. It is first reported in twelfth-century England. Philip IV of France (1285–1314) was notorious for his choice of plebeian councillors. Like Louis XIV, he has been credited with 'absolutist' appetites based on titbits of Roman law with which they tempted him. Louis' originality, if any, lay not in refusing to appoint great nobles to high office but in awarding his officials the same social status as if he had. Saint-Simon's exaggerated emphasis on the low origin of the new secretaries was not because it was new but because it was being obscured.[31]

A twin élite therefore dominated central government under Louis XIV. The secretaries of state were robe nobles whose relatively low social status was appropriate to their close association with clerks and files of paper. They were, sniggered contemporaries, 'men of pen and ink'. Though the dazzling marriages which the king arranged for them would ultimately launch a great dynasty, a social gulf separated them from the princely landowners whose power in the provinces could not be ignored. Both these groups, with their clients planted in every crevice in the kingdom, were the monarch's own faction. The reintegration of the sword nobility into the ruling circle defused one of the grievances which had caused the Fronde. It also explodes the picture of Louis as the monarch whose bourgeois bureaucrats marginalised feudal nobles and inaugurated 'absolutist' centralisation, herald of the modern world. It was painted by Toqueville in 1856, and though faded is still with us.[32] Modern research has proved that corporate and noble bodies were an integral and not an obsolete part of the system of government. But Toqueville's view survives – and for an obvious reason. Noble-dominated institutions must be presented as outside the system: the system is 'absolutism' and if they are inside they destroy it. Neither centrally nor locally were nobles deprived of power. Harding has shown the continued importance of aristocratic governors as allies of intendants, Mettam of sword nobles as advisers of the king and Kettering of patronage-brokers as fixers of everything. *Intendants* worked through regional bosses who wielded influence and authority in their own right: they were not a substitute for them. Had they tried to be they would have swiftly discovered the limitations of royal authority without local allies. Nobles were still in charge in the provinces.

INSTRUMENTS OF SELF-GOVERNMENT

The machinery initially considered posed a lesser threat to royal control, since it owed its power and existence to the king's commission. More deadly, if mishandled, were the agencies endowed with ready-made authority of their own. The assemblies and councils of province, town and village, nobles, clergy and professions, owed their power to their representative and corporate status. In that sense they existed independently of the king. They are crucial to any evaluation of 'absolutism', which is still alleged to have marginalised or crushed all organizations apart from its bureaucrats and standing armies.[33]

A vital feature of 'absolutism' is the erosion of the independence of the judiciary. In order to establish it once and for all the *parlements* had to be crushed. Historians of 'absolutism' find the achievement conveniently symbolised by the 1673 decree removing their right to remonstrate *before* registration. Yet it should by now be apparent that there was no requirement for such drama. The pushy behaviour of the *parlement* under Mazarin was its response to an unusual situation – a minority government dominated by a foreign favourite, and arguably an incompetent and despotic one. From 1661 neither condition obtained. By ending the rule of a chief minister and governing alone, Louis satisfied one of the dearest wishes of the *frondeurs*. It is true that he firmly forbade the *parlement* ever again to interfere in matters of state. But he also initiated a policy of compromise and cooperation. The quiescence of the courts is explained by the crown's avoidance of issues over which to quarrel and by its delegation to them of an active role in its reform programme.[34] Investigation of the financiers, the policing of Paris and the abuse of noble powers in the remote Auvergne absorbed them more than disputes with the crown. The *parlement* of Toulouse was assigned a flattering role in the management of Languedoc.[35]

Between 1667 and 1673 royal policy had elicited not a single remonstrance and there was no expectation of a return to the provocations of Mazarin. The loss of the right to remonstrate was evidently not regarded by the judges as a major constitutional deprivation. They made no fuss and viewed the modification in the way it was presented, as a temporary wartime measure aimed at irresponsible provincial *parlements*. War had just been declared against the Dutch and the government was anxious to forestall obstruction of its financial necessities. In fact Louis' fiscal policy was constitutionally impeccable. He imposed new levies only in war emergencies, checked their legality with the judges and withdrew them when war ended. There is no evidence that the king intended the 1673 decree to be permanent, but as war continued until 1713 it lasted for the rest of his reign.[36]

Apart from the increasingly desperate hunt for tangible steps on the ascent to 'absolutism', there is no reason why significant constitutional change should be read into the restrictive rules of 1673. Mettam draws attention to what few have noticed – that they related only to letters patent, a form of legislation mainly affecting grants to individuals. Ordinances, edicts and declarations, which covered the majority of legislation, were not involved.[37] Retention of *parlementaire* teeth is indicated by their discreet sabotage of royal edicts which were disliked and by their vigorous opposition when a row did erupt over papal power in 1713. The *parlements*' stated aims and responsibilities in this respect were identical to those enunciated in the wrangle over the Pragmatic Sanction of Bourges, which raised the same issue in 1438.[38] Nor did their judicial role lack the spirit of independence. Though in other countries the outcome of state trials was rarely in doubt, Louis XIV could not secure a death sentence for Fouquet, the disgraced finance minister. The independence of the judges was assured since they had purchased their offices: whatever they said or did, the king could not dismiss them. If they had accepted a newly humbled role in an 'absolutist' state, it was not apparent. For its own part, the crown never fundamentally dissented from the *parlement*'s claim to vet royal legislation and verify its consistency with existing law. Louis also relied on its backing against the Pope and in all matters concerning the royal succession; and before he died he left his will in its care. He did not therefore regard it as merely a judicial court.[39]

If the judiciary preserved its integrity so, by seventeenth-century standards, did civil liberties. They are popularly supposed to be one of the chief casualties of 'absolutism', and Richelieu's regime was certainly not forward in the provision of health care. Again the contrast with Louis XIV is marked. The judicial murders which disgraced the cardinal's management of the nobility were not a feature: in a long reign there were no executions for treason. Whatever the identity of the Man in the Iron Mask, it is perhaps significant that he was kept alive and not accommodated more cheaply in a coffin. In spite of his divine right claims of omniscience, Louis tolerated political – though not religious – dissent. Even here his intolerance is exaggerated. He presided over no *autos-da-fé*, such as the burning of eighteen heretics eagerly witnessed by his Spanish cousin Charles II in 1680. He made no serious attempt to suppress the infidelities of writers such as Bayle and Fontenelle, who were members of academies of which he was patron.[40] The circle of critics which emerged in the 1690s around the duke of Burgundy advocated grandees in government, representative Estates in every province and free trade for economic growth. The group's theorist, Fénelon, made stinging personal criticisms of the king. Yet no attempt was made to terminate the influence of these malcontents on the heir to the throne, nor to deprive them of their place among Louis' closest advisers. Far more ordinary people were unafraid to grumble, either to the king about his ministers or to ministers about their subordinates. A few developed a sophisticated complaints procedure, exploiting the knowledge that some measures were backed with more enthusiasm by some ministers than by others.[41]

'Absolutism' may be a moot point in just over half France. But Louis XIV was certainly not an 'absolutist' monarch in the *pays d'état*. That is no trifling exception. Too often historians implicitly compare French provinces with English counties. It is the wrong analogy. Languedoc's separatist traditions and institutions were more formidable than those of the most self-conscious English county. Furthermore, Languedoc was nearly twice the size of Wales. Provincial Estates were a major governmental preoccupation and the king's approach was as traditional as Richelieu's. There is a clear distinction between employing them and promoting their obsolescence, but few historians are anxious to make it. Instead of suppressing or bypassing them he adopted the usual policy of manipulating them through the brokers. But the scale of the operation marked a new advance in royal control. Previously a few royal clients were planted in the Estates. Louis XIV and Colbert nobbled most of the bishops and nobles who attended the Estates of Languedoc, and to make assurance doubly sure they put the deputies of the third estate on their pension list as well. Where numbers were so great that bribes would have required an increase in the national revenue, they squared a prominent noble such as Rohan. He then packed the Estates of Brittany with his own clients. Another effective trick was to change the place of assembly at the last minute and inform only the government's followers. While disaffected elements rambled round trying to find the meeting, the crown's allies were taking the lead.

Colbert raised previous manipulation techniques to a fine art. He relied more heavily than his forerunners on the intendants, most of whom were his own clients. Fundamental to all his methods was what one of them called 'sweetness and fear' – a subtle blend of persuasion and intimidation achieved by the flow or withdrawal of royal favour. In Provence the redoubtable Oppède managed the Estates as dependably as the *parlement*. His inconvenient death – in the middle of an assembly – led to the swift substitution of Grignan, who became involved in a power struggle with Janson-Forbin, Oppède's kinsman. Competition for government recognition as the crown's broker could lead to serious feuding – a drawback of patronage as a method of control. Grignan nevertheless managed the Estates success- fully for decades, and Colbert leaned on similar allies in the other *pays d'état*.

The problem of control varied according to the constitutions of the different assemblies. In most the Estates met and voted separ- ately: the clergy and nobility could therefore outvote the third estate. In Languedoc the third estate had twice the deputies of the other two and they all voted together: it could therefore outvote the other two. Some met only three or four times a decade, while others presented the crown with an annual problem.[42] Major argues that the extent of royal control over the *pays d'état* indicates the final establishment of 'absolutism'. Yet on his own evidence the Estates were reborn under Louis XIV in terms of the nobles attending them. Between ten and thirty-one participated in the Estates of Brittany under the Valois. Under Louis XIV the number rose to 500.[43] Nor is there any evidence that the Estates had become a rubber stamp. The meticulous preparations made by royal agents before their meetings suggest that co-operation could not be taken for granted. Tactful handling, bribery, bargaining and the avoidance of controversial issues were as responsible for their apparent quiescence as for the *parlements*'.[44]

In 1600 Estates met regularly to consent to taxation in two-thirds of France. By 1700 they met regularly in one-third of France. In Normandy, Guyenne and Auvergne Estates ceased to meet in Louis XIV's reign, owing to the hostility of royal officials and jealousy among the members who composed them. There is little record of local protest against their demise. And nowhere do the king's *Memoirs*, prepared for the guidance of the dauphin, advocate the *élus* favoured by Sully and Marillac as an alternative to the Estates. When Colbert criticised the Estates it was usually on the grounds that they oppressed the local people, not that they stood for a principle of consent uncongenial to 'absolutism'. There is therefore little evidence that the crown desired their disappearance on principle. In its continued habit of convening assemblies of all kinds and for many purposes, there is ample evidence that it did not.

The impression during and after Louis XIV's reign is of a regime trying to find a satisfactory substitute for consultative mechanisms which had been lost. In areas where they no longer met regularly assemblies of the three Estates were summoned in 1694 and 1710 to discuss the new war taxes, the Capitation and the Tenth. In 1700 the larger towns received their first directive since 1596 to send deputies to a special meeting on the lines of the Assembly of Notables of that year. Estates were revived in territories recently added to the realm, such as Artois, Hainault and Lille. Long after regular Estates meetings disappeared in Anjou and Poitou, districts were represented by a permanent syndic in continuous collaboration and contact with the royal administration.[45] Towards the end of his reign the king assembled a council of commerce, in what its historian has dubbed an important demonstration of the consultative principle.[46] All these forms of consultation were ignored by nineteenth-century historians who considered that national assemblies alone merited attention.

On a national scale there was admittedly little representation to attend to. The absence of the Estates-General between 1614 and 1789 is a well-publicised feature of French 'absolutism'. Its failure to meet more than twice between 1460 and 1560 is less celebrated. This suggests that there was no objection to the body in principle, but to its lamentable performance in practice. Its disappearance was due to its uselessness as a consultative mechanism rather than to its effectiveness. Most historians nevertheless take literally the confident assertions of some seventeenth-century political theorists that the king could tax without consent. This fits snugly as a central plank of autocratic 'absolutism'.[47] In fact such publications had a polemical purpose, were exploited by the government as propaganda which it did not necessarily believe and were a far cry from political reality.[48] The crown gained consent to taxation by negotiating individually with a multiplicity of corporate groups such as provincial Estates and *parlements*, as well as ecclesiastical, municipal and aristocratic assemblies. What it lacked was any national consensual voice to make decisions binding on the realm.

A further channel of participation in public affairs was provided by parish and village assemblies. Though the crown may have regulated more than previously their mode of operation, they continued to meet as before to manage their affairs. Assemblies usually met about once a month after Sunday mass, in the church or the square before it. Any inhabitant could attend, though the vote was confined to heads of households including widows. A quorum of ten was necessary for valid deliberation and the *curé* or seigneur's judge presided. Had Louis XIV summoned the Estates-General, this body would have drawn up the *cahier* of complaints for the king's attention and subsequently embodied them in a more comprehensive document incorporating the grievances of the whole area. It would also have nominated two representatives to speak for them in the selection of deputies of the third estate. Village assemblies could participate in the compilation of local custom.

Though justice was the prerogative of the lord of the manor (*seigneur*), clichés about downtrodden peasants should be approached critically. The village community collectively brought lawsuits against the *seigneur*: it sought legal advice, appointed attorneys and often won. It was not invited to discuss national issues but elected the assessors and collectors responsible for raising the tax charged upon the community. The only exemptions from this onerous distinction were the old, sick and destitute, schoolmasters and fathers of eight children. The community owned communal property in the form of local lands and resources; it could also impose local taxation. Matters of economic regulation, poor relief, health care, education and policing were handled by the assembly. It fixed local wages and prices, maintained roads and bridges, and paid the village crier, schoolmaster and midwife. Thus purely local matters were left to local people and they participated in precisely what must have been of most concern to them.[49] Many historians seem to imagine that these matters came within the national scope of Colbert's economic and social planning. In fact he had no interest whatever in parochialism unless it also carried national implications. Only those determined to discover Stalin's role-model in Colbert could have imagined otherwise.[50]

Much the same is true of the towns, whose repression under the royal jackboot has been predictably exaggerated. They were distinguished from the Estates by the frequently irresponsible attitudes of the elected élites who ran them. Resources were more likely to be squandered than directed to the social administration for which they were intended. Though the crown had no wish to take over municipal duties, it was anxious that someone should. It also wanted to raise more revenue from a notoriously tight-fisted source. Consequently the crown enlisted the support of local bishops and nobles and attempted to influence council elections. By an edict of 1692 the king established the right to choose a sympathetic mayor; but he had no intention of ending local participation in elections and in practice central control was less than the government's already modest aspirations. Two months later, Dijon was permitted to buy the right to elect its mayor.[51]

A neglected instrument of government under Louis XIV was the Church.[52] It was the greatest of the corporate bodies with its own source of independent power which was nevertheless an integral part of the state. Its assemblies were consulted over taxation and its bishops were exploited as a means of administrative control. Archbishop de Bonzi of Narbonne was as noted for patronage-broking as for lechery: he was Colbert's invaluable ally as president of the temperamental Languedoc Estates. The Church owned at least a tenth of the land, and on the strength of its tithe it advanced enormous loans to government which were rarely repaid. Every five years it made to the crown a free gift (*don gratuit*) which was invariably pronounced inadequate. Francis I had asserted control over ecclesiastical appointments, though Louis XIV failed to beat the Pope over the *régale* (right of appointment to empty bishoprics). Education from university to primary level was in its hands and its pulpits were the main media of communication in each of the parishes of France. *Curés* read out royal ordinances and letters patent when they preached, even after the edict of 1695 which relieved them of the obligation. The Church's importance as a government agency necessitated royal intervention. The monarch's absolute power was emphasised to establish his independence of any superior authority. Of these the most conspicuous was the Pope.

Louis XIV's handling of institutions with independent sources of power establishes the status of 'absolutism' as a problematic concept. As a system of government it is supposed to marginalise them: they are kicked into subservience or bypassed and left to rot. The Sun King did neither. He treated them as agencies of consultation and consent – showing that his regime was not autocratic. He treated them as guardians of corporate rights and liberties – showing that it was not despotic. And he treated them as agencies of administration – showing that it was not bureaucratic. It is true that he denied them any right to meddle in matters of state: policy was made by the royal prerogative alone, with the help of those whom the king chose to advise him. In this he consummated the work of Francis I and Richelieu, and confirmed that never again would feudal lords share prerogative rights with the king. Is that all 'absolutism' means? If so, we have another problem. For the king of England did the same.

REFERENCES

1   Mettam R 1988 *Power and Faction in Louis XIV's France*. Basil Blackwell, pp. 96–7, 179
2   Mettam R 1988, pp. 95–9
3   Rule JC 1969 King and Minister: Louis XIV and Colbert de Torcy. In Thomson MA *William III and Louis XIV*. Liverpool University Press, pp. 214–15
4   David R and de Vries HP 1958 *The French Legal System*. Oceana, pp. 9–12
5   Isambert FA 1822–33 *Recueil général des anciennes lois françaises depuis l'an 420 jusqu'à la révolution de 1789*
6   Goubert P 1972 *Louis XIV and Twenty Million Frenchmen*. Vintage, pp. 55–6
7   Bluche F 1990 *Louis XIV*. Basil Blackwell, p. 354
8   Mettam R 1988, p. 48
9   Bluche F 1990, p. 351–2
10 Anderson MS 1988 *War and Society in the Europe of the Old Regime*. Fontana, pp. 29–32
11 Mettam R 1988, pp. 36, 216–24, 239; Parker D 1983 *The Making of French Absolutism*. Arnold, p. 137; Duffy M 1980 *The Military Revolution and the State 1500–1800*. Exeter University Press, pp. 30, 40; Scott SF 1978 *The Response of the Royal Army to the French Revolution*. Oxford University Press, p. 27
12 Munck T 1990 *Seventeenth-Century Europe*. Macmillan, pp. 344, 347–8; Goubert P 1972, p. 96
13 Bonney R 1978 *Political Change in France under Richelieu and Mazarin, 1624–1661*. Oxford, *passim*; Mousnier R 1984 *The Institutions of France under the Absolute Monarchy 1598–1789, volume 2: The Organs of State and Society*. Chicago University, p. 159; Knecht RJ 1991 *Richelieu*. Longman, pp. 144–7
14 Mettam R 1988, pp. 214–15
15 Campbell PR 1988 *The Ancien Régime in France*. Basil Blackwell, p. 52
16 Mettam R 1977 *Government and Society in Louis XIV's France*. Macmillan, *passim*
17 Mettam R 1988, pp. 211–12
18 Harding RR 1978 *Anatomy of a Power Elite: the provincial governors of early modern France*. Yale University Press , pp. 189–90
19 Emmanuelli F-X 1981 *Un myth de l'absolutisme bourbonien: l'intendance du milieu du xviie siècle à la fin du xviiie siècle*. University of Aix-en-Provence, pp. 174–6
20 Mettam R 1981 Two-Dimensional History: Mousnier and the Ancien Regime. *History*, **66**, p. 229
21 Campbell PR 1988, pp. 57–8

22 Kettering S 1986 *Patrons, Brokers and Clients in Seventeenth-Century France.* Oxford University Press, pp. 68–97
23 Beik W 1985 *Absolutism and Society in Seventeenth-century France: state power and provincial aristocracy in Languedoc.* Cambridge University Press, *passim*; Anderson P 1989 *Lineages of the Absolutist State.* Verso, pp. 15–42
24 Campbell PR 1988, pp. 59–60
25 Campbell PR 1988, p. 54
26 Campbell PR 1988, p. 60
27 Kettering S 1986, pp. 40–67, 104–11
28 Kettering S 1986, pp. 138–9
29 Kettering S 1986, pp. 104–11
30 Mettam R 1988, pp. 81–91
31 Fawtier R 1960 *The Capetian Kings of France: Monarchy and Nation 987–1328.* Macmillan, pp. 41–7; Bluche F 1976 The Social Origins of the Secretaries of State under Louis XIV. In Hatton R (ed.) *Louis XIV and Absolutism.* Macmillan, p. 95;
32 De Toqueville A 1966 edn *The Ancien Régime and the French Revolution.* Collins, pp. 63–5, 83–8
33 Subtelny O 1986 *Domination of Eastern Europe.* Sutton, pp. 55–7
34 Hamscher AN 1976 *The* Parlement *of Paris after the Fronde.* Pittsburgh, pp. 200–2
35 Beik W 1985, pp. 309–10
36 Mettam R 1988, pp. 264–8
37 Mettam R 1988, p. 267
38 Shennan JH 1974 *The Origins of the Modern European State 1450–1725.* Hutchinson, pp. 47–9
39 Shennan JH 1968 *The* Parlement *of Paris.* Eyre and Spottiswoode, p. 283
40 Bluche F 1990, pp. 491–2
41 Mettam R 1988, pp. 91–2, 185–6
42 Major JR 1980, pp. 622–72; Kettering S 1986, pp. 167–75; Mettam R 1988, p. 271
43 Major JR 1980 *Representative Government in Early Modern France.* Yale University, p. 671
44 Miller J 1984 The Potential for 'Absolutism' in later Stuart England. *History,* **69**, pp. 199–200
45 Major JR 1980, pp. 631–6; Parker D 1983, p. 139; Mousnier R 1979 *The Institutions of France under the Absolute Monarchy 1598–1789, Volume 1: Society and the State.* Chicago University Press, p. 611
46 Schaeper TJ 1983 *The French Council of Commerce 1700–1715: a study of mercantilism after Colbert.* Columbus
47 Koenigsberger HG 1987 *Early Modern Europe 1500–1789.* Longman, p. 182
48 Mettam R 1988, pp. 29–32
49 Mousnier R 1979, pp. 551–7
50 Mettam R 1988, pp. 15–16, 188–9; Cole CW 1964 *Colbert and a Century of French Mercantilism.* Archon
51 Mettam R 1988, pp. 276–7
52 Campbell PR 1988, pp. 52–3; Mousnier R 1979, p. 552

CHAPTER THREE
A Highroad to Revolution?

In an influential article Elton berated those who view history backwards. He focused on the depiction of early seventeenth-century parliamentary opposition as a series of rehearsals for its challenge to the king in the Civil War. He might with equal justice have criticised those whose real interest in eighteenth-century France lies in locating the causes of the Revolution. The chief culprit is of course the creaking 'absolutist' structure erected by Louis XIV. What has traditionally been depicted as a royal monopoly of power was increasingly resented by the thrusting classes excluded. Simultaneously the administrative disorder characteristic of all early modern states has been magnified through the Revolution's lens into structural defects leading to the monarchy's collapse under its own deadweight.

This travesty is the result of the rear-view driving mirror approach to history. Historians career into the past with their eyes glued on the present, or at least on the end of the story, in this case the spectacular fulfilment of all things eighteenth-century – the Revolution. The result is a historiographical pile-up. Most of the issues and tensions of 1789 and after were probably generated by the revolutionary dynamic as it unfolded, but they have been read back into the preceding period. *Ancien régime* studies have been dominated by the search for revolutionary classes, movements, ideologies and institutions: a historiographical agenda has been drawn up with one eye on the future. Any historical event larger than a blip produces a crop of explanations about why it was bound to happen. This is to ignore the wafer-thin line which divides regimes between success and failure: there is nothing inevitable about either. Until late in the 1780s revolution was widely expected – but in England rather than France.[1]

It is possible to argue that the Revolution was produced by a series of fortuitous coincidences – a sequence of events in an unpredictable order. While each of these, like the royal bankruptcy of 1788, may have a long-term cause, they do not have the same causes. Nor are such causes the origin of the French Revolution. If it had never happened they would be the long-term causes of a sequence of random events which led to nothing. Its occurrence owes more to the mishap of two ditheringly despotic rulers than to the structural defects of the old regime. Obsessive digging for deep roots is an activity more suited to landscape gardeners than historians.

FACTION AND IDEOLOGY

The rulers of eighteenth-century France were ill-fitted to cope with the eternal faction struggle. The Regent Orléans suffered from the same infirmities as the cardinals. Fleury, who followed as unofficial chief minister, has not been the subject of a modern biography and remains mysterious. Louis XV was active and intelligent but lacked the confidence in his own judgement which enabled Louis XIV to keep the same ministers in office for decades. He switched constantly from one faction to another to keep himself out of their pockets, but merely emerged as a ditherer. Louis XVI was well-meaning, but without the personal authority to suggest that his decisions were final. Political leaders became convinced that they could topple any minister if they pushed hard enough. The increased resistance of *parlements* and Estates to royal wishes may conveniently be interpreted as their response to an increasingly unacceptable 'absolutist' regime, which was paying the price for inability to adapt while times changed. It can more plausibly be read as a signal that the monarchy had changed rather than the times. Adroit political management had succumbed to heavy-handed bungling, a nice equilibrium of factions to imbalance, comfortable tradition to a dizzy rate of innovation and prudent moderation to trigger-happy despotism. Corporate bodies were more troublesome after the Sun King's death because his successors simultaneously created issues *and* disaffected groups to exploit them. Thus faction feuding, which was normal, reached danger level, which was not.

Constitutional conflict was inseparable from court faction. There was never one official view of the nature and extent of royal power. The court was always divided: contemporary and current historical usage which equates it with the government line is often wide of the mark. For the division was not merely between courtiers in office and courtiers out of it. Even royal ministers usually disagreed over constitutional and policy issues. Unanimity in government circles was highly unlikely, since Louis XV emulated Louis XIV by deliberately encouraging divisions among his ministers in order to avoid domination by one faction. Had Burgundy lived, Louis XIV would have been succeeded by a grandson whose advisers favoured the establishment of more effective mechanisms of consultation. The confrontations between Machault and d'Argenson in the 1740s, and between Choiseul and Maupeou in the 1760s, are merely the most spectacular examples of rivalries based partly on differing evaluations of royal power. This even extended to musical appreciation. The court feud between supporters of French and Italian opera reflected opposed political philosophies – the one ceremonial and imperial and the other informal and egalitarian.[2] Louis XVI attempted less successfully to balance the clashing constitutional priorities of Calonne, Breteuil and Vergennes. The intense rivalry between court factions made it inevitable that they would espouse conflicting views of the constitution. Rival ministers had to be overthrown by any means that came to hand: denouncing them for exceeding their rightful powers simultaneously undermined their legitimacy and attracted support from interests offended by their policies. Constitutional ideologies were weapons in the power struggle: they offered a menu of options which monarchs and politicians could select as appropriate.

The crown's ability to manipulate faction in order to secure compliance with its policies is only half the story. Faction could also sabotage them. Opposition from corporate institutions was usually the result of factional quarrels overflowing the confines of the court and polarising other political arenas. Nor was this accidental. Once a minister had been appointed, his rivals directed all their efforts to eroding royal confidence in him; even his colleagues would gain by replacing him with a relative or client. No one was safe. Administrative gifts alone were insufficient for survival in this jungle of vendettas: a minister needed manipulative skills, cool nerve, deft footwork and devoted friends. Something could be achieved by sniping at the offender in council meetings, though it was known to annoy Louis XV. Court intrigue based on gossip and innuendo could be effective if the victim lacked an intelligence network and counter-smear agents of his own. The ultimate weapon was the corporate bodies. There policies could be obstructed and sabotaged so that their author was comprehensively discredited in royal eyes. Clients in *parlements* and Estates consequently became a vital requirement for those engaged in the power struggle.

Small wonder then that few reform plans survived in this scrum: too many had an interest in their failure. The merits and demerits of particular reform schemes were seldom the real issue among the politicians involved. They would support or, more usually, oppose them after coolly calculating the political benefit to themselves. Few politicians were interested in policy as such: its promotion or destruction was a means to an end, that of capturing the attention of the monarch and winning his favour. The power and prestige of faction and family could then be promoted with sensational speed. There is formidable evidence that among the élite power-seeking factions were the primary allegiance, overruling corporate and ideological loyalties. Too many groups out of office jettisoned their beliefs once they were in office.

The crown clashed repeatedly with corporate bodies. On every occasion faction lurked beneath the constitutional rhetoric spotlit by the history books. Whispered conversations in antechambers are tricky historical materials – or non-materials. Until recently historians considered the evidence conjectural and the subject matter trivial, compared with the social and economic forces which were the true motor of history. Court faction was written up as a titillating mixture of historical journalism and salacious gossip, the preserve of Hollywood and Nancy Mitford. As court politics are charted by scholars it becomes clear that they illuminate much that was previously obscure. The conflict of the 1750s can now be shown to reflect the successful attempt of a Jansenist and court party to bounce the Paris *parlement* into opposition. In the crisis of 1770–71 the show-down with the *parlement* was the direct consequence of the ferocious feud conducted across the council table by Maupeou and Choiseul. Opposition from the *parlement* alone could never have destroyed Turgot in 1776. Behind it skulked his own intriguing colleague in the ministry, Miromesnil. Price's research demonstrates the crucial impact of factional politics in precipitating the final crisis of 1787–89. A faction in the *parlement* was virulently opposed to Calonne and his reform schemes. It was largely created by the subversive intrigues of Breteuil, Calonne's colleague in the ministry. The excavator of this subterranean perspective errs only in believing the situation unusual.[3]

The most neglected element in the political history of the eighteenth century, as in the seventeenth, is therefore court faction. It is too often forgotten that monarchy was still personal. Under the influence of the Enlightenment the French government, like most others, assumed greater responsibilities and embarked on elaborate reform schemes. Administration became more professional and complex, and it was impossible for one man to master and monitor everything. But whether the ruler closely superintended the operation of government himself or left his ministers to get on with it, government was still carried on in his name. Political decisions and patronage were ultimately the king's. Politics therefore revolved round persuading him and undermining his confidence in rival advisers.

But because all depended on the royal person there was a risk that opposition to his ministers would be perceived as disloyal, if not treasonable. Few political gangs found it safe to operate without the blessing of a prominent member of the royal family or court nobility. As in the seventeenth century the princes of the blood were crucial. Another indication that power was seen as the personal delegation of the monarch is that successful opposition to the king's minister could be justified only by the convention that he was guilty of malpractice. Politicians were no longer playing for each other's heads, as before the mid-seventeenth century and again after 1789. In addition to loss of place and preferment, their fate was usually dignified exile to their estates. As well as creating a political tidal wave, the fall of the gregarious Choiseul in 1770 disrupted the social lives of half the population of Versailles.

Monarchs were aware of a shift in the resources of the nobles on whom they depended. In 1660 a duke's household might number a hundred servants and hangers-on, mostly designed to impress. A century later he would probably be down to a dozen needed to run the establishment – cook, coachman, maids, keepers and stable boys. The entourage of a hundred armed retainers with which his ancestors had travelled was mere nostalgia. Since there is evidence that many nobles had difficulty mobilising their forces during the Fronde, this change cannot be wholly attributed to the policies of Louis XIV. However, his permanent residence at Versailles after 1682 tempted about 250 grandees to move in on a semi-permanent basis. Their châteaux were maintained by a skeleton staff while most of their income was lavished on maintaining their prestige in Paris. Politicians now had to be courtiers. Opposition was therefore conducted more peacefully and less overtly but it was regarded by kings as almost as dangerous. They now lived in a world of palace coups, backstairs intrigue and treacherous courtiers, powdered, bewigged and reptilian.

Recent scholarship indicates that French monarchs and their court were the decisive generators of political action. It was not the only focus of power, but it remained the only central institution and from it radiated the networks which enmeshed all the rest. The problem in eighteenth-century France was therefore not the rise of a revolutionary class, ideology or institution. It was the same problem which periodically afflicted seventeenth- and sixteenth-century France – the failure of political management. The circumstances in which the monarch found himself were crucial in determining his successful control of competing groups besieging him – his character and abilities, his age, health and succession, his susceptibility to favourites and ability to be his own man. Resistance by corporate bodies was secondary to the crown's handling of court factions. What has previously been viewed as a constitutional drama can now be res-cripted as a gangland feud between operators pulling strings in every direction. This perspective necessitates much rewriting of history and the results are currently available, if at all, only in the learned form of Ph.D. dissertations. Campbell's useful introduction is so far almost alone among published works.[4]

DESPOTISM OR CONSENT?

Two threads are interwoven throughout this period. One is the government's Enlightened drive to rationalise, liberalise and equalise. It wished to increase personal rights and liberties and extend the organs of consent which defended them. Equally Enlightened was its response when existing organs of consent obstructed its progressive intentions. Autocratic fiat was employed in the belief that the higher law of Reason justified all – whether lesser mortals agreed or not. These twin inspirations of Enlightenment were incompatible. So were the Enlightenment's simultaneous attack on privilege in the name of equality and defence of it as one of the rights which constituted liberty. Had the monarch possessed the 'absolutist' powers with which he is credited, there would have been no dilemma. He would have wielded his legislative sovereignty to abolish a few tax exemptions, smooth away anomalies in the geographical distribution of the fiscal burden and eliminate vested interests among the collectors: that would have been the end of the matter. No one thought it that simple.

Most historians have recognised the practical difficulties of ignoring consent in a state based on co-operation, but it was also a question of the legitimacy of government action. The vital point is that in addition to its physical infirmity in the face of robust corporate institutions the monarchy lacked any theoretical basis for such initiatives. The royal prerogative did not extend to the private law which guaranteed the personal and property rights of subjects. According to the 'fundamental laws' of France their defence was the ruler's first domestic duty. Consequently the government felt unable to undertake the serious modification of those rights necessitated by fiscal reform without the consent of those involved. There is a growing scholarly consensus, still too little publicised, that the crown could not impose new taxation or fundamental reforms without consulting some form of representative assembly.[5] Political theorists might argue about whether the king was above or below the law, but in practice there was no doubt: private rights were defended by private law, which could not be altered without consent. The only alternative was despotism. Though the concept was an eighteenth-century obsession which left no cliché unturned, the disgust it encapsulated was real. Almost always pejorative, like 'fascist' today, it indicated the antithesis of legitimate monarchy.

The absence of consultative mechanisms in eighteenth-century France has been grossly exaggerated. Historians have partly taken their cue from official government propaganda, which chose instead to stress the absolute power of the crown. An exception is Burley, who has drawn attention to the respect paid to individual and corporate rights and to the persistent official interest in forms of representation which embodied them.[6] In 1774 a secretary of state admonished an incredulous British ambassador on the wildly inaccurate assumptions of his press and public. Louis XVI, the official was informed, could not order an arrested merchant to be freed: if he overruled legal decisions he would not be a monarch but a despot. The crown, contrary to the pronouncements of historians, had never gained the formal right of taxing without consent. By custom only the Estates-General had the constitutional right to give it. The permanent *taille* was levied by extension of its consent in 1439.[7] Too often written out of the story after 1614, its reappearance in 1788–89 is treated as the abandonment of the old order. The Estates-General was *part* of the old order. That is why, when George III's subjects celebrated the end of French despotism in 1789, Louis XVI had just held a more democratic election than any held up to then in England or France.

Not a decade had passed since its last meeting without a call for it to be reconvened, often from within government circles like Burgundy's early in the century. The government always took care not to encroach on its powers when drafting its own legislation. The proof of its survival as a living force rather than a relic was the ease with which elections were held in 1789. While the Estates-General was absent, however, its authority was wielded by the *parlement*. In this way a real financial limitation was placed on royal power, however absolute in its own prerogative areas. As well as legitimating interference with subjects' rights, consent was also perceived as having severely practical implications. Painful comparisons were drawn between the tax yield in *pays d'élection* and *pays d'état*. Normandy was one of the richest provinces but subject to a government *élu* it yielded its tax quota laboriously. Languedoc was one of the poorest but its tax was granted and collected by the provincial estates with embarrassing facility. The proceeds from both were the same.

Such considerations were present as ministers made repeated attempts during the century to clear blocked and inefficient channels of consultation. Burgundy's circle envisaged a major role for the Estates and in many ways provided a blueprint for the rest of the century. A major initiative by Laverdy in 1764–65 established a system of municipal assemblies designed to cut back the centralisation represented by Louis XIV's appointment of mayors. It institutionalised participation by local people in matters which most closely affected them and about which they knew best. Power was entrusted to assemblies of notables elected by deputies, who were themselves selected by occupational groups, crafts and corporations. The notables were to submit three candidates for the post of mayor, from which the king would select one. In 1771 the reform was rescinded by Terray, the new controller-general, who claimed it reduced royal power and clearly cherished an alternative concept of the constitution. Estates were established in Lorraine and Corsica on their annexation to France as a principal means of giving the government a sense of the province and winning its loyalty for the crown. Sweeping reforms in 1778–79 and 1787–88 established provincial assemblies, first for Berry and Guyenne and then throughout the *pays d'élection* which lacked them. In all of them third estate numbers were doubled and voting was by head, in order to prevent domination by nobles and clergy. Usually dismissed as the last wriggle of a doomed regime, this string of consultative initiatives prompts one to wonder how early it acquired precognition.

When consent to its reform proposals was not forthcoming, the crown's response was rather different. While with one hand it extended institutions which checked despotism, with the other it practised it.

A FORMATIVE MINORITY

The regime which followed the death of Louis XIV poses profound questions about the shape of eighteenth-century French history. The regent Orléans was a prince of the blood – the most deadly of the species, descended from the brother of a king. Like all his descendants, and most of his ancestors, he was playing for the throne, if a trifle more scrupulously than his seventeenth-century predecessor – and his great-great-grandson got it. It is odd that historians have not taken the family's machinations more seriously. They have shown more interest in Orléans' financial and administrative reforms than in his factional and dynastic self-seeking. Yet one without the other furnishes an inadequate explanation of the opposition he encountered. Reform schemes invariably offended corporate vested interests, but corporate bodies needed encouragement from friends at court before finding the will to resist. Such support was forthcoming from the gangs excluded by Orléans' *polysynodie* arrangement, which placed randy drinking cronies such as Biron and Brancas on the committees which replaced each secretary of state. According to Shennan it was merely a seductive façade designed to reward personal friends and win the support of grandees. The regent continued to consult old ministers such as Torcy and La Vrillière behind the scenes; and once the system had served its purpose by buying time for him to consolidate his authority it was wound up.[8] Since Biron and Brancas were principally noted for their energetic performance in the regent's orgies, this may reassure the historian. But it can hardly have comforted those left out.

Louis XV was five in 1715 and opposition could be more wholehearted, since policy was clearly not in any sense the king's. Orléans was hampered by frequently expressed suspicions that affairs, especially foreign, were conducted for the benefit of the house of Orléans and its kingly ambitions. He vainly attempted to buy support by restoring the right of remonstrance which Louis XIV had denied the *parlement*. Re-equipped with teeth, it used them. The major row was ignited by the regent's support for the financial schemes of the alleged financial wizard, John Law. In 1717 the *parlement* demanded a comprehensive account of the crown's financial situation – a clear case of trespass on matters of state. Having digested the regent's flat refusal, in 1718 it maintained its high profile by issuing an *arrêt* forbidding circulation of his newly coined money. Since control of the coinage of the realm was one of the most hallowed of royal prerogatives, this confirmed the impression of a political takeover. It then challenged Orléans' authority with a decree effectively blocking his support for Law's schemes: all foreigners, even if naturalised Frenchmen, were forbidden to participate in financial administration. It also informed him that no enactment was valid unless registered in the *parlement*, though it acknowledged the crown as sole legislator. This was consistent with its previous claims, to which it adhered until 1789: the crown was the initiator of legislation yet the *parlement* participated in the law-making process. The crown's position was not far removed, since it claimed to be sole legislator but simultaneously acknowledged its obligation to submit its decrees for approval. Only when the *parlement* encroached on the royal prerogative was the gap unbridgeable. In tones reminiscent of Louis XIII a century before, the *parlement* was forbidden to discuss any matter of state unless specifically invited to.

This offensive has been interpreted as a prompt move by the *parlement* to retrieve powers lost under Louis XIV. Again we have the picture of a corporate body, cowed by the heavy hand of 'absolutism', lying in wait for the moment to encroach. This all slots neatly into the 'absolutist' scenario. The alternative approach is to recall that royal minorities were inherently unstable. Since no one had an interest in weak monarchy, strong and active rulers were more likely to create satisfaction than sow seeds of future trouble. The *parlements* had no desire to trespass on the prerogatives of kings ruling personally and responsibly. Orléans offended on both counts. He was not a king and his methods were contemptuous of the *parlement* and of legality. He was caught in the same vicious circle which trapped Mazarin: the more a ruler was challenged, the more autocratic he was tempted to be. The misuse of prerogative, as usual, evoked an equal and opposite reaction. It was the old attempt to encroach on prerogative matters of state, once more ceasing to be seen as a no-go area in the alluring glow of a royal minority. Factions and the corporate bodies round which their tentacles wrapped had no need of 'absolutism' to keep them in check. All they required was skilful management and a little statesmanship. Shennan suggests that they did not get them from Orléans. Nor from Fleury, who followed the regent with a similar battery of *lits de justice*, arbitrary arrests and sentences of exile. He also made the fundamental mistake of allying himself with the Pope against Gallicanism, a tradition of national ecclesiastical independence which was built into French law. Not only was the policy perilously novel but it was forced on the *parlement* in an arbitrary manner with little regard for normal process of law.[9] It was an ominous prelude to the new reign.

LOUIS XV AND LOUIS XVI

The Revolution is traditionally presented as the outcome of preceding developments – a declining monarchy, a disaffected and ineffectual nobility, a rising bourgeoisie with revolutionary potential, if not intentions, and an Enlightened revolutionary ideology. Furet argues that this misses the point.[10] Marxism is fundamentally flawed in suggesting that revolution is the predictable result of social and economic change. The uniqueness of the 1789 Revolution is that it created a practice and ideology of political action which was totally unrelated to anything that came before. It was a bolt from the blue which transformed the language and experience of politics. A sudden change in political climate bounced developments into a new groove, which then launched a new set of chain reactions. The explosion of the people on to the political stage initiated democratic culture, as speeches and motions ceased to be aimed at educated people and addressed the masses. Their mobilisation unleashed unprecedented political forces. But the unique importance of the French Revolution in European history does not impart unique importance to its origins.

The administrative problems encountered by the French crown in its last years were common to most eighteenth-century monarchies. Even its celebrated financial embarrassments were less calamitous than usually asserted, though there were intractable problems. The receivers who collected and disbursed royal taxes were private business men, who between these operations lent the government its own money at interest. Much energy was devoted to making nobles, most of whom were poor, pay more. Meanwhile the principal tax-dodgers, the bourgeoisie, paid nothing. Nevertheless, by 1774 Terray had increased revenues by forty million *livres*, cut the deficit and halved anticipations on future income.[11]

Above all, the traditional interpretation of the Revolution has focused on a rising tide of conflict – between crown and *parlement*, crown and Jansenists, crown and *philosophes*, nobles and bourgeois, nobles and peasants. While this provides a resonant ensemble for the revolutionary chorus, it ignores the capacity of the *ancien régime* for absorbing and harmonising conflict. None of this was peculiar to the later eighteenth century and earlier confrontations were resolved as those of the reign of Louis XVI could have been – by political management and the resilient elasticity of the political system. Nor was it peculiar to France. Austria experienced widespread rejection of aristocratic values. A small but significant example is Mozart's *Marriage of Figaro* of 1786. Opera had previously preserved a theatrical apartheid. Aristocrats and lower orders were given contrasting styles of music, the one florid and graceful and the other dependent on plebeian dance rhythms. For the first time Figaro, a servant, was given a recitative with a princely orchestral accompaniment.[12] Equally, government attempts to extend consultation and participation were common after 1760 from London to St Petersburg. Pitt introduced parliamentary reform and Catherine II established assemblies to represent nobles, bourgeoisie and even peasants. There is no need to view similar French initiatives as the desperate measures of a doomed regime. The spread of literacy and political information accounts for them more plausibly.

Nor was the French monarchy, as is often claimed, uniquely musty and fuddy-duddy. Louis XVI was a modern-minded king who suffered attacks of antiquarianism at vital moments, such as his coronation and his meeting with the Estates-General in 1789. His reign bubbled with innovation. The main response was resistance rather than any wish to promote it more rapidly. Whether initiating plans for equalising taxation or releasing industry and commerce from economic shackles, the government's reforming tendencies ran into trouble. Religion was a central problem. Toleration for Protestants in 1787 was popular with progressive opinion but with no one else. In spite of the Bourbons' subsequent exclusion from the Enlightened Despots' club, they chose to present themselves as Enlightened. Yet when they soft-pedalled religion and tradition as their justification and embraced reason and humanity, they dangerously narrowed the basis of their authority. Catholic counter-revolution after 1789 was widespread and royal relics were treasured after 1793. This suggests that a safer foundation would have been to invoke sacred loyalties and trust to the throne and altar alliance.[13]

THE WAGES OF DESPOTISM

The most convincing evidence for French 'absolutism' has always been the persistent campaign mounted by the *parlements* against royal power in the decades before the Revolution. While there is still strong support for this view, it now appears that it may be in error. The first difficulty is the early date at which 'absolutism' was apparently being rejected. The *parlements* said or did nothing after 1750 which they had not said or done before. The Paris *parlement* mounted two of the most savage attacks of the century on Louis XIV over the Pope's *Unigenitus*

Bull and on his successor, the regent Orléans, over finance. If the *parlements* rejected 'absolutism' so soon, it seriously attenuates the period when it was accepted.

The second problem is the *parlements*' consistent willingness to accord the king undivided sovereignty. In attributing to them the intention of proclaiming the nation a new focus of loyalty, historians have probably fallen victim to the propaganda of the government. It levelled exactly those charges against the *parlements*, which indignantly repudiated them.[14] Apart from rare occasions when the crown's excesses provoked an equally extreme reaction from the *parlements*, in the shape of an assault on its prerogative, the theoretical claims of the antagonists were not far apart. It may be that crown rather than *parlement* was trying to change the constitution. Increasingly despotic tendencies (and inexpert management of faction) can account for their struggle, without recourse to theories of subjects' changing expectations of government. If 'absolutism' did not exist, there was no reason to challenge it. This perspective has the added intellectual advantage of not viewing the *parlement*'s confrontations with the crown as training sessions for the Revolution. They were arguably not seeking to change the traditional constitution but to implement it.

If we forget the revolutionary agenda and instead approach the old order on its own terms, we shall not view the *parlements* as the standard-bearers of a new political culture. This allegedly found 'absolutism' increasingly unacceptable and lodged sovereignty in the nation rather than the king: a large volume has recently been devoted to the premise that it existed.[15] Instead we shall depict the *parlements* as guardians of an old culture, based on the crown's sovereignty and defence of subjects' rights and privileges against royal despotism. When the *parlements* opposed their monarch, it was not as a representative of a hated system of government. They lectured him on the danger of legitimate monarchy degenerating into despotism. Nor shall we present the French Enlightenment as hostile to the existing political system. Contrary to the usual assumption, it was directed less against the *ancien régime* than against its abuses – against despotism rather than absolute monarchy. But because the men of 1789 assembled a revolutionary ideology from snippets of the moderate Enlightenment, it is all too easy to radicalise Montesquieu and Voltaire by viewing them through the filter of the Revolution.

It is arguable that the regimes of the regent and Fleury were a more important turning point than the rise of a new political culture after 1750. Their repeated recourse to arbitrary methods suggests that the crown had turned a corner carefully avoided by Louis XIV in the direction of despotism. When the ministers of Louis XV were thwarted, despotic responses achieved the status of an automatic reflex. In 1753 the *parlement* of Paris was exiled for its defence of Jansenist heretics; in 1763 it was forced to register Bertin's *vingtième*; and in 1766 the *parlement* of Brittany was dismissed after reminding the king that only the Estates-General could authorise new taxes. Most famously, on 20 January 1771 between one and four in the morning each member of the Paris *parlement* was awakened by two musketeers beating at his door. He was handed a *lettre de cachet* effectively offering the choice of deferring to royal policy or immediate exile. The result was the replacement of former magistrates by non-venal, non-hereditary judges appointed and paid by the king. It produced a permanent 'patriot' opposition to despotism and the conviction that only the Estates-General could defend liberty.

Having demonstrated the frailty of traditional safeguards of its subjects' rights, the monarchy, in the person of Louis XVI, proceeded to new extremities. It *talked* of widening the organs of consent by establishing more local Estates. It *acted* to push through by despotic *lit de justice* Turgot's Six Edicts freeing the Paris grain trade and abolishing the gilds. In 1788 the *parlements'* rights of remonstrance and registration were arbitrarily abolished. This proved the nemesis of the regime, since the aristocratic revolt which followed precipitated the stoppage of loans to the crown and the suspension of its payments. The grievances recorded by all the orders of society in the *cahiers* of spring 1789 reflected the universal conviction that the French monarchy had degenerated into despotism. What they requested was not the abolition of the monarchy but a return to its true principles. There was hardly a wisp of ideas destined to blaze forth in the Declaration of the Rights of Man in August 1789 – the sovereignty of the people and their right to establish a new order drawn from rational principles. Outside Paris the *cahiers* looked to the traditional constitution and invoked the authority of precedent and the past. Their language was that of the *ancien régime*.[16] The Tennis Court Oath of June 1789 did *not* propose a new constitution for France. It declared itself a pact to consolidate the old one.

THE DOMINANCE OF COURT FACTION

If the issue was the ancient one of despotism, it was exploited by the factions which competed at the Bourbon court. To the end of the old regime the court was the main centre of political life and the political networks of the great noble families provided its dynamic. The bourgeoisie was not yet politicised as a force in its own right.[17] It is now fairly clear that its values, ambitions and forms of investment were identical to those of the nobility[18] – a correspondence confirmed by their similar demands in the *cahiers* of 1789. The purchase of office acted as an escalator on which huge numbers of the middle classes rose to the top. The French nobility was a young and open social class. A quarter of its 25,000 families in 1789 were ennobled in the eighteenth century and two thirds of them in the seventeenth and eighteenth centuries together. Most of the nobility had recently ascended from the bourgeoisie, 2,477 bourgeois families having bought their way into the nobility in the fifteen years before 1789 – at a time when the English nobility numbered 200.[19] Nor can a flicker of middle-class aggression be assumed from their frustration at an alleged 'aristocratic reaction' in the later eighteenth century. Nobles certainly dominated government, administration at central and local levels, the Church, the army, the diplomatic service and cultural patronage. But they had *always* done so.

There was therefore nothing new about the decisive role of the nobility, and especially the grandees, under Louis XV and Louis XVI. What *was* new was the inability of these monarchs to match Louis XIV's handling of his nobles – to manage their intrigues and play them off so that power remained in their own hands. Under Louis XV decisions were frequently influenced by the *dévot* faction, representing the cause (*thèse royale*) of undivided royal sovereignty and favouring the ultramontane Jesuits. It was dominated by the queen, the dauphin and the king's daughters. Against them were arrayed Louis' mistress, Madame de Pompadour, and the ministers whose careers she promoted – Bernis, Marigny, Machault, Bertin and Choiseul. They stood for the *parlement* as a participant in royal government (*thèse parlementaire*) and the more Enlightened gallican cause of the Jansenists.

The king's vacillation between these factions was bad for the continuity of policy and reform. Both Frederick of Prussia and Joseph of Austria noted the disastrous result of the factional free-for-all at Versailles. On grounds of financial necessity Louis favoured the Pompadour entourage, which had the best chance of extracting the necessary concessions from the *parlement* during years of almost unremitting warfare. But the *dévots* joined forces with the clergy and other privileged groups to resist new tax demands: they pulled strings in the *parlement* and the result was resistance. Another group at court, led by Conti, joined forces with a group of Jansenist magistrates, who between 1754 and 1764 hijacked the *parlement* for their own purposes.[20] The monarch's usual response to confrontation was initially a hard line followed by capitulation. Plans for equalising taxation associated with Machault and Bertin therefore foundered when their architects were dismissed. Louis XV's Controllers-General of Finance were a short-lived species, with an average life span of under three years. On the other hand, their master succeeded in maintaining some sort of balance between competing factions. Though less skilful than Louis XIV and universally identified as a ditherer, he never made the mistake of allowing one gang to monopolise power indefinitely and thus encouraging the others to unite against him. Only Louis XVI understood court politics so little as to commit that error.[21]

Admittedly Louis XVI started with a problem. Court factions usually hitched their fortunes to members of the royal family believed to have access to the king – younger brothers, heirs apparent or royal mistresses. The new monarch boasted none of these accoutrements. He had no mistress and no heir (for similar reasons), and his brothers were too young. The primary means of access to him was therefore through Marie Antoinette, his wife, who instantly began to alienate most of the court nobility by spurning their attentions and confining her favours to a tiny circle of friends and admirers. Playing at shepherdesses in the Petit Trianon with Polignac, Lamballe and Vaudreuil, she denied those outside her coterie the offices, pensions, sinecures and influence essential to the maintenance of their own position. In spite of her nickname of *Madame Déficit*, it was the recipients rather than the amount of her largesse which attracted criticism. Maria Theresa thundered from Vienna about the terrible risks run by her daughter. Among the earliest victims of her slights were some of the oldest and most powerful noble families in France – Noailles, Rohan and La Rochefoucauld and the princes of the blood, Orléans, Condé and Conti. It was they who eagerly subsidised the publication and distribution of pornographic *libelles* against the queen. Through them was communicated to the people at large the titillating picture of a monster whose sexual appetite was indiscriminate and insatiable. The rabid hatred of the offended nobility is evident from the breathtaking depths to which they sank. The obscenities which they sponsored embraced *inter alia* their queen's lesbianism and nymphomania, spiced with speculations on the size of equipment needed to satisfy her lust.[22]

More sinister, if that is possible, was the impact on the location of opposition. The political significance of the royal court was reduced as leading nobles reassessed its potential for advancement. It ceased to perform its function of earthing the political heavyweights to the centre – and with them the main currents of political activity. Versailles was becoming a provincial town. And there were other factional reasons for a shift of the centre of gravity twelve miles up the road to Paris. In 1786 the crown's faction or *parti ministériel* in the *parlement* moved into opposition. Louis XVI had lost control of the faction battle between Breteuil and Calonne in the ministry. It spread to the *parlement*, destroyed the smooth running of government and precipitated the financial and political crisis of 1787–89.[23]

The names of alienated members of the court nobility may be compared with those whose initiatives precipitated the Revolution. The correlation is devastating. A group of the queen's enemies started the *révolte nobiliaire* in 1788. In the crucial summer and autumn of 1788, when the crown's bankruptcy and the imminence of elections for the Estates-General had raised the political temperature to boiling point, some of the highest nobles in France turned their homes and salons into political clubs dedicated to sabotaging the court. The Society of Thirty was formed at the same time to repudiate the *parlement*'s pronouncement that the Estates-General was to meet in the same form as in 1614 – with a third of the deputies for the entire third estate instead of representation equal to that of the clergy and nobles put together. This was an old issue with seventeenth-century precedents: what made it dangerous was the subversion of this noble pressure group. Their propaganda whipped up feeling among the third estate against the allegedly privileged position of the other two: they created class antagonism where it had not previously existed and thus politicised the bourgeoisie. Twenty-one out of the twenty-three sword nobles in the Society of Thirty were court grandees. Its leaders read like a roll-call of absentees from the queen's revels – La Rochefoucauld, Lauzun, Lafayette, Noailles, d'Aiguillon and the three Lameth brothers.[24] In June 1789 they were the first members of the noble estate to join the bourgeois National Assembly.

Nor does the trail of catastrophe end there. Orléans, Louis' cousin, strove tirelessly to destroy the credibility of the king and queen. He hired Choderlos de Laclos, the scandalous writer of *Les liaisons dangereuses,* to produce vicious propaganda. He accused Louis to his face of despotism in the Royal Session of *parlement* in 1787, thereby wrecking the financial deal which had just been negotiated.[25] His Palais Royal was a hotbed of political disaffection, protected by the duke's status from the government's police. From it he muckraked and plotted, directing the mob violence which eventually produced the attack on the Bastille in the summer of 1789. He was awarded a leading role in MGM's *Marie Antoinette* of 1938, but has barely merited a line in serious analysis of the monarchy's collapse.

Several members of the Society of Thirty went on to greater things. Mirabeau led the National Assembly. Lafayette became the first commander of the National Guard. Noailles introduced the decrees abolishing 'feudalism'. Talleyrand proposed the secularisation of Church land. The Lameths helped to found the Jacobin Club. Above all, nobles alienated by Louis and Marie Antoinette played a crucial role in the collapse of the monarchy's last line of defence – the army. Ségur's army reforms of 1781 and Guibert's of 1788 were intended to loosen the grip on the juiciest appointments of court nobility who used their wealth to purchase commissions. In the forefront of their sabotage were the Lameth brothers, Lafayette and Lauzun. When the regiments were called to Paris in June 1789 the king had the worst of all worlds. The army was enough of a threat to incense the population but too mutinous to use against them. In this sense the Revolution was a military *putsch*.[26]

The crisis which preceded the end of the *ancien régime* was typical of that regime throughout its life. It was an affair of Estates and factions, of 'ins' and 'outs'. It spoke the traditional language of liberty, privilege and despotism, employed conventional modes of political conduct and denounced the abuse of power.[27] It is therefore unlikely that rejection of 'absolutism' was a significant component. The French Revolution began as an old-style revolt within the old order against its abuses. There was no thought of abolishing a system from which most of its protagonists benefited. They could not know that it was a revolt which would go wrong. The masses were called out in the time-honoured way to strengthen the arm of élite factions. This time they refused to go home.

REFERENCES

1   Jarrett D 1973 *The Begetters of Revolution*. Longman, pp. 1–2
2   Cranston M 1987 *Jean-Jacques*. Penguin, pp. 275–8
3   Price M 1989 The Comte de Vergennes and the Baron de Breteuil: French Politics and Reform in the Reign of Louis XVI. Unpublished Ph.D. dissertation, Cambridge University
4   Campbell PR 1988 *The Ancien Régime in France*. Basil Blackwell
5   Burley P 1989 *Witness to the Revolution*. Weidenfeld and Nicolson,

pp. 16–20; Campbell PR 1988, p. 8; Behrens CBA 1962–3 'Nobles, Privileges and Taxes in France at the end of the *Ancien Régime.*' *Economic History Review*, xv, p. 462; Roberts JM 1978 *The French Revolution.* Oxford University Press, pp. 5–6

6 Burley P 1989, p. 18–20

7 Durand D 1976 What is Absolutism? In Hatton R (ed.) *Louis XIV and Absolutism.* Macmillan, p. 20; Burley P 1984 'A Bankrupt Regime.' *History Today*, vol. 34, January 1984, p. 41.

8 Shennan JH 1979 *Philippe Duke of Orléans.* Thames and Hudson, pp. 81–90

9 Shennan JH 1968 *The Parlement of Paris.* Eyre and Spottiswoode, pp. 306–7

10 Furet F 1981 *Interpreting the French Revolution.* Cambridge University Press, pp. 22–4

11 Black J 1990 *Eighteenth-Century Europe.* Macmillan, p. 353

12 Mann W 1977 *The Operas of Mozart.* Cassell, pp. 427–8

13 Schama S 1989 *Citizens.* Viking, pp. xv, 259

14 Rogister J 1986 *Parlementaires*, Sovereignty and Legal Opposition in France under Louis XV. In *Parliaments, Estates and Representation*, **6**, no. 1, pp. 26–7

15 Baker KM 1987 *The Political Culture of the Old Regime.* Pergamon, pp. xvi–xviii

16 Taylor GV 1972 Revolutionary and non-revolutionary content in the *cahiers* of 1789: an interim report. *French Historical Studies*, vii, pp. 479–502

17 Doyle W 1980 *Origins of the French Revolution.* Oxford University Press, pp. 128–38

18 Lucas C 1976 Nobles, Bourgeois and the French Revolution. In Johnson D (ed.) *French Society and the Revolution.* Cambridge University Press, pp. 90–8

19 Chaussinand-Nogaret 1984 *The French Nobility in the Eighteenth Century.* Cambridge University Press, pp. 25–31; Behrens CBA 1985 *Society, Government and the Enlightenment.* Thames and Hudson, p. 52

20 Swann J 1989 Politics and the *Parlement* of Paris, 1754–71. Unpublished Ph.D. dissertation, Cambridge University

21 Wick DL 1980 The Court Nobility and the French Revolution. *Eighteenth-Century Studies*, xiii, pp. 267–9

22 Schama S 1989, pp. 221–7

23 Price M 1989, pp. 253–74

24 Wick DL 1980, pp. 264–6

25 Doyle W 1989 *The Oxford History of the French Revolution.* Oxford University Press, pp. 79–80

26 Blanning TCW 1987 *The French Revolution: Aristocrats versus Bourgeois?* Macmillan, pp. 37–8

27 Campbell PR 1988, pp. 71–82

CHAPTER FOUR

France and England: Absolutism Versus Limited Monarchy?

The one certain thing about 'absolutism' is that it was never English. Whatever it was, England had the opposite. There prevailed the diametrically opposite constitutional arrangements of limited monarchy, civil liberties and the politics of parliamentary parties and popular electioneering. In 1973 Jarrett broke new ground by arguing that English and French politics revolved round many of the same issues, which were fought out in a not dissimilar framework.[1] Despite its originality, the book was ignored. But if we forget for a time that France was supposed to be 'absolutist', *was* it so unlike England – even in the eighteenth century when it is usually supposed they had drastically diverged?

Historians observing monarchy in France and England have a problem. They cannot help being aware that one crown has a future and the other has none. In the nineteenth century it was assumed that because they ended differently they must have been different from the start. Most of the fundamental differences between the 'absolute' and 'limited' monarch have proliferated retrospectively. Historians tend to pounce on all conflict in France as a symptom of incipient revolt; in England it is recognised as a sign of stable institutions which could defuse tension.

MONARCHS

In both countries personal monarchy was central to government. A change of monarch was a devastating political event, usually spelling disaster for the henchmen of the old and triumph for the friends of the new. The accessions of Louis XVI in 1774 and George III in 1760 both heralded retirement for their predecessors' ministers. The importance of his personal wishes made the monarch's household or court the central institution and his dynasty the principal issue of domestic and foreign policies. In France and England until the late eighteenth century opposition was therefore tainted with disloyalty to the dynasty; and since Hanoverians suffered from a Jacobite cast waiting in the wings the accusation was more meaningful on their side of the Channel. Unity was assumed between men of goodwill, and party divisions were considered disloyal – an attitude usually attributed unfairly to the fanaticism of the French Revolutionaries. Parties were considered sectional interests conspiring against the common good represented by the monarch.

Relationships between members of the royal family were politically crucial, since the king's disaffected relatives could partially legitimise opposition. One of the main generators of political conflict was the activities of the French princes of the blood and rival twiglets of the Tudor and Stuart branches. Nor did the parallel end after 1688. Rows between all three Georges and their eldest sons mirror feuds between Bourbon monarchs and successive dukes of Orléans. In the 1780s the Prince of Wales and the duke of Orléans were good friends, swopping racehorses and mistresses and encouraging each other in their respective rebellions against tyrannical regal relatives. Both acted as a safe focus of opposition, one shielding the increasingly republican-minded Fox and the other the menacing alliance of malicious courtiers and gutter press whose calumnies were corroding the prestige of Louis XVI and his Queen.

Both monarchs were absolute under the law. The French king was not, however, legally answerable if he broke it; nor was the English king, either before or after 1688. This has generated immense confusion, principally because historians of Tudor and Stuart England have deployed the word 'absolute' in a nineteenth-century 'absolutist' sense. Thus Coward denies that James I and Charles I ever claimed to be absolute monarchs.[2] They did, repeatedly, and even their enemies made the same claims on their behalf. But they used the word in a different sense from Coward. They simply meant that as true monarchs the Stuarts were subject to no man. Like the Bourbons, they had no intention of submitting their decisions to a committee of grandees. And also like them, English monarchs asserted their independence of Pope and Emperor, harking back to Henry VIII's Break with Rome in the 1530s and Francis I's Papal Concordat of 1515. To claim absolute power was to possess 'imperial' status –

independence from any higher authority. Most of the French king's subjects nevertheless belonged to the Roman communion. But 'the only supreme head in earth of the Church of England' could claim to be truly absolute in matters spiritual and temporal. The relevant legislation had been careful to vest ecclesiastical supremacy in the king alone and not king-in-parliament.[3] In this respect the personal power of Tudor monarchs and their successors was awesome. It was one of the most absolute monarchies in Europe which installed in parish churches royal coats of arms instead of rood crosses.

Yet, for both Tudor and Valois, laying claim to absolute power was a defence mechanism, aimed at external threats to monarchs. Both had recently terminated the feudal dispersion of sovereignty, when local lords enjoyed prerogative or regalian rights. England had started the process long before France, but had not yet finished it. The marcher lordships were stripped of their regalian rights in 1536. Absolute power did not imply that either monarch could do what he liked. Each had similar prerogative powers, against which there was no legitimate resistance or appeal, and for the conduct of which he was answerable to no earthly authority. Parliament or Estates might try to make his *ministers* answerable: there was an ancient tradition of parliamentary impeachment. But that was someone else's problem. The monarch himself was above the law and under it, though no paradox was intended. He was below the law because he was supposed to recognise the subjects' rights which it guaranteed. It has often been pointed out that if the French king chose not to he could not be made to. This is correct: but neither could the king of England. He could not be made to submit to his own writ. As the source of justice he could not simultaneously be subject to it, and in that sense both kings were above the law. The English crown still is. Until 1947 it was not even liable for damages inflicted in its name. Not until the 1980s were prerogative decisions subject to judicial review.[4]

In 1756 Louis XV commissioned a report on the power and resources of his rival George II. His spy left him in no doubt about the nature of royal authority in England: 'The king does all he wants, peace, war, treaties and alliances, he can levy troops, equip fleets providing it is at his own expense and not the people's. . . . He disposes of all the ecclesiastical dignities, of all offices civil, political and military and justice is done in his name.'[5] Throughout the period French and English monarchs tried to promote a beatific vision of prerogative affairs (matters of state). They were presented as arcane mysteries beyond the intellectual grasp of mere mortals. In France it was in effect *lèse-majesté* to take an interest in politics without the king's express invitation: Calonne once apologised to Louis XVI for mentioning the dreaded word. British historiography has long chosen to believe that the conduct of government was, at least after the 1688 Revolution, a matter of legitimate public interest. It was not. The role of the press and public opinion has invariably been exaggerated to make Georgians sound more comfortably like Victorians. Black and Clark have begun to replace wishful thinking with historical accuracy. As late as the 1750s politics were too private to permit accurate popular scrutiny. The court at St James's and parliament at Westminster were hermetically sealed worlds of which few signals were intercepted outside. Political reporting in newspapers was confined to a sparse record of changes of office: comment and speculation was minimal. Parliamentary debates could not be reported until the 1770s. Most politicians deplored public discussion of issues which were too subtle for common people to understand. Popular protest carried little weight because other politicians were assumed to have incited it – as they usually had. Chatham and Wilkes are often treated as though they had wandered into the age of Gladstone. The mass following they commanded owed more to rent-a-mob tactics than to their mastery of the Hanoverian media. The War of Jenkins' Ear is reputed to have begun in response to the popular outcry when Spanish coastguards severed the ear of a sea captain. It is now clear that international negotiations were of far more weight than the clamour of parliament and press – or the ear of Robert Jenkins, left or right, boxed or bottled.[6]

Neither country had a written constitution in the sense of the Swedish document of 1772 and the American of 1788. By the 1770s and 1780s this was the requirement, and states without a formal statement of the rights of monarch and people were informed that they lacked a constitution. Even fortunate peoples in possession of such a document were to discover it no safeguard against differing interpretations, but there was wider scope for argument over the airy arrangements prevalent elsewhere. Neither the English nor French constitutions were described in any single document. Yet more precise statements existed than have been acknowledged – in coronation oaths, law books, statutes and (in France) treaties made by the crown with separate provinces. Disagreement was within a set of shared conventions rather than between adherents of different ideologies.

Both conventions incorporated similar guarantees of subjects' rights. England had its 1215 Magna Carta, 1689 Bill of Rights and 1701 Act of Settlement. France's 'fundamental laws' were more tangible than some historians seem to imagine. Though the phrase was affixed to any principle a politician believed vital, certain axioms were accepted by all. The monarch could not change the succession or alienate the royal demesne. He could not deprive his subjects of their life, liberty or property: there was no taxation without consent and no imprisonment without trial. The revolutionaries of 1789 naturally announced that these blessings were absent in the *ancien régime* and drew a lurid portrait of the sort of 'off with his head' tyranny previously associated with Turkey and Russia. But had the Bourbons been able to tax at will they would have had no financial problem. Nor was the infamous, *lettre de cachet* an instrument of despotism. It was intended to prevent the flight of criminals while an official writ was being prepared. Only its *abuse* was despotic and Louis XVI introduced reforms to prevent it. On the whole historians have believed the revolutionaries.

Both monarchs delegated their prerogative powers to ministers and chose between alternative policies rather than initiating them personally. In this respect also the 1688 Revolution is irrelevant. Louis XV and XVI were as accustomed as the Georges to playing second fiddle to their ministers. Modern scholarship has revealed that this was not because they were lazy or weak, or spoke the wrong language or had to choose from the majority party in parliament. It was because they could not rival the expertise of their advisers in their increasingly specialist fields. The expanding size and activities of central government pushed all monarchs into the administrative background. The excruciating details of finance were as much beyond Louis XVI as George III, though military and diplomatic affairs were usually subjected to more detailed royal attention.

Sometimes monarchs pursued personal foibles and exploited similar strategems to promote them. George II's fixation with Hanover worried his ministers in 1727–28, when he sent secret agents to negotiate with Saxony and Austria.[7] It is tempting to see this as the sort of humiliating subterfuge to which a 'limited' monarch was reduced, in comparison with the freedom to dominate policy of his 'absolutist' cousin. Then we recall that Louis XV, less lethargic than is usually supposed and frustrated by his foreign secretaries' failure to share his enthusiasm for Poland and Sweden, conducted a Secret Diplomacy through his own agents. 'Backstairs influence' was a common cry when monarchs conferred with those who lacked the public responsibility of office. Elizabeth I's ministers constantly moaned about her habit of taking advice from others: they claimed a monopoly of advice but could not enforce it.[8] George II continued to consult Granville and George III Bute after those ministers had resigned. Louis XIV had his unofficial think-tank and was discreet about who composed it. All such behaviour indicates that monarchs felt in some sense constrained by their official ministers.

COURTIERS

Considering its huge expansion in the period, the court and its occupants have been neglected by French historians, with their eyes glued to the official machinery of government and to the economic and demographic realities with which it was allegedly struggling to cope. Mettam has now begun to fill the gap. He has emphasised that the great household offices carried far more than merely ceremonial weight. French courtiers could wield political influence without holding political office because the court was the centre of politics. Anyone who could capture the attention or affection of the ruler was assured of influence and therefore of power. The courtiers most likely to succeed were those in attendance on the monarch in his more intimate activities: factions consequently competed frantically for such posts. A rigid line between courtiers and politicians is impossible.

Historians of the English court were earlier in the field. In the 1970s Starkey began to put the court back at the centre of government.[9] He drew attention to the significance of physical proximity in the arrangement of royal and governmental apartments. This administrative geography pins down previously disembodied political processes and 'gives to airy nothing a local habitation and a name'. The result puts in doubt Elton's older contention that Cromwell's reforms in the 1530s ended the court's significance as an agent of national administration; but in an influential article he himself shifted it on to firmer ground as a 'point of contact' reconciling the interests of crown and political élite.[10] The English court thus achieves the same political status as the French. Tudor courtiers and politicians not only pursued similar goals by similar methods. They were often the same people. Elizabeth I made courtiers like Dudley, Hatton and Essex into politicians and politicians like Cecil and Knollys into courtiers. In England as much as France a minister needed a courtier's skills if he was to please his master and courtiers needed political address if they were to profit from their talent to amuse. Cromwell allegedly entertained Henry VIII with sixteenth-century executive toys.

From the monarch's point of view the court was a central clearing-house where the political nation (those involved in central or local government) was gratified with royal favour. Its management was a major challenge. The surviving archives of ministers are crammed with requests for posts and perquisites. Lord Burghley received between sixty and a hundred letters a day. Louis XIV achieved much by dispensing words of thanks, letters signed by himself and often just simple courtesy – at which he had no equal. Since there were never enough resources to satisfy everyone ministers had to be selective. The essential task was to earth the political heavyweights to the centre of government.

After the 1688 Revolution the position in England was rather different. Instead of one political centre there were two, since parliament now met every year, and historians have assumed that the main focus shifted to Westminster. Academic research has followed it. The spotlight was beamed on parliamentary parties, elections and anything else with reassuring pre-echoes of modernity. Consequently much work remains to be done on the Hanoverian court, traditionally dismissed as a social and political backwater. Evidence is now accumulating that it remained the political centre where power was won by time-honoured methods – attendance on and manipulation of the monarch.[11] It is certainly true that in the eighteenth century parliament was the surest road to office for ambitious politicians. But as Elton has observed the same route congested with rising Tudor statesmen, it is unclear what that proves. Parliament as a ladder to power seems to have been confused with parliament as a repository of power. Post-Revolution monarchs such as Queen Anne obstinately refused to play the part assigned to them by future-minded historians. She maintained her prerogative of appointment and declined to restrict herself to those with a majority, or even a following, in parliament. Instead, as historical novelists knew all along, the vital manoeuvres were executed between the royal closet, bedchamber and backstairs.[12] This topographical shift brings English power politics more into line with French.

The French court also remained the centre of administration, while in England by the eighteenth century they had drawn apart. This can be seen as evidence for the diminishing centrality of its monarchy. At Versailles the council of state met next door to the king's bedchamber, as did the privy council in the palace of Whitehall. But in 1698 most of that palace was destroyed by fire and William III moved instead to the remodelled residences of Kensington and Hampton Court. He left most of the government departments dotted around Whitehall, where they remained until the building of Somerset House in the 1760s provided additional accommodation for some of them. The secretaries of state were physically separated from the king, who was arguably becoming less of an administrative driving force. Yet an alternative explanation is possible. The 'Royal Kalendar' for 1784 listed secretaries of state and Lord Privy Seal with the personnel of court and household. Their control of the Signet and Privy Seals which authenticated royal orders had made them the main agents of royal administration since the fifteenth century. Their appearance on the court list was not quaint antiquarianism but recognition that they still derived their powers from the monarch and operated in a close physical relationship with him, in the manner of his household officials.[13] Government was still the king's personal affair. Government and palace are more likely to have split because of the inadequacy of royal premises in Georgian London.

This in itself might suggest the dwindling significance of the English monarchy, had parliament or law courts been accommodated with greater magnificence. Instead an indignant observer noted 'an inadequate senate house' and 'oracles of law . . . delivered from wooden booths run up in the corners of an old Gothick Hall'. The head of a mighty empire was proclaimed to be worse lodged than the chief magistrate of Glarus or Zug in the Swiss Confederation. He required a palace roomy enough for 'the departments of the executive power, that are more immediately connected with the crown, such as those pertaining to the Privy Council and the Secretaries of State; the latter of which are at present scattered in different corners of the town, and some of them hired by the week'.[14] In Paris the courts were sumptuously established in neo-classical splendour in the same period. The lack of a suitably grandiose palace was considered a disgrace to the nation and a symptom of a bigger problem – England's apology for a capital city, without exciting vistas, baroque public buildings or heroic equestrian statues. We need not read profound constitutional implications into a matter of national style. French governments evaluated lavish public display as worth every *sou*. English pennies were pondered over for longer. George IV showed what a monarch with taste and vision could still do in England. Carlton House, Brighton Pavilion, Buckingham Palace and Windsor Castle leapt from the drawing board at a speed which left parliament speechless.

The French monarchy was personal: the king's response to influence and manipulation therefore determined the course of politics. Louis XIV functioned like a stiff wind, his favour as it blew hot and cold depositing the factions where he wanted them. Louis XV behaved more like a weathercock. In spite of a valiant attempt to prevent a take-over by one faction, he was no match for seasoned intriguers who exploited his diffidence. English government reflected the same crucial range of reaction, from Henry VII who was the nearest thing to his own man in early modern monarchy to Henry VIII and Charles II who thought they were but jumped all the more unknowingly into politicians' pockets, to James I and George II who for different reasons became the prisoners of faction.

Monarchs did not make policy decisions in a vacuum: instead they were enmeshed in the complex web of relationships which character-ised court society.[15] This meant they were subject to intense pressures which few could resist. Nor was it desirable that they should resist such pressures, for conciliation was the essence of patronage. But it does make the quest for the monarch's personal opinions elusive. Contemporaries were shrewder than many historians when they attributed unpopular policies to 'evil councillors' rather than to their masters. Long interpreted as an excuse for treasonable opposition, it now seems an accurate description. The eighteenth century's ritual complaint of 'ministerial despotism' reveals the same awareness of the monarch's submission to his advisers – even if only as amateur to expert. American attribution of the crown's iniquities to George III's ministers could be taken as confirmation that the 1688 Revolution had finally pushed the king out of politics – until we find the Pilgrims of Grace making the same assessment of Henry VIII in 1536.

Royal mistresses and consorts were another crucial influence. Their 'reigns' in France have long been celebrated, from Diane de Poitiers to Mesdames de Pompadour and du Barry. Now that court politics are back on the English agenda, similar influences are discovered. The decisive role of Anne Boleyn in the break with Rome is now well established: by a mixture of relentless pressure, sexual blackmail and well-timed pregnancy she effectively kick-started Henry VIII.[16] Pepys' verdict on James II was to the point: 'in all things but his codpiece, led by his wife'. Nor did such influences end after 1688. The Duchess of Kendal, mistress of George I, and Queen Caroline, consort of George II, played vital roles in maintaining Walpole's support at court. The king had to be kept steadily behind his ministers and the Duchess acted as an energetic link, broaching delicate subjects and briefing the ministers on probable royal reactions.[17]

After the rise of the royal court as the centre of patronage in the late middle ages, courtiers became the focus of keen interest. If some observers like Castiglione produced treatises of advice on courtly conduct, others condemned the whole charade of greed, hypocrisy and duplicity. The courtier's smile was a stock ingredient of drama in every early modern monarchical state. Shakespeare alluded to the courtier as a sponge 'that soaks up the king's countenance, his rewards, his authorities'. Many who sounded the anti-courtier note were themselves disappointed courtiers and were not dangerous. The vitriol hurled at the eighteenth-century Bourbon court was notable for its obscenity rather than its originality.

DESPOTS

'Despot' is perhaps the most overworked cliché in the eighteenth century's political vocabulary. Levelled against monarchs and ministers, it requires cautious evaluation. Transports of zeal for infringed liberties were often the rage of 'outs' against 'ins'. They have traditionally been accepted at face value as a description of the French system of government and dismissed in relation to England, where they were marginally more obsessive. The evidence suggests a strong element of ballyhoo in both. Charges were shrillest when a ministry's tenure of power was apparently unshakeable. The regimes of Wolsey, Buckingham, Walpole and Pitt raised the issue most acutely in England, as did those of Richelieu, Mazarin, Fleury and Maupeou in France. Concern for liberty was fleeting. The enthusiasm of late seventeenth-century Whigs for reducing the armed forces evaporated in office. Brienne denounced Calonne's proposals as despotic in 1787 and implemented them himself in 1788, just as the opposition to Brienne was recognised as coming from the malcontents in the *parlement* eager for office in their turn. 'Despotism' was the language of rivalry: it engaged with men and their measures. Declarations of war on arbitrary power issued from those understandably miffed by royal policies. Huguenots and Englishmen, alarmed by the intentions of Louis XIV, identified despotic features in his system of government which they had unaccountably overlooked in the days of their co-operation. The Austrian ruler's assaults on his Hungarian subjects were viewed as the just depredations of a good ally.

Yet some fears for liberty were warranted. Louis XV and XVI did themselves no favours with their frequent recourse to despotic short cuts when challenged. *Lits de justice* were held to force royal legislation through the *parlement*, and *lettres de cachet* were issued illegally to imprison offenders without trial. The *parlements* were abolished in 1771 and again in 1788: new courts were established but judges could now be sacked and the judiciary lost its independence. All such acts were justifiably abhorred as invasions of subjects' rights and challenged by the courts – in spectacular fashion by the *cour des aides*, watchdog for public liberties threatened by executive action. In 1767 the obscure Monnerat was arrested for tobacco smuggling. A *lettre de cachet* confined him for six weeks in an underground dungeon without light and with a fifty-pound chain round his neck. He was imprisoned for over two years without trial before the authorities announced that they had got the wrong man and released him. The *cour des aides* authorised him to sue the government officers who had wrongfully arrested him and awarded 50,000 *livres* damages.[18]

French 'absolutism' at its most Dickensian, no doubt. Yet, four years before, one of George III's secretaries of state had sent king's messengers to ransack the house and papers of Wilkes' publisher. The courts did not agree with his interpretation of the royal prerogative and the case of *Entick* v. *Carrington* permanently defines one of its limits. French and English parallels were remarked at the time. In 1771 a Bristol newspaper noted a striking similarity between the politics of England and France:

> in both their Parliaments have been essentially suppressed, the one by force, the other by fraud; in both their Princes do not rely on the affections of their subjects, but on large standing armies; in both the King's will and pleasure is the only law; in both the just and constitutional rights and liberties of the people have been infringed and trampled upon; in both there have been frequent remonstrances to their Kings, which have been totally disregarded; and in both there is such a general ferment and discontent, they may probably bring on a confusion, and end in a change of their forms of government'.[19]

The mistake lies in supposing that only 'absolutist' rulers had unpleasant tendencies. These cases prove that despotism had nothing to do with 'absolutist' regimes. There was little difference between George III's persecution of Wilkes and Louis XVI's vindictive treatment of the defendants in the Diamond Necklace trial twenty years later. Both became *causes célèbres* and symbols of government despotism to an extent out of all proportion to their intrinsic importance. All rulers pushed out the limits of their power and it was the function of law to stop them. In France we should recognise not the existence of 'absolutism' but of its opposite – a constitution which respected legal rights and triggered an early warning system when they were endangered. The thrust of the action was not to attack an 'absolutist' system which trampled on rights but to implement an existing constitution which defended them. Despotism was not a system of government but a malfunction: it related to a ruler's policies rather than his constitutional position. The defence of individual and corporate liberties is one of the most continuous refrains of the late medieval and early modern periods. If we smell 'absolutism' every time a ruler needs reminding of the limits of his prerogative, the term will embrace most rulers in the pack.

BUREAUCRATS

In one respect England was undoubtedly more 'absolutist' than France. There was little about Bourbon government that can helpfully be described as bureaucratic. Justice and finance were in the vice-like grip of officials who had bought their posts and felt entitled to run them as a private undertaking as much as a public service. The motive of private profit dominated the outlook of the tax-farmers and revenue contractors. They were as distant as possible from the dedicated bureaucrats of 'absolutist' legend, for Dessert has shown that the contractors who battened on to the state's financial necessities were closely related to the court nobility. So were the government's creditors.[20] Serious money to invest came from the largest landed estates in France and the opportunities to invest it from connections at court. The rest of local administration was mostly in the hands of regional, municipal or ecclesiastical corporations. Bureaucratic performers were therefore relegated to walk-on parts, since the leading roles had already been taken by those with more naked self-interest to pursue. The state was a partnership, based on mutual benefits, between crown and élites: an expanding range of governmental activities was delegated to private enterprise.

The publication of Brewer's important book enables us to see clearly the contrast with England. Before the Revolution England scarcely had a bureaucracy, however loosely defined. Elizabeth I employed about 1,200 officials to govern a population of five million – one for every 4,000 subjects. The early Bourbons had 40,000 on their payroll for sixteen million – one *officier* for every 400 subjects. Thus the bureaucratic density of France was ten times heavier than England's.[21] After 1688 England soon overtook her rival. Brewer notes the rise of a 'fiscal–military state' based on a large standing army, high taxation, heavy government borrowing and the establishment of a large body of public servants. Before the Revolution officeholders considered themselves the clients of leading nobles or politicians. They shuttled between government and private employment and felt no exclusive loyalty to the crown or any particular government department. When they retired they kept their papers, as did Colbert. But from the 1690s more professional and bureaucratic attitudes are perceptible. Departmental documents stayed put; heads of department paid their clerks with departmental funds rather than their own; and the sense of working for a government department rather than a patron intensified. One of the ways this was achieved was by putting offices into commission. A single Lord Treasurer was replaced by a committee of Treasury Commissioners, so that the loyalty of officials was less to a personal empire and more to a department as a whole.

The most spectacular development was in the Excise service. By the eighteenth century it was the biggest government department and it had the most contact with the public. The 5000 excisemen of the 1780s were no private contractors but bureaucrats under close government control, both centrally and locally. Everything about them smacks unmistakably of Prussia. Entrants were required to pass a written examination, rather than learning on the job, like all French officials. They had to use decimals, cube roots and slide-rules. They worked long hours and had to make their precisely delineated tours of inspection carrying their books and seven instruments, with pen and inkpot attached to their lapels. Their jurisdiction knew nothing of due process of common law. It was geared to the fiscal needs of the crown rather than the rights of its subjects and the excise commissioners in London were judges in their own prosecutions of defrauders. Blackstone regarded their arbitrary proceedings as incompatible with the temper of a free people. Active in every town and village where tea was retailed or ale brewed, as well as in the ports and on the coasts, the excisemen were hated and ubiquitous.[22] They focused popular hatred of authority and inspired a colourful demonology which survived until yesterday in boys' adventure books. Public rage exploded into violence against the excise scheme of 1733 – a fair parallel to the French population's rough handling of its own less obnoxious and only faintly bureaucratic tax officials in 1789.

ARISTOCRATS

Early modern France was an aristocratic society until 1789, and some would say until after that. The aristocratic nature of English eighteenth-century society became headline news in the mid-1980s, owing to Clark's polemical talents. The wide currency of his views has been in a way counterproductive: not everyone believes the popular press. The first volume of the *New Oxford History of England* is defiantly entitled *A Polite and Commercial People*. We learn that the depiction of Georgian England as an aristocratic society mistakes appearance for reality: blue blood without property was of small consequence. Few could disagree, but on that analysis France was also non-aristocratic. There a noble title was no guarantee of entry to the ruling class. Every member of a noble family enjoyed noble rank, and barons who had fallen on hard times could be found sweeping the streets – literally. Noble shopkeepers, peasants, shepherds and labourers are a little-known feature of most eighteenth-century states. Everywhere wealth was the *entrée* to power. In that respect Georgian England and Bourbon France were identical.[23]

In France the nobility, robe and sword, dominated all corporate bodies, as well as the lusher pastures of the army, the Church and political office in general. Cannon has demonstrated that much the same was true of England – and in some respects it was more exclusively aristocratic. We owe to the Marxists the misplacement of bourgeois supremacy from the nineteenth to the seventeenth centuries. Such shifts have to be violent and the English Civil War is the grandest upheaval available. Caught between the two, the eighteenth century has been twisted out of recognition. The English nobility consisted almost entirely of what the French called grandees: it was so impermeable to pressure from below that Stone has seriously questioned its celebrated status as an open élite. Its monopoly of the top posts was the more unacceptable as it could not be broken into. Purchase of office lasted longer in England than anywhere else, owing to the manic veneration of inherited rights.[24] Commissions on merit were not introduced until 1871, two centuries after Louis XIV established them in France. Up to the Revolution the French nobility was far easier to penetrate: by 1789 nearly half its members had been recruited since the mid-seventeenth century.[25] Many were elevated because government service generally conferred a title of robe nobility: they became noble because they were senior administrators. In England, by contrast, they became senior administrators because they were noble. English social snobbery compared unfavourably with French attitudes, if James Watt is to be believed. He wrote that contempt for 'us poor mechanics' contrasted strongly with the respect he was accorded in France.

Fiscal policy confirms that if any country was run for the benefit of the nobility, it was England rather than France. Generations of students have clung to the certainty that French nobles were exempted from the *taille* – and so they were. But so also were the bourgeoisie of most towns, while many peasants coolly deducted their *taille* payments from their rent. And if nobles did not pay that tax, at least not directly, after 1749 they were paying three simultaneous doses of *vingtième*. In England a far greater proportion of revenue was raised from indirect taxes on beer and ale consumed by those with plebeian tastes and, presumably, pockets. Its nobles and gentry declined throughout the early modern period to pay significant direct taxation. Under Elizabeth I they enjoyed the perk of assessing themselves for tax purposes. At his death Lord Burghley was still assessed at £133 6s 8d, the same as thirty years before. His actual income has been estimated at £4,000 a year. Little had changed by the 1790s, when Earl Fitzwilliam was paying £721 on an income of £20,000. So total was dominance of political and economic power by the English nobility that, given a free hand, they could scarcely have constructed a society more to their liking.[26]

Both French and English government machines were colonised by nobles at every level. Government departments were family businesses for centuries. The tenure of the Osmonds and Fanshaws as Royal Remembrancers extended from the mid-sixteenth to the late-seventeenth centuries. An endless innings was unsurprising since venality of office was as immovable, though less conspicuous, in England as in France. By the Tudor period the crown was losing control over appointments, through selling offices or granting life tenures and reversions (by which a queue of hopefuls fixed the order of succession to a vacancy and so deprived the monarch of choice). Sitting officials were even able to prevent the crown creating new offices on the grounds that they infringed their property rights.[27] A handful of dynasties dominated royal ministries. Townshends, Pelhams, Pitts, Grenvilles and Temples were adequate counterparts for Phélypeaux, Noailles, Lamoignons and Briennes. And a bald recital of names conceals the fact that most of them intermarried and ramified into all sorts of branches and sub-branches. Those not in the know easily miss the fact that Maurepas, de Vrillière and Pontchartrain all belonged to the same Phélypeaux clan. The élite was tightly knit and aristocratic kinship and friendship were the strongest bonds and motives of politics. Representative bodies were also a noble preserve, the Grosvenor family holding one of the two Chester parliamentary seats without a break for 159 years. Though they differed in detail, both French and English élites used them as a point of contact through which they could conduct their relations with the crown.

Nor did nobles dominate only the formal machinery of government. The easy access to court enjoyed by French grandees and English lords enabled them to maintain the local influence on which the crown relied. Tudor historians have recently stressed the importance of informal contacts between crown and governing élites. Before the inauguration of the Lords Lieutenant in the 1550s the nobility had no official positions in the English counties. Yet Henry VII and his son could not rule without them. Their local role has been the subject of debate, historians such as Stone and Williams detecting a royal preference for breaking up the regional power structures of magnates like Howard and Percy and relying instead on lesser men who owed more to the monarch.[28] Though careful to avoid 'rising middle-class' clichés, these writers nevertheless believe that the stronger monarchy of the sixteenth century depended for local control on a new type of royal servant who lacked regional authority in his own right. Other authorities like Bernard argue that the crown's aim, as in France, was to hijack local clout which it did not itself have. The most satisfactory choice was therefore a man with major influence to borrow.[29] But we cannot assume that there was an unlimited supply of powerful regional lords who were also adult, loyal and competent. Where they were lacking, substitutes had to be found. The continued importance of such families as the Talbots and the Stanleys suggests that a distinction must be made between an onslaught on the nobility in general and attacks on individual noblemen who had attracted royal displeasure.

There is no indication that the position had changed substantially by the eighteenth century. Stone has constructed an impressive picture of the declining economic, social and military power of the nobility. One of the casualties was allegedly patronage, the keystone of noble power, now yielding to 'possessive individualism' – every man for himself instead of clinging to sentimental loyalties. The hypothesis should be evaluated with caution. Contemporary lamentations to this effect have perhaps been too readily believed, since patronage was seen as vital to social stability and fears for its continuing prominence were correspondingly overplayed.[30] And loyalty had rarely been sentimental. Clientage and patronage now seem no less prominent under the Hanoverians – though the rise of the Georgian standing army obliged lords to offer peaceful sponsorship rather than military backing. George II's ministers prized nobles with local influence as much as Elizabeth I's – probably more so in view of the greater regularity of parliaments and elections. The local operations, social, military or electoral, of a Lowther in Westmorland or a Fitzwilliam in Yorkshire could not be ignored. Key governmental positions in the localities were therefore still in their hands.[31] When Pitt flashed the red alert sign in the revolutionary 1790s, his mechanisms of local control and intelligence were local aristocracy and justices of the peace – the same as Cromwell's during the Reformation crisis of the 1530s.

In this England mirrored France. There was never an attack on the nobility as such. Their deadliest enemy was allegedly Richelieu; yet Bergin has recently demonstrated that he devoted much energy to making his family the aristocratic equal of any. It was their obedience he wanted, not the destruction of their power and prestige. The Noailles of Languedoc did not cease to matter as the seventeenth century gave way to the eighteenth. As in England so in France: neither ruler could wield power through formal institutions and bureaucratic agencies alone. Not until the late nineteenth century were habits of obedience to government so ingrained as to permit the abandonment of patronage mechanisms.[32] Both regimes depended heavily on triangles of clientage with their base in the localities and their apex at court.

Yet if clientage continued in both countries, its basis was transformed. Since political and military prerogatives were now focused on the French court, along with ultimate power over patronage, grandees increasingly sought civil or military office under the crown. They were consequently obliged to spend more of their time in the capital. Formerly, the position occupied by lesser nobles within a great man's household was the main means of cementing their mutual dependence. But the skeleton staff which maintained grandees' establishments in the provinces reduced their households from political to merely domestic mechanisms, as their physical absence narrowed opportunities for attendance by a well-born retinue. Domestic service became the work of menials. By 1700 the grandees' entourages, for war as much as display, had disappeared.[33]

English nobles, blessed with less narcissistic monarchs, were deemed to have stuck doggedly to residence on their estates – thus presenting a satisfying contrast to their French counterparts, absentee, court-bound and doomed. But since we now know that the behaviour of English nobles was identical, French 'absolutism' probably had little to do with it. The Reformation triggered a property boom, as episcopal residences between the Strand and the Thames were converted into town palaces for peers. Though the concentration of prerogatives in the English crown was an older trend, the early modern period was the first in which nobles began to neglect their provincial households. As in France, they were sometimes disbanded for years on end and their servants became fewer and lowlier. By 1700 noble households were as politically impotent as the women who largely staffed them. The reduced status of servants allowed practical considerations to prevail. The introduction of servants' backstairs ensured that a gentleman ascending the grand staircase was not met by the spectacle of his last night's faeces descending.[34]

The result in both countries was remarkably comparable. In England households exceeding forty were rare after 1660, while the court nobility of late eighteenth-century Paris managed with establishments of under thirty. In 1561 Stanley, earl of Derby, ran a household of 120; by 1702 his descendant was down to thirty-eight. In the mid-seventeenth century the establishment of a duc d'Epernon numbered seventy-three, excluding his guards. A century later the comparably endowed prince de Lambesc had a staff of twenty-nine.[35]

Both English and French regimes also relied for their success on expert management and balancing of power groups. As neither Louis XV nor George II *was an* expert manager, both were repeatedly victims of ministerial and factional pressure. Both succumbed to the manoeuvres of politicians who were adroit enough to compel a reluctant monarch to appoint them or dismiss those he preferred. Crown patronage usually guaranteed a dominant following in parliament, *parlement* or provincial Estates, which then, among other vital duties, obediently voted supply. But if individual leaders were offended, corporate sensibilities wounded or contentious issues mishandled, the result could be steering failure by the ministerial group in the assembly. Other political bosses could then outbid the ministerial party for the support of the majority. If the monarch wished to retain the support of the institution, he then had to start making concessions. In 1742 George II was forced to part with Walpole – a minister whom he wanted to keep – and in 1746 to keep the Pelhams – ministers he wanted to part with. In 1759 Louis XV was obliged to sack Controller-General Silhouette so fast that he gave his name to the new craze for sketches of which one caught only the profile. In 1763 he was advised to buy peace with the *parlement* by appointing as Controller-General Laverdy, leader of the Jansenist opposition within it. Historians have always seized on such episodes in England, since they can be presented as an early appearance of that sophisticated blessing, parliamentary government. Yet these political upsets were really not very different from what could equally well go wrong in France, where Laverdy's appointment has occasioned no interest whatsoever in a country which looks for symptoms of the present

97

only since 1789. The cause in both cases was not that legislative bodies had collectively begun to dictate to the monarch on his choice of ministers: they explicitly disavowed any such intention. It was that corporate institutions were manipulated by all interested parties, monarch included, and in mediocre reigns he was not always the most skilful practitioner.

French and English nobles claimed to be the mediators between monarch and people. Blackstone and Montesquieu justified their predominance in identical terms, namely to shade the people against the power of the monarch. From the 1760s this rhetoric was modified in both countries by the demand for wider representation. Aristocratic bodies were progressively discredited. In England the scandal of Wilkes' triple expulsion after the Middlesex election stimulated a movement to form extra-parliamentary associations. In France the impotence of the *parlement* in the face of the 1771 coup started a search for a more independent alternative.[36] It is too easy to offer such responses as evidence of crumbling French 'absolutism' and ignore the same criticisms of the English political establishment. The extent of anti-aristocratic feeling is hard to estimate. In France the Low Enlightenment depicted the nobility as socially parasitic and morally degenerate twenty years before the Revolution.[37] It has attracted attention because it interlocks neatly with that Revolution's rejection of the aristocratic principle and thus finds its niche in the framework of declining 'absolutism'. A similar attack on noble values in England from the 1750s has until recently been ignored.[38] It levelled the same charges of effeteness, moral contagion, lack of patriotism and selfish disregard for the nation's destiny. Yet in neither country does the aristocratic ethic seem to have been deeply dented before 1789. Aristocratic duels were aped, coaches coveted and fashions followed. The lowly hero of most eighteenth-century novels and *romans* secured the well-born lady of his heart only by the timely discovery that he was a gentleman. Only thus did Tom Jones not woo in vain.

REFERENCES

1 Jarrett D 1973 *The Begetters of Revolution*. Longman
2 Coward B 1980 *The Stuart Age*. Longman, p. 81
3 Guy J 1988 *Tudor England*. Oxford University Press, pp. 369–78
4 Wade HWR 1961 *Administrative Law*. Oxford University Press, pp. 809–13; Turpin C 1985 *British Government and the Constitution*. Weidenfeld and Nicolson, pp. 343–4

5   1756 *Etat actuel du royaume de la Grande Bretagne*. BL Add. MSS 20842, 406, A22
6   Black J 1987 *The Origins of War in Early Modern Europe*. Donald, pp. 185–209; Clark J 1982 *The Dynamics of Change*. Cambridge University Press, pp. 10–14
7   Black J 1985 *British Foreign Policy in the Age of Walpole*. Donald, p. 38
8   Haigh C 1988 *Elizabeth I*. Longman, p. 88
9   Starkey D 1987 *The English Court from the Wars of the Roses to the English Civil War*. Longman, p. 102
10   Elton GR 1953 *The Tudor Revolution in Government*. Cambridge University Press; Elton GR 1976 Tudor Government: the Points of Contact. III The Court. *Transactions of the Royal Historical Society*, XXVI
11   Beattie JM 1967 *The English Court in the Reign of George I*. Cambridge University Press; Gregg E 1980 *Queen Anne*. Routledge & Kegan Paul; Black J 1987 *The Collapse of the Anglo-French Alliance 1727–1731*. Alan Sutton, p. 214
12   Holmes G 1987 *British Politics in the Age of Anne*. Hambledon, p. 217; Elton GR 1974 Tudor Government: the Points of Contact. I The Parliament. *Transactions of the Royal Historical Society*, XXIV; Gregg E 1980, pp. 403–4
13   Ehrman J 1969 *The Younger Pitt: the Years of Acclaim*. Constable, pp. 169–70
14   Stuart J 1771 *Critical Observations on the Buildings of London*, pp. 32–8, 51–2
15   Elias N 1987 *The Court Society*. Oxford University Press
16   Ives EW 1986 *Anne Boleyn*. Basil Blackwell
17   Beattie JM 1967, pp. 247–8
18   Echeverria D 1985 *The Maupeou Revolution*. Baton Rouge, Louisiana, pp. 12–13; Black J 1986 *Natural and Necessary Enemies*. Duckworth, p. 190
19   Black J 1986, pp. 192–3
20   Dessert D 1984 *Argent, pouvoir et société au grand siècle*. Fayard
21   Williams P 1979 *The Tudor Regime*. Oxford University Press, p. 107
22   Brewer J 1989 *The Sinews of Power*. Unwin Hyman, pp. 79–85, 102–14
23   Clark J 1986 *English Society 1688–1832*. Cambridge University Press; Langford P 1989 *A Polite and Commercial People: England 1727–1783*. Oxford University Press, pp. 742, 690; Bush M 1983 *Noble Privilege*. Manchester University Press, p. 207
24   Hatton R 1969 *Europe in the Age of Louis XIV*. Thames and Hudson, p. 199; Stone L 1986 *An Open Elite? England 1540–1880*. Oxford University Press, pp. 303–6
25   Campbell PR 1988, p. 34
26   Cannon J 1984 *Aristocratic Century*. Cambridge University Press, pp. 125, 140–7, 177; Williams P 1979, p. 74
27   Williams P 1979, p. 93; Brewer J 1989, p. 17
28   Williams P 1979, pp. 428–51
29   Bernard GW 1985 *The Power of the Early Tudor Nobility*. Harvester, pp. 197–205; Gwyn P 1990 *The King's Cardinal: the Rise and Fall of Thomas Wolsey*. Barrie and Jenkins, pp. 212–35
30   Coward B 1988 *Social Change and Continuity in Early Modern England 1550–1750*. Longman, pp. 28–9; Stone L 1965 *The Crisis of the Aristocracy 1558–1641*. Oxford University Press

31 Cannon J 1984, pp. 115–23
32 Campbell P 1988, pp. 58–62
33 Kettering S 1986 *Patrons, Brokers and Clients in Seventeenth-Century France.* Oxford University Press, p. 217
34 Girouard M 1978 *Life in the English Country House.* Yale University, p. 138
35 Kettering S 1986, pp. 215, 218; Mertes K 1988 *The English Noble Household 1250–1600.* Basil Blackwell, p. 191
36 Jarrett D 1973, pp. 123–4
37 Darnton R 1976 The High Enlightenment and the Low-Life of Literature in Pre-Revolutionary France. In Johnson D (ed.) *French Society and the Revolution.* Cambridge University Press, pp. 53–87
38 Newman G 1987 *The Rise of English Nationalism.* Weidenfeld and Nicolson, pp. 68–9

CHAPTER FIVE

France and England: Absolutism Versus Parliamentary Liberties?

> The nations not so blessed as thee
> Must in their turn to tyrants fall
> While thou shall flourish great and free
> The dread and envy of them all
> (James Thomson, 1740)

PARLIAMENTS, ESTATES AND *PARLEMENTS*

Parliamentary liberties are still a sacrosanct portion of England's heritage. So they were to Georgians. Eighteenth-century critics of the Bourbons were quick to deny the *parlement*'s claims to a role similar to the English parliament's. Historians have believed them too readily. For other contemporaries discussed their inadequacies in the same terms and many, including Burke, thought the institutions comparable. Hanoverian newspapers spelled '*parlement*' as 'parliament' and discerned a similar function.[1] Both bore the name of '*parlement*' in the French-speaking thirteenth century, and the same appellation is unlikely to have been hitched to different contrivances. Subsequently they diverged, but not as much as Stubbs would have us believe when he set out to discover in the thirteenth and fourteenth centuries the parliament he knew in the 1870s. When stood on its head, historical methodology generates odd selection procedures. Stubbs excluded assemblies which called themselves parliaments and pronounced only foreign assemblies of social orders or estates to be comparable with the English parliament. This narrow definition disqualified France's *parlement* and left only its Estates-General and the German diets and the Spanish cortes.[2] Nineteenth-century historians arranged that France had never had a viable representative body simply by rigging their definitions.

Yet the English parliament was never an assembly of estates. In its earliest phase it represented only nobles, clergy and lawyers. Greater and lesser nobility finished in separate houses, the gentry rubbing shoulders with a minority of burghers and professionals. Admittedly the *parlement* was not elected, but neither was the senior body of the English parliament, the House of Lords. Many Frenchmen, including Voltaire, were contemptuous of the suggestion that the *parlement* represented anything but itself. Yet its 190 judges were a weighty segment of the robe nobility, and similar samples were represented in the twelve provincial *parlements*. The forty-nine grandees, who joined the Paris *parlement* when important political issues were at stake, were imposing specimens of the sword: yet they are usually overlooked. They bore roughly the same relationship to the rest of the French nobility as the 150 members of the English parliamentary peerage to the Hanoverian gentry. Their presence alongside the judges makes the *parlement* a good parallel to the House of Lords. Tocqueville considered the *parlements* representative – presumably of the nobility as a whole. As he was otherwise rude about them, there is no reason to suspect a biased judgement.

The English parliament in this period arouses less debate. It was a committee of landowners, representing in democratic terms only a few thousand people. But the obsession of English historians with borough franchises and distribution of seats has imposed an anachronistic mode of analysis, familiar to few Georgians apart from a minority of radicals. Eighteenth-century representation did not depend on democratic mechanisms. In a society textured by patronage and clientage, the English House of Lords and French *parlements* were obliged and happy to represent interest groups and individuals other than themselves, as well as corporations and localities. In this respect their role was comparable. As the embodiment of the ruling élite, both bodies were perceived as a barrier preventing the power of the crown from degenerating into despotism. Lamoignon de Malesherbes, the liberal-minded censor and official guardian of civil liberties, declared that the *parlement* was necessary to the preservation of the constitution: it was the guardian of the laws which regulated citizens' interests and safeguarded them against despotism. The princes of the blood used the same formula in 1771 when they protested against its abolition: the judges' independence guaranteed public liberty against arbitrary power.

Parliamentary liberties became the cornerstone of the unique heritage of the English nation from an early date. They may have existed in practice: it is quite certain that they have dominated the national myth for half a millenium. Fortescue in the fifteenth century is the first to mention them, as an object of national pride separating English from Continentals. By the fourteenth century financial need had induced most European rulers to establish assemblies of estates which could bind the realm by giving consent to taxation. Fortescue equipped his countrymen with totally unjustified grounds for smugness by informing them that parliaments were uniquely English. The popularity of this flattering misconception has never dimmed. Since it quickly became part of the national consciousness, the myth in a sense became reality and influenced English attitudes and behaviour. But we have less excuse than Tudor and Stuart Englishmen, who were too close to the euphoria, for not taking a hard look at the whole matter. Since the mid-1970s a group of revisionists, led by Elton and Russell, have examined the impact on our historiography of reading history backwards. Their target is Whig history, which starts with the triumph of parliament in the nineteenth century and then trawls preceding centuries for developments which made the happy outcome inevitable. The result has been to downgrade the importance of parliament in the sixteenth and seventeenth centuries, though the status of their verdict is controversial. Clark has extended their approach into the eighteenth century with similar results, though his conclusions are deemed even more speculative.

Nevertheless, it is now clear that the contemporary significance of England's parliament has been inflated. In the sixteenth and seventeenth centuries it was an intermittent and abnormal instrument of government. It had an undoubted monopoly of granting taxes, subject to the strategems devised by Tudor and Stuart ministers for evading it. Forced loans, benevolences and ship money were disputed but effective means of finding urgent cash. When parliamentary consent was sought, it was an exceptional event: taxes were voted for emergencies like war or invasion and not for the ordinary expenses of government. Two recent studies further deflate high claims for parliament's financial authority.[3] One suggests that under the early Tudors taxes were cleared with great councils (usually the Lords without the Commons) rather than parliaments. The other argues that under Elizabeth parliament's approval of taxation was a formal ritual: it was never withheld, and on one occasion an official was told to prepare an engrossed subsidy bill (one entered in the parliamentary record) *before parliament had met*. Both shift Tudor parliaments nearer to the rubber stamp model which some historians prefer for the French provincial Estates.

There is no doubt of the English parliament's grip on law-making: on the strength of it a neat distinction has been made with France, where the king made the laws. But law-making in England was a rare event: law was made exceptionally, to remedy abuses. Using it to effect permanent change in the name of improvement made little sense to a society which saw in the passage of time decay rather than progress.[4] In France the pronouncements of monarchs and political theorists prove that law-making was something different. It embraced much of the conduct of government, from the making of treaties to the granting of charters and the maintenance of the coinage of the realm. If these functions are renamed the royal prerogative, it appears that the king of England had the same powers. In neither country was executive and administrative action the business of parliamentary bodies, unless things were going wrong. Tudors and Stuarts spent as long as Bourbons warning their parliaments off prerogative matters of state. Elizabeth and James I have been accused of hypersensitivity in their jealous regard for their prerogatives: some historians even seem to believe that they invented the whole business. Yet from the Middle Ages the distinction between mysteries meet for kings and matter fit for subjects was one of the oldest in the business. In one respect, however, the French monarch was more generous. Letters patent, the form taken by certain categories of grants and orders, were subject to registration by the *parlement*. In England letters patent were a prerogative matter which never went near parliament: they were unparliamentary law-making.[5] Because of the all-embracing connotation of his law-making, the French monarch allowed his *parlement* to vet far more of what would in England have been placed in the hands-off category of royal policy. In France foreign treaties, royal charters and peerage grants were hands-on.

Compared with most Continental assemblies, the powers of England's parliament were surprisingly limited. Its summons was part of the king's prerogative rights. It met at royal will and had no right of regular or even periodic meeting. Nor had it the right to maintain any permanent presence between meetings: no standing committees or permanent officials oversaw royal government or monitored the spending of the taxes they themselves had granted.[6] In these respects it occupied a less prominent position than the provincial Estates in France, with their annual meetings and permanent syndics to speak on their behalf between sessions. And because it had no permanence, it did not enjoy the legal status of a corporation.

All this changed after 1688. England's parliament met annually and became a permanent political factor with which the country's rulers had to reckon. Yet this fails to invalidate comparisons with France, since the *parlement* had been in permanent session since the thirteenth century. But the English institution had the advantage of not being abolished as an abuse in 1790: it survived the *ancien régime* and successfully adapted to democracy. It has been retrospectively endowed with a more exalted role than it possessed and the parallel with France's *parlement* has been concealed. Neither French nor English monarchs imposed new taxes or made significant changes in the law without their participation. Both institutions were an *entrée* to power in which the rich could buy seats and seek further office. Scions of good families regarded both as a stepping stone to place and preferment: both were enmeshed in a network of élite patronage and kinship. England's parliament was in significant ways self-appointing. The landed gentry and peerage selected an overwhelming proportion of the House of Commons, their control making it one of the most exclusive assemblies in eighteenth-century Europe. The myth of a vigorous political life stimulated by parliamentary elections evaporates before the chill fact that in 1761 only forty-two out of 203 boroughs and four out of forty counties were contested – nor was this untypical. Many borough seats were as much their owner's property as seats in the French *parlement*. Cannon notes a relentless increase in the proportion of the Hanoverian Commons selected by the Lords. After a period of fluidity and confusion in Queen Anne's reign, the nobility steadily tightened their grip. In 1715, 105 seats were under their control – one-fifth of the House of Commons. By 1747 the number had risen to 167 and by 1784 to 197. The parliamentary patronage of the peerage had probably quadrupled since the beginning of the century. In 1784, 304 out of 558 MPs were related to peers. The opening of most Georgian parliaments resembled a family reunion.[7]

Both institutions were a forum for faction rivalry originating outside them – usually at court, since political information gathered elsewhere was an inadequate basis for intrigue.[8] Much of this was stage-managed by politicians avid to displace ministers of the crown. In these bodies most French and English ministers started their careers: skilful operators could use them as a power base to force themselves on the monarch, although the practice was officially deplored. In 1763 Laverdy, leader of the opposition in the *parlement*, was promoted to be controller-general of finance. Recent research has uncovered unexpected rivalries behind the scenes.[9] Foreign secretary

Choiseul was eager to replace controller-general Bertin. He persuaded the Jansenist opposition in the *parlement* to come up with a replacement and on the shortlist of three was imposed a competitive examination. Laverdy produced the best essay on the problem of combining increased revenue with *parlementaire* peace of mind. In a similar way George III's favoured minister Shelburne was ousted by Fox in 1783. (The parallel is inexact, since Fox was not a colleague of Shelburne; he had, however, been one six months before and the two were essentially rivals in government.)

Until recently, modern assumptions about cabinet solidarity blinded historians to this treachery by ministers towards their monarchs and colleagues. They frequently wanted their clients in posts occupied by fellow-councillors. Suitably manipulated, corporate bodies could be exploited as levers to supplement ministerial pressure on rulers. The *parlement*'s resistance to Turgot was initiated by his opponents in the ministry. Breteuil whipped up opposition in *parlement* to the reforms of his rival, Calonne. The lack of governmental unity which has emerged in France is mirrored in England throughout the period. Revisionists now note how Elizabeth I's ministers employed parliament as a fall-back mechanism when they had failed in a courtly context to coerce her into marrying a suitable husband or decapitating the Queen of Scots. Comparable stabs in the back by rival colleagues led to parliament's impeachment of Bacon and Cranfield in the 1620s. Nor did the danger evaporate with the supposed rise of the office of prime minister in Hanoverian England. The real threat to Walpole during the Excise Crisis of 1733 came from disaffected ministers such as Cobham and Chesterfield, who intrigued against him with the parliamentary opposition.[10] In both countries conflict between crown and corporate bodies was frequently the result of disagreement between the king's advisers, not of institutional opposition to royal policies. The main threat to ministers was from their colleagues.

French and English corporate bodies were also manipulated by the crown. Parallel to the clients maintained by Bourbon ministers in the *parlements* were the Hanoverian monarch's followers in both houses of parliament. The danger of royal financial dependence on the whims of members was neutralised by the distribution of crown patronage. 'Making a parliament' was essential if the English king's government was to be carried on. In this non-adversarial context, annual meetings were more blessing than curse, since no Georgian parliament ever refused supply or made it dependent on redress of grievance. But both monarchs preferred not to risk it and avoided appointing ministers so distasteful to these bodies that they refused taxation. The threat remained tacit in England but noisier in France. Louis XV was obliged to jettison Machault, Silhouette and Bertin as they were unable to obtain funds from the *parlement*. The technique which avoided this embarrassment in England is known as 'management'. It is unclear why the same technique, which often failed to prevent it in France, is known as 'absolutism'.

English and French representative bodies differed in many ways, but in the context that mattered most they were similar. They provided a medium through which the crown could conduct its relations with the ruling élite.[11] This will displease those who see French 'absolutism' as the institutional underpinning of a different social order from that of England. Yet recent studies viewing early modern institutions against the interplay of forces which gave them life conclude that the social basis of authority in England and France looks increasingly the same.[12] Relations between crown and representative bodies thus displayed a strong resemblance in both countries. Beyond rhetoric about checking royal power, they interpreted their role as co-operation with the monarch's government. They embodied a bond between centre and locality, crown and élite, which was beneficial to both and had nothing to gain from breaking it. There is little evidence that monarchs viewed them negatively. The availability of consent extended royal power into a wider context and bound the realm, or parts of it, to decisions reached collectively. The English parliament had the advantage of embodying a united state, itself the creation of a strong monarchy at an early date. The French *parlements* and Estates reflected a decentralised and composite state: consequently they were weaker *vis-à-vis* the crown, the sole embodiment of national unity, and less useful as royal agents. Yet Estates remained what they were when monarchs had called them into existence – an asset, not an outdated obstacle for the destruction of which supposedly 'absolutist' regimes relentlessly plotted.

Much of this contrast disappeared after 1603, when the Union with the crown of Scotland threatened to relegate England's parliament to the status of provincial Estates and destroyed its claim to represent the whole realm. In British terms it was as much a provincial assembly as the cortes of Castile. Ireland already had its own parliament and the addition of a separate parliament in Scotland made the constitutional position of the Stuarts comparable with that of the Bourbons. Henceforth relations between crown and parliament were destabilised by a novel factor. A parliament of England, which had no responsibility for the rest of the British Isles, had to partner a king of Great Britain, whose responsibility for the multiple kingdom was not even shared with his English Privy Council.[13] Historians have recently become interested in the problem of instability in composite states – a category which included most of the European monarchies.[14] Each was an empire of constituent provinces, all with their own laws and customs embodied in their own representative assemblies. The only principle of unity was the monarch, who ruled each of the theoretically equal provinces by a different title and under a different constitution. The problem was that in practice formal equality was nudged aside by the emergence of the ruler's home province as the dominant centre, containing the royal court and providing most of the resources. The French state, though not the most intractable example, managed relations with its constituent parts with more success than her rival. Significant, though unremarked, was England's final solution. It was not the 'absolutist' French but the 'limited' English regime which cut the knot by dissolving the peripheral assemblies.

1688: THE GREAT DIVIDE?

Modern historical opinion still endorses the Whig view that in or shortly after 1688 England acquired a parliamentary monarchy. The monarch had to delegate his power to ministers chosen by parliament: henceforth his views were subordinate to theirs. England diverged from 'absolutist' Europe and became one of the few realms where representative assemblies ruled the state.[15] Eighteenth-century government was parliamentary government. Macaulay announced in 1835 that from the Revolution England's parliament 'appointed and removed ministers, declared war and concluded peace'.[16] Namier corrected a bundle of Whig fallacies about party, but his impact on the role of parliament was less decisive. He himself stated that the first two Hanoverians had to base their government on the leaders of the majority party in the House of Commons.[17]

We have subsequently been alerted to the tendency to exaggerate the historic role of parliament.[18] To argue that by the eighteenth century authority lay with king-in-parliament is to ignore the authority that lay exclusively with the crown. Georgian parliaments claimed no powers and took no initiatives unknown to medieval assemblies – and in some respects fewer. Medieval parliaments had claimed to appoint and dismiss ministers and oversee policies on which taxes should be spent. Once a Georgian parliament had granted funds, the king could spend them how he liked. Even annual meetings were not new and they conferred on members no more ambition to run the government than was displayed by their more periodic predecessors. Parliament met every year under Edward III and vetted his expenditure. But that did not make him a parliamentary monarch. What mattered was not how often parliament met but whether it regarded itself as ally/critic of monarchy or as substitute for it. The attitudes of eighteenth-century MPs described by Namier are identical to those of their Tudor ancestors in Neale's analysis. Local, family or personal ambition predominated with both rather than the desire to initiate national policies. That was the prerogative of the king and his ministers.[19] Except when they were grossly incompetent, parliament was expected to support them.

A mass of evidence is emerging to make clear the personal power retained by Hanoverian monarchs.[20] Most of parliament's energies were devoted to managing the private and local affairs of the landed classes. Most legislation was private members' bills, of the kind which exercised provincial Estates in France. Three million acres were enclosed by parliament in the eighteenth century, while hundreds of public acts inaugurated canals and turnpikes. In contrast the crown had little interest in legislation and rarely required new laws. Its executive powers in the eighteenth century were almost entirely derived from the royal prerogative.[21] Overwhelmingly its greatest concern was for foreign policy and that fell within its prerogative. When in 1788 George III lapsed into insanity, the conduct of foreign policy ceased: negotiations were suspended and ambassadors left without instructions.[22] Only treaties which necessitated the voting of supply had to be made the subject of an act of parliament, unlike in France where all treaties were registered in the *parlement*. In peacetime, when subsidies were not required, most diplomacy was beyond parliamentary control and knowledge.[23] Hanoverian parliaments were interested in foreign policy and not without expertise, but so were the parliaments of Elizabeth I two centuries before.[24] No permanent parliamentary standing committees, conspicuous on the Continent, were created by the Revolution Settlement to monitor foreign policy. No restriction was placed on the monarch's right to declare war without parliamentary consent. The Scottish parliament's ban on such prerogatives in 1703 shows what could be done when assemblies had a mind to it. The English parliament had no new role in the formulation of eighteenth-century foreign policy. As in the 'absolutist' states, it was made at court.[25]

The 1689 Settlement was stated at the time to have restored the old constitution, not created a new one. Though this has recently been challenged it has been argued with equal conviction that the real revolutionary was James II, with his despotic disregard for property rights in the guise of university fellowships, benefices, army commissions and enclaves of local power. The Glorious Revolution was little more than a successful counter-revolution.[26]

The changes introduced by the Declaration of Rights were minor compared with what mattered from the monarch's point of view. It is true that in forbidding abuses (as with the dispensing power) the Convention Parliament made limitations explicit which in France remained implicit – and therefore easier to ignore. But the royal prerogative was left intact. Making war and peace, summoning and dissolving parliament, appointing and dismissing ministers were under the absolute control of the crown, as in France. Thus, though parliament had the satisfaction of forbidding armies in peacetime without its permission, it made no attempt to deprive the king of *control* of the army. The Triennial Act permitted up to three years between parliaments, which was more than the medieval average.

No parliamentary monarchy was established in the sense that the king could no longer choose his own ministers. Contrary to the usual assumption,[27] the 1688 Settlement posed no threat, direct or indirect, to this most vital of royal prerogatives. Eighteenth-century prime ministers (whose existence was long denied) were not invited to form an administration of their own choosing. The term looked back to Gaveston, Wolsey and Burghley, not forward to Major. It indicated one who monopolised royal favour, not one who used his command of parliament to dictate to the king.[28] As in France ministries usually included members who were opposed to the leading minister and whom it was impossible for him to discipline.[29] Nor did the rise of party prove a threat to royal control in the century following the Revolution. All seventeenth- and eighteenth-century monarchs refused to countenance it. Queen Anne declined to allow parliamentary majorities to dictate her choice of ministers.[30] Party had little significance as a device for managing the electorate or disciplining a faction in parliament. It gained ground in the 1790s but the Younger Pitt repudiated party and never tried to turn his followers into one.[31]

The only safe basis for political power was therefore royal favour. With it came access to royal patronage which would ensure management of parliament. As in France, the expansion of the state machine and the armed forces in the late seventeenth and early eighteenth centuries presented new opportunities for binding the élite to the monarchy. The crown undoubtedly lost independence by relying on parliament for servicing its debts in the great wars against France between 1689 and 1713. Like many European monarchs with the same problem, it regained it by deploying its military and civil employments to procure political goodwill. The result was state asset-stripping on an unprecedented scale. Hundreds of London jobs and over 6,000 local ones provided grazing for politically significant families. By the 1790s there were 14,000 fiscal officers, all obliged to use their influence on behalf of the government in elections. The creation of a large standing army gave employment to the nobles and gentry who manned the new officer corps: many were simultaneously MPs voting for the government.

Eighteenth-century governments therefore lost divisions rarely and elections never. Ministers who enjoyed the king's confidence had the moral and material means to command a parliamentary majority. They were appointed before and not after winning general elections. George II's failure to exercise his personal choice was largely self-inflicted. His subservience to a faction of Old Corps Whigs left him little room for manoeuvre. In 1744 he had to part with Carteret because no colleague would serve with him and in 1757 to appoint the Elder Pitt because no colleague would serve without him. Parliament had little to do with it. Faction could also impose on Louis XV a minister he did not want. The appointment of Laverdy in 1763 reflected the strength of the Jansenist opposition rather than the inclinations of the king.

The power with which ministers were endowed was the king's: he appointed and dismissed them. They rarely attempted to use their command of parliament to dictate policy to him.[32] They regarded themselves as responsible to the monarch and not to parliament. Its right of impeachment no more gave it the right to choose ministers and policies than did the same right in the fourteenth century. After 1832 royal powers were increasingly placed at the disposal of ministers chosen by the electorate, but until then the king's personal choice was crucial and of greater concern than parliament to politicians. This restores the centre of political gravity to the court, where it was in France.[33] Parliamentary debates might be important to Walpole and the Elder Pitt, but the decisive battle ground was the king's closet. Godolphin and Harley based their power from 1702 to 1714 on the queen's closet: neither led a majority party in the Commons.[34] Court intrigue undermined Walpole in 1733 and victory there was vital to his final survival. Bute, George III's Groom of the Stole, survived as chief minister for two years on the strength of court favour alone. Yet the Hanoverian court is almost totally neglected by historians.

As in France there were grey areas. Neither constitution was written and each was ambiguous. The Tory view stressed the king's unrestricted right to choose his ministers, while Whigs talked increasingly of his obligation to choose those enjoying the confidence of parliament.[35] So in France there was a *thèse royale* which placed absolute sovereignty firmly in the king's hands and a *thèse parlementaire* which awarded a more prominent role to the *parlements*. Just as the French court of the 1780s was split between the constitutional views of Breteuil and Vergennes, so was the English between those of Pitt and Fox.

Nor was there a shift to parliamentary monarchy after 1688 in England in the sense that a parliamentary title replaced divine right. In 1534 and 1544 parliament had set a powerful precedent for altering the succession by statute, and election to kingship was not considered to compromise the divine origin of the office. If the idea was to establish an earth-bound, quasi-republican regime, William III was unaware of it. He sat under a canopy like the best of the Tudors, was portrayed on horseback by Kneller as a slimmer version of the Sun King and built a palace at Hampton Court which is merely Versailles-on-Thames.[36]

ECONOMIC AND FISCAL POLICY

Comparison of economic policies supplies further correctives to platitudes about French 'absolutism' and English 'limited monarchy'. Both crowns used their assemblies to guarantee loans, English monarchs borrowing on the credit of the Westminster parliament and French on that of the provincial Estates, especially Languedoc. In spite of the usual assumption that this was a unique strength of the English crown, the Bourbons' credit was substantially extended by their ability to register major loans in the *parlement*. Both parliament and Estates took more interest in economic development than did their governments. They also constructed roads and canals, though the French crown had to pick up the bill where local Estates no longer existed.

Economic regulation is usually dragged into the discussion as it sounds like the sort of thing an 'absolutist' government should be doing. If so England and the Dutch Republic were as 'absolutist' as France for they controlled trade and industry to an equal extent, though without the comprehensive plans on paper to which Colbert was addicted. And it is possible to exaggerate his intentions. There is no evidence of his determination to regulate every morsel of economic activity, from the initiatives of great trading companies to the weaving of village crones. Nor, if this is the criterion, was France 'absolutist' for much longer. After 1760 it rapidly dismantled its mercantilist controls. Choiseul's edict of 1763 permitted foreign ships to carry goods to and from the French colonies: it was the first major breach in the old colonial system. Another edict of 1764 took a daring plunge towards free trade in grain. While France experimented with *laissez-faire* economics, England stuck for another generation to her mercantilist guns. The role of government in her industrial revolution has been underrated. State intervention in the shape of parliamentary statute was crucial for the security of capital investment.[37]

Scrutiny of French fiscal policy also fails to establish satisfactory 'absolutist' credentials. In France as much as England one of the greatest limitations on royal power was the refusal of taxpayers to provide the crown with what it considered an adequate revenue. The Bourbons could tax at will no more than the Stuarts and Hanoverians. For Louis XIV the moment of truth came with the Capitation (1695) and the Tenth (1710). These were new taxes based on a revolutionary principle – ability to pay. Levied on grounds of state necessity in wartime, they were subject to the judges' pronouncement that they should end with the emergency. The king's failure to render them permanent advertised royal inability to encroach on property rights. The belief that the French people were crippled by a tax burden imposed by an 'absolutist' monarch is a myth. The Hanoverian government extracted the same revenue from a population one-third of the size and producing half the GNP, while the nobility paid less than its opposite number in France.[38]

Brewer gives a neat twist to this. He stresses that it was precisely because England was a parliamentary state after 1688 that it created its fiscal–military apparatus so smoothly. Between 75 and 85 per cent of annual expenditure went on the armed forces – the same as in Prussia and more than in France. One man in thirty-six was in the army – more than in France or Russia. George II's army used 65,000 tons of flour annually for powdering wigs. He deployed more tax officials than either Prussia or France.[39] This is meant to prove that parliamentary institutions were more successful than 'absolutism' in mobilising resources for war. It can as easily indicate failure to *succeed* with organs of consent as failure to try. All Brewer proves is that representative bodies made monarchs strong and not weak. That is why they were introduced in the thirteenth century. French rulers were not unaware of their beauties: they often revealed their desire for effective ones. A new agenda is required for the period of French 'absolutism' – one which presents it as a quest for viable means of consultation in a mosaic state where jurisdictions overlapped, anomalies were the norm and the requirement was for management of thinly concealed chaos.

CIVIL LIBERTIES

Inseparable from representative assemblies are the liberties they guard. It is a historical commonplace that individual liberties were safer in England than pre-revolutionary France. French attachment to 1789 and English pride in occupying a land of liberty explain its origin. Yet Samuel Johnson disabused James Boswell at their first meeting: 'The notion of liberty amuses the people of England and helps to keep off the tedium vitae.'

The wraiths of the free-born Englishman and the French slave vanish before the chill facts. The relative freedom and importance of the press is a significant indicator. The English press is widely believed to have outclassed the French in political influence. This is partly in deference to the English national myth and partly owing to the assumption that the Hanoverian monarchy had lost its power. The French press seems to have exerted as much influence or more. Between 1750 and 1763 the Enlightened Malesherbes was the government's *directeur de la librairie*, who decided which books should be published. Under his relaxed interpretation of the rules Diderot and d'Alembert's *Encyclopédie* was published, along with Rousseau's more subversive volleys. Most texts got through, short of exhortations to regicide. Nor was the French government responsible for most of the bans imposed: they were usually the responsibility of corporate bodies. Rousseau's *Emile* was proscribed not by Louis XV but by that celebrated opponent of 'absolutism', the *parlement* of Paris. By the 1770s the Enlightenment had conquered most of the institutions of intellectual life and the Bourbons presided over one of the most vigorous political cultures in Europe. There are no grounds for the belief that 'absolutism' closed down political life until 1789. The revolutionary ideology was assembled from commonplaces of progressive opinion in the *ancien régime*.

The English press enjoyed no more freedom in the sixteenth and seventeenth centuries than the French. Charles I deprived Prynne of his ears for attacking the Church, and it was no untypical display of

Stuart despotism. Queen Elizabeth shared the attitude but confiscated a different member when Stubbs lost his right hand for criticising her matrimonial fantasies. A Star Chamber decree of 1583 subordinated press freedom to the inspired judgement of the Archbishop of Canterbury. Nor was liberty of the press more secure after the 1688 Revolution. The end of the Licensing Act in 1695 did not establish formal freedom of the press: the decision not to renew it was taken for practical rather than idealistic reasons. The liberalism of a regime does not depend on the existence or non-existence of a libel law. It depends on its scope, and from that test Hanoverian England emerges badly. Hints of dissatisfaction with government or its servants were treated as seditious libel. The opinion of one of Queen Anne's judges scarcely places the law on the side of freedom of expression: '. . . it is very necessary for all governments that the people should have a good opinion of it. And nothing can be worse to any government than to endeavour to procure animosities, as to the management of it; this has always been looked upon as a crime and no government can be safe without it be punished.'[40]

Both Whig and Tory governments viewed an unbridled press as a threat to political stability. Repression took two forms. The Stamp Act of 1712 imposed taxes to raise the cost of newspapers, while the libel laws were interpreted broadly and tyrannically. In 1716 Townshend had the publisher of a Tory pamphlet arrested. He was sentenced to six months imprisonment and whipped from the jail to Smithfield market. A few years after the regent Orléans relaxed censorship, Walpole tightened it: his 1737 Act made short work of stage libels and was not as exceptional as often assumed. Until stopped by the Wilkes judgement, secretaries of state could order a search for anyone associated with publication of a libel: where names were unknown a General Warrant was used. Offenders often behaved more amenably after confiscation of their goods and papers, rough treatment at the hands of the messenger, a gruelling examination, residence in Newgate and a bill for accommodation.[41]

It is also assumed that the physical liberty of the individual was safer in England than France. In the last fifteen years a group of Marxist-inspired historians has emphasised the ruthlessness with which an élite of eighteenth-century nobles and squires repressed the lower orders. A brutal regime lurked behind the cool Palladian portico and the family posing gracefully on the lawn for Mr Gainsborough. Scepticism has been aroused by the determination of these historians to present poachers, smugglers and wreckers as protesters against a class conspiracy. In most cases they clearly were not – and one of the most enterprising smugglers of the century was Robert Walpole.[42] But the bland acceptance of Hanoverian England as a land of liberty has been successfully challenged. By 1800 several 'absolutist' states had reduced the number of capital offences or abolished the death penalty altogether. In England, though the law was administered erratically, it is notorious that over 200 crimes were capital. The Game Laws prohibited the killing of game to all save substantial landowners. More particularly, the Black Act of 1723 prescribed death for anyone appearing armed or disguised in a gentleman's park. It was unnecessary to prove that he had actually poached any deer.[43]

This seems a fair parallel to better-publicised stories of feudal hunting rights in France. Defoe was confident that the strong tradition of English liberties would have been a match for the troops who opened fire on a crowd at Versailles. His faith was touching: it failed to stop an act which in 1715 made it lawful for English troops to fire on demonstrators who refused to disperse after due warning. Royal troops were billeted on non-taxpayers in England and Scotland as well as in France, and the Hanoverian army's biggest role was the containment of bread riots and political unrest.[44] The English populace displayed an alarming tendency to detest tax collectors, protect smugglers and deride the law. Politicians were widely regarded as criminals and criminals as heroes. Condemned highwaymen were the pop stars of Georgian London and their last journey to Tyburn was reminiscent of the triumphal return of Cup Final winners. When order collapsed in London during the Gordon Riots of 1780, the mob made as straight a beeline for Newgate prison as Parisians did in similar circumstances for the Bastille.

Informed opinion in Continental Europe regarded England as a haven of religious liberty and France as a hotbed of persecution. There were strong reasons for the more relaxed attitudes of the Church of England after, though not before, the Toleration Act of 1689. This broke the Church's official monopoly and made it hard for Church courts to maintain ecclesiastical discipline: parishioners who were harassed tended to leave one church and join another. But Roman Catholic and Jewish worship did not fall within official toleration, and participants were excluded from public life and political rights. Nonconformist worship was permitted but Protestant Dissenters were theoretically barred by the Test and Corporation Acts from municipal and civil rights. In their case enforcement is a complex process to unravel: it mainly depended on local attitudes, and in the right places Dissenters could dominate local oligarchies.

But as Clark has stressed, *ancien régime* England was a confessional state and could be uncomfortable for outsiders.

Much the same was true of France, where the degree of toleration afforded to Protestant Huguenots varied according to time and place. For much of the sixteenth and seventeenth centuries their rights of worship and citizenship were far more substantial than those enjoyed by Catholics in England. Before the persecution of the 1670s and 1680s Huguenots were to be found presiding over municipal councils, officiating in bi-partisan courts (*chambres mi-parties*) and prominent in gilds, tax farms, the magistracy and the professions. After the removal of all their rights by the Revocation of the Edict of Nantes in 1685, they gradually fought their way back to the previous position. In the 1760s the youthful de la Barre and the aged Calas were helpless victims of religious bigotry, the one condemned to have his tongue ripped out and his head cut off for blasphemy and the other to be broken on the wheel for arousing the prejudices of the Catholic community of Toulouse. Again the persecuting bodies were the *parlements* rather than the government. The significance of these infamous episodes lies less in their occurrence than in the repugnance aroused, which suggests their rarity. In 1787 Lamoignon restored full civil rights to Protestants – a noble gesture of which the significance is often missed. It gave them a status denied at that time to Catholics *and* Protestant Dissenters in England. In 1789 Lord Stanhope unsuccessfully moved the repeal of the Test and Corporation Acts. He argued that unless something was done English Dissenters would enjoy greater civil liberty in France than in their own country.[45] The myth of England's well-advertised religious freedom was exploded, just in time, by the last ministers of France's *ancien régime*.

REFERENCES

1   Black J 1986 *Natural and Necessary Enemies*. Duckworth, p. 191
2   Sayles GO 1975 *The King's Parliament of England*. Arnold, p. 33
3   Holmes PJ 1986 The Great Council in the Reign of Henry VII. *English Historical Review*, **401**; Dean and Jones (eds) 1990 *The Parliaments of Elizabethan England*. Basil Blackwell, pp. 101–2
4   Sharpe K 1989 *Politics and Ideas in Early Stuart England*. Pinter, p. 91
5   Hinton RWK 1957 The Decline of Parliamentary Government under Elizabeth and the Early Stuarts. *Cambridge Historical Journal*, XIII, 2, pp. 125–6

6   Bush M 1983 *Noble Privilege*. Manchester University Press, p. 112

7   Cannon J 1984 *Aristocratic Century*. Cambridge University Press, pp. 104–15

8   Black J 1990 *Robert Walpole and the Nature of Politics in Early Eighteenth-Century England*. Macmillan, p. 100

9   Swann J 1989 Politics and the Parlement of Paris 1754–71. Unpublished Cambridge Ph.D. thesis, pp. 192–6

10 Black J 1990, pp. 36, 61–2

11 Miller J 1984 The Potential for 'Absolutism' in Later Stuart England. *History*, **69**, p. 204

12 Kamen H 1984 *European Society 1500–1700*. Hutchinson, p. 305; Clark JCD 1985 *English Society 1688–1832*. Cambridge University Press, pp. 42–118; Jones C 1989 France and England: How We Saw Ourselves. In *A Tale of Two Cities*. Comag, pp. 12–26

13 Russell C 1983 The Nature of a Parliament in Early Stuart England. In Tomlinson H (ed.) *Before the English Civil War*. Macmillan, pp. 134–5; Russell C 1982 Monarchies, Wars and Estates in England, France and Spain, c. 1580–c. 1640. *Legislative Studies Quarterly*, VII, pp. 205–20

14 Koenigsberger HG 1987 *Early Modern Europe 1500–1789*. Longman, pp. 48–9;

15 Doyle W 1978 *The Old European Order*. Oxford University Press, p. 37; Dickinson HT 1981 Whiggism in the Eighteenth Century. In Cannon J (ed.) *The Whig Ascendancy*. Arnold, p. 40

16 Macaulay TB 1907 *Critical and Historical Essays*. Everyman, p. 323

17 Owen JB 1973 George II Reconsidered. In Whiteman A, Bromley JS and Dickson PGM (eds) *Statesmen, Scholars and Merchants*. Oxford University Press, p. 115

18 Sayles GO 1975 pp. 3–20; Elton G 1986 *The Parliament of England*. Cambridge University Press, p. ix, 377–9

19 Miller J 1983 *The Glorious Revolution*. Longman, pp. 73–4; Pares R 1953 *King George III and the Politicians*. Oxford University Press, p. 2

20 Gregg E 1984 *Queen Anne*. Routledge & Kegan Paul; Clark JCD 1986 *Revolution and Rebellion*. Cambridge University Press, pp. 68–91; Owen JB 1973

21 Clark JCD 1982 *The Dynamics of Change*. Cambridge University Press, p. 451

22 Pares R 1953, pp. 7, 163–4; Blanning TCW and Haase C 1989 George III, Hanover and the Regency Crisis. In Black J *Knights Errant and True Englishmen*, John Donald, p. 135

23 Gibbs GC 1970 Laying treaties before Parliament in the Eighteenth Century. In Hatton R and Anderson MS (eds) *Studies in Diplomatic History*. Longman

24 MacCaffrey WT 1981 *Queen Elizabeth and the Making of Policy 1572–1588*. Princeton University, pp. 485–90

25 Black J 1984 *Britain in the Age of Walpole*. Macmillan, pp. 168–9; Black J 1991 *A System of Ambition? British Foreign Policy 1660–1793*. Longman, pp. 19, 30, 43–58

26 Speck WA 1988 *Reluctant Revolutionaries*. Oxford University Press, pp. 139–65; Harrison G 1990 Prerogative Revolution and Glorious Revolution: Political Proscription and Parliamentary Undertaking,

1687–88. *Parliaments, Estates and Representation*, **10**, no. 1, pp. 29–43

27 Speck WA 1988, 163–5; Miller J 1983, pp. 76–8

28 Kemp B 1976 *Sir Robert Walpole*. Weidenfeld and Nicolson, pp. 4–7

29 Black J 1990, p. 63

30 Gregg E 1984, p. 403

31 O'Gorman F 1982 *The Emergence of the British Two Party System*. Arnold, pp. 23, 51–3; Ginter DE 1967 *Whig Organisation in the General Election of 1790*. California University Press, xlv–xlvi

32 Black J 1985 *British Foreign Policy in the Age of Walpole*. Donald, p. 36

33 Beattie J 1967 *The English Court in the Reign of George I*. Cambridge University Press, p. 217

34 Coward B 1980 *The Stuart Age*. Longman, p. 361

35 Peters M 1988 Pitt as a Foil to Bute: the Public Debate over Ministerial Responsibility and the Powers of the Crown. In Schweizer K (ed.) *Lord Bute. Essays in Reinterpretation*. Leicester University Press, p. 111

36 Summerson J 1977 *Architecture in Britain 1530–1830*. Penguin, p. 246

37 Langford P 1989 *A Polite and Commercial People*. Oxford University Press, p. 391

38 Braudel F 1984 *Civilization and Capitalism, Volume III: The Perspective of the World*. Collins, pp. 383–4

39 Brewer J 1989 *The Sinews of Power*. Unwin Hyman, pp. 40, 42, 128

40 Williams EN 1960 *The Eighteenth-Century Constitution*. Cambridge University Press, p. 402

41 Hyland PJB 1986 Liberty and Libel. *English History Review*, **401**

42 Cannon J 1981 *The Whig Ascendancy*. Arnold, p. 183

43 Thompson EP 1977 *Whigs and Hunters*. Peregrine, pp. 21–2

44 Childs J 1982 *Armies and Warfare in Europe*. Manchester University Press, pp. 177–91, 197

45 Jarrett D 1973 *The Begetters of Revolution*, Longman, pp. 257–8

CHAPTER SIX
A Theory of Absolutism?

Most critics of 'absolutism' as a concept have focused on the practice of governments. They have exposed the extent to which rulers failed to achieve their programmes. But the theory of 'absolutism' has been assumed rather than examined. The question is whether such a theory existed in early modern times. We start with the three ruler classifications used in early modern Europe – monarch, republic and despot. Then we shall see if we require another to make sense of the story.

PROBLEMS OF EVIDENCE

Forms of government were regulated by a constitution, which laid down the distribution, procedures and limits of public power. Constitutions were usually customary, resulting from tacit agreement by the community about the best way of satisfying its collective needs. They might include written items, such as the English constitution's Magna Carta and Declaration of Rights, but their weight rested on the acceptance of a customary way of doing things. Nineteenth-century European Liberals considered customary constitutions to be no constitutions at all, since they had benefited from what they considered the superior arrangements of the late eighteenth century – getting fundamentals on paper.

The lack of written constitutions before the 1770s has an important consequence for historians. A definitive statement about the source and limits of power was beyond the capacities of contemporaries. Controversy rumbled at the time and subsequently. Before we enter the fray, let us be clear that the Bourbon constitution had little objective existence. It was merely the sum total of what people said and thought about it at the time. Nor did the monarchs of seventeenth-century France ever make an official statement about the extent and nature of their power. A few one-liners are attributed to Louis XIV, including the notorious 'L'état, c'est moi' – which can be made to fit any theory of Bourbon power that one chooses. His motto was *nec pluribus impar*, which is Versailles-speak for 'I'm the greatest'. It scarcely amounts to a political theory. He also wrote his *Memoirs*, but these tips for a Dauphin in no way amount to a systematic treatise.

Contemporary theory about how political systems operated requires examination at three distinct levels. The standard clichés of 'the free-born Englishman' originated among the politically illiterate. 'Popery and wooden shoes' was the complacent slogan with which seventeenth-century Protestant mobs mocked the servile penury of Catholic peasantry: the enthusiastic support for absolute power by Protestant writers in Germany and Scandinavia underlines its divorce from reality. By the eighteenth century Englishmen revelled in what Wilberforce described as the special privilege of being born an Englishman.[1] Popular awareness in France appreciated the merits of strong monarchy but dwelled lovingly on 'the liberties of the French'. Early modern Frenchmen did not regard themselves as slaves, much as the fact would have astonished their English contemporaries.

These archetypes were echoed and exploited at a higher level by political hacks and activists for blatantly propagandist purposes. Tens of thousands of ephemeral tracts and pamphlets, the status of which as historical evidence is dubious and the authors of which are forgotten, are dismissed by some historians as dictated by political convenience. Others, led by Pocock and Skinner, view them as the intellectual matrix out of which the major texts of Harrington and Hobbes emerged. For they could not have worked as propaganda if they failed to acknowledge norms widely regarded as acceptable. At the first two levels the traditional picture of England as a 'limited' monarchy and France as 'absolutist' is to some extent sustained. One loses count of English writers' acclamations of the capacity of their constitution for safeguarding subjects' life, liberty and property. By the same token France was found wanting. All three desirables were depicted as subject to the whims of Bourbon tyrants. The French disagreed and denounced English sneers as a travesty of their constitution.

At the highest level political philosophers like Hobbes are sometimes misleading as academic authorities on working constitutions, or even on the theory of absolute power as understood by contemporaries. As Skinner has pointed out, the great texts are often the least representative of the political thought of an age.[2] A different picture emerges if we accept Mousnier's advice to attend to the comments of those involved in the operations of government – to ministers' memos, bishops' sermons and Estates' declarations. French and English are then found to agree about fundamentals.

THE CONCEPT OF THE STATE

In the Middle Ages there was no 'state' – at least not in the modern theoretical sense of the word. It denotes a unique association characterised by sovereignty, the existence of a supreme law-making power. The state concentrates the individual wills and interests of the community in a central authority with power over their collective affairs. Such was the '*res publica*' of Ancient Rome – public affairs. For centuries after the Fall of Rome these conceptions were blurred by a return to what were essentially tribal societies. Larger units returned in the Middle Ages, but if they boasted any 'state' it was the state of Christendom, ruled in theory by the Holy Roman Emperor and the Pope. They were the only rulers who could legitimately claim supreme power.

Even these heavyweights scarcely ruled sovereign states, since the medieval notion of making law was not ours. We envisage the conscious will of a legislator, whether the whole community or a single ruler. So did the Romans. But in the Middle Ages law meant habit or custom and the nearest thing to legislation was compilation or codification of what already existed. The legal codes of medieval rulers are the customs they confirmed. Their so-called 'law-making' is often what we regard as the executive and judicial functions of government. They made no distinction between these and legislation, much of which was their assent to the judicial petitions of their subjects. This intermingling of government functions survived until the eighteenth century, though Montesquieu's division of them into executive, legislative and judicial has obscured the fact.

At the same time public authority was diffused. In the period of the barbarian invasions and settlement it fell to the noble dominant in each area. Feudal ties bonded lord, vassal and serf in mutual obligation and counts, marquises and dukes wielded kingly prerogatives of commanding armies, 'making' laws and minting money. Again there was no focus of sovereignty, since power had passed from the king to those who wielded it in their own right. Feudal society was a pyramid in which the monarch retained nominal status at the apex but real authority had slipped to the base. From the king's point of view feudal theory was accordingly contractual and non-autocratic.

Modern ideas of the state resulted directly from renewed study of Roman law. By the fourteenth century two ideas were proving useful. One was a snippet from the Roman lawyer Ulpian, misleadingly famous only for its first clause: '*quod principi placuit legis habet vigorem*'. The whole passage creates a somewhat different impression. 'What the prince has decided has the force of law, inasmuch as by a special enactment (*lex regia*) concerning his government the people has conferred on him the whole of its government and power.' This made available the notion that somewhere in the community, whether in the people or in the prince, is located the ultimate will which is the essence of the state, and that law-making in the creative sense was the expression of its power. The other idea proceeded from the first. The supreme power within the state must not be subject to a higher power without. The Roman '*imperium*' or supreme power was borrowed from the Holy Roman Emperor and appropriated by half the kings of Europe. By the sixteenth century the concept of the modern state existed.[3]

THEORIES OF ROYAL SOVEREIGNTY

Monarchy was absolute by definition. That was the point of it. 'Monarchy' is Greek for 'rule of one', and 'absolute power' implies that one man made decisions of high policy without the need to defer to anyone else: the tautology of 'absolute monarchy' was spotted several times in the early modern period. Since monarchy concentrated power in the hands of one individual and denied anyone else the legitimate right to overrule him, it was a political commonplace that it was the most effective form of government. It was contrasted with republican arrangements, in which executive power was entrusted to a committee or assembly and consequently vulnerable to paralysis and delay.

Before the fourteenth century absolute monarchy could scarcely exist, since the rulers of the European states were theoretically subject to Pope and Emperor. But from that time they began to claim the *imperium* or imperial power which put them on a level with the

Emperor, subject to none. Roman law was raided for tags flattering to concepts of kingship and *rex in regno suo est imperator* made the headlines: 'the king in his kingdom is an emperor'. Monarchs began to wear the arched crowns which signified supreme as opposed to lesser power. For 200 years the coin of the realm portrayed English kings in an open crown, before Henry VII appeared resplendently in arched headgear on the gold sovereign. From Philip IV of France to Henry VIII of England the theme was the same. The king was independent of any higher or equal power and his authority was absolute.

Monarchs simultaneously asserted their power against the feudal authority of the landed nobility. Their theorists claimed for the crown a monopoly of law-making and jurisdiction, of war-making and taxation: seigneurial powers which survived were delegated by the crown and not independent rights. Feudal relationships had been contractual. Service was conditional on satisfaction. Hence the famous oath of the cortes of Aragon: 'We who are as good as you swear to you who are no better than we, to accept you as our king and sovereign lord, provided you observe all our liberties and laws; and if not, not.'

From the sixteenth century this feudal right of rebellion was rejected by royal theorists. In France Du Moulin's '*Commentaries*' of 1539 insisted that royal demands were absolute and that none could share his theoretical monopoly of sovereignty or '*imperium*'. He dismantled the feudal pyramid of independent powers and mutual rights and obligations.[4] This coincided with Francis I's drive to eliminate nobles who levied taxes, made laws, declared war, raised rebellion. By 1500 England, France and Spain had all emerged from civil wars incited by overmighty subjects. The absolute authority of the crown was seen as a liberating and not a repressive force. It was preferable to the tyranny of the local magnate. A Spanish royal councillor noted that men 'wanted to leave lordship and place themselves under the freedom of the king'.[5]

Many historians have mistaken the objective of the theory of absolute power.[6] It targeted those who threatened royal authority, both internally and externally. It was *not* a conspiracy to enslave the people. This is clear from a simple juxtaposition. The first references to absolute power are accompanied by continued emphasis on subjects' rights and representative institutions. In the Spain of Ferdinand and Isabella the crown's absolute authority had been recognised since the fourteenth century. Yet though only the crown could make laws it did so in the presence and with the consent of the representative cortes. Though the crown was declared absolute it could not tax its subjects without consent. Palacios Rubios, an early sixteenth-century jurist, pronounced the king to be 'entrusted solely with the administration of the realm, not with dominion over property'. The crown was absolute yet the king was subject to the law and could be cited before the courts. It was absolute yet it had to respect the fundamental laws of the realm, such as not alienating its own property. Though absolute it allowed free discussion of political affairs. A contemporary historian commented that Spain and her rulers would lose credibility if subjects were not allowed to speak freely.[7] Nor was Spain an exception. French monarchs were called 'absolute' at a time when the Estates-General was summoned with untypical regularity.

So in what sense was the power of French and Spanish kings alleged to be absolute? Clearly it implied no challenge to subjects' rights or the representatives who upheld them. It was part of the bulwark erected to make the monarch independent of Church and nobility. The more monarchs asserted their rights against these rivals, the more they defined those of their subjects. While royal power was limited by foreign superiors, guarantees of subjects' freedom remained implicit. When it became imperial and sovereign, guarantees were spelled out and parliaments and Estates mushroomed all over Europe. The republican virtues of freedom, self-government and the rule of law were effectively preserved beneath the surface of monarchy by the device of corporate bodies charged with the representation of subjects' rights. The motive was not royal altruism but self-interest. As the crown's authority grew, the obstacle of subjects' rights could be legitimately surmounted with their consent. It was one of several ways in which Estates enhanced monarchy rather than diminishing it. With them the ruler bargained over taxes and negotiated changes in the law. Estates in turn were eager to defend his new authority against the old adversaries. From Charles VII's Pragmatic Sanction of Bourges to Henry VIII's Act of Supremacy, corporate and representative bodies were the staunchest upholders of absolute power.

Absolute power – but not despotic. Rulers sometimes *did* trample on the rights of their people. When they did so, 'despot' was the name with which they were stigmatised. Until the late eighteenth century, when a clique of Enlightened intellectuals discovered undetected possibilities in the concept, it was a dirty word. This vital point has been obscured by the current obsession with judging which eighteenth-century rulers win the 'Enlightened Despot' award. Few early modern monarchs would have wanted it.

BODIN AND ABSOLUTIST THEORY?

In the 1570s Bodin's *Six Books of the Republic* popularised the word 'sovereignty' and defined it as an absolute and irresistible power. His Gallic logic could not tolerate the contradiction of a final authority which could be challenged. Bodin is seen as the crucial thinker in the development of 'absolutist' theory. He is credited with destroying the medieval theory of the 'mixed' constitution and substituting that of 'absolutism'. The first was based on shared power and mutual obligations, the second on monopolised power and royal autocracy. The discovery that law could be enacted by a legislator as well as enshrined in custom was apparently charged with 'absolutist' tendencies. Did law come from the people or from a king? We are informed that a vital principle was at stake: was government to be constitutional or absolute?[8]

Historians of political thought have tended to seize on the original features of his work and marginalise the discrepant elements as inconsistencies. His sovereign makes the law and is therefore not bound by it (*legibus solutus*), since supreme power cannot be subject to itself. But his power is not arbitrary and lawless: that would be a contradiction in terms. He is subject to the laws of God and nature. Nor can he alter the fundamental laws which establish the constitution, such as the law of succession. Above all, he must respect his subjects' right to their property and cannot tax them without their consent. Bodin thus ensures that his sovereign is no despot.[9]

There is a further limitation which has passed unnoticed. He endows his sovereign with law-making power and emphasises that because it is not to be shared it is to be exercised without consent. Most modern commentators assume that he refers to the creation of law in the modern sense, which sounds sinister. But when it is reduced to its components, it consists of royal prerogatives which Bodin was anxious to buttress against noble challenge. He was also eager to refute theorists such as Hotman and Beza, the so-called monarchomachs or king-killers.[10] These scary scribblers drew up a grim scenario which envisaged assemblies of estates supervising matters of state, appointing ministers, declaring war and peace, determining public law and deposing wicked kings. Significantly, Bodin's definition of law-making embraces all the irresistible prerogative powers of royalty which they had conferred on the Estates – appointing councillors, declaring war, coining money and so on. He is still failing to distinguish what we should consider the separate legislative, executive and judicial functions of government. The modernity of his analysis of sovereignty has distracted attention from his regression: he continues to think of law-making in a medieval manner. In Bodin, and writers such as Loyseau and Le Bret who followed him, 'law-making' is little more than the prerogatives enjoyed by the crown for centuries.

The mistake is to see Bodin in the context of developments which occurred long after him rather than as part of the intellectual destruction of feudalism. Henceforth there was allegedly a polarisation between those who placed above all other considerations the absolute authority of the crown and those who would ultimately sacrifice it to the rights of the people. No such polarisation existed. Away from the political extremities the crucial concept was that of a *balanced* constitution which preserved harmony between subject and sovereign. This was a favourite theme of those 'correspondences' which gave such satisfaction to early modern media-watchers. Harmony in the commonwealth (the body politic) mirrored harmony in the microcosm (the human body) and the macrocosm (the heavenly bodies and the music of the spheres). Most regimes were based on a theory which stressed both the sovereign authority of the crown *and* the rights of the people. Absolute and limited ('mixed') power were not alternatives. They were two aspects of the same political system. To regard them as mutually exclusive betrays a nineteenth-century perspective (see Chapter 9). In prerogative matters the crown was absolute; in matters touching subjects' rights it was limited by law – and the need for consent if it was altered. Bodin advocated absolute power for the king and a strong role for the estates: a prince who abolished them would embark on a barbarous tyranny and ruin the State. This duality is a fundamental aspect of so-called 'absolutist' regimes – and one of the most underplayed.

It is incorrect to present Bodin's thought as leading straight to 'absolutism'. Salmon has shown it was exploited for widely different ends. He changed his mind so often and festooned his basic principles with so many glosses that it was hard to be sure of his intentions. Some commentators fused his concept of sovereignty with divine right kingship to engender a near-despotic theory of monarchy. Others deployed it as an argument for the supremacy of parliaments. Translating Bodin in 1606, Knolles praised his theory of sovereignty as compatible with the English common law.[11] Emphasis on other parts of the text suggested that, though legislative sovereignty was indivisible and located in the state, the practical arrangements of government might divide and distribute power in a variety of ways. The monarch could therefore govern through aristocratic and representative elements.[12] It is these diverse interpretations of Bodin which dominate the next century. The most famous of them, Loyseau, Le Bret and Bossuet, reproduce faithfully the balance he achieved between royal prerogatives and subjects' rights.

TWO SPHERES OF ROYAL AUTHORITY

Theory in both France and England stressed the coexistence of absolute power on the one hand and limited, shared or mixed power on the other. In about 1470 Fortescue described the government of England as *regimen politicum et regale* – a famous term which has been misunderstood. It did not mean mixed government. *Politicum* signified mixed and *regale* royal government. Fortescue did not suggest that the king had one power which he shared with parliament. He had two, one shared with parliament and one his alone. *Rex in parliamento* taxed and legislated. *Rex solus* wielded the royal prerogative. The distinction is usually ignored. The balance between the two was praised a century later by James Morice. He contrasted 'the sovereign authority of one, an absolute prince, great in majesty' with 'the subjects of this kingdom . . . enjoying by limits of law and justice our lives, lands, goods and liberties'.

Historians have often obscured this duality. An expert on the English ideology of liberty presents it as incompatible with absolute power, which is equated by the author with despotism.[13] Yet absolute prerogatives and subjects' rights were *not* normally perceived as rivals. In the parliament of 1610 Thomas Hedley rhapsodised on their interdependence. Remarking that the law guaranteed the king his prerogatives and the subject his land and goods, he extolled the virtues of both: 'This kingdom enjoyeth the blessings and benefits of an absolute monarchy and of a free estate. . . . Therefore let no man think liberty and sovereignty incompatible, that how much is given to the one is taken from the other; but rather like twins, that they have such concordance and coalescence, that the one can hardly long subsist without the other.' The reason is explained. Subjects secure in their liberty and property can sustain a powerful king who is in turn 'able to stand of himself without the aid of any neighbour princes or states and so to be an absolute king . . . able to defend himself and his subjects against the greatest monarchs in the world'.[14] The same sentiments were repeated a century later in Swift's comment on the Tories: 'They believe that the prerogative of a sovereign ought, at least, to be held as sacred and inviolable as the rights of his people, if only for this reason, because without a due share of power, he will not be able to protect them.'[15]

Similar sentiments were expressed in contemporary France. Forty years after Bodin, Loyseau addresses the same theme. 'Sovereignty is the form which gives being to the State . . . it consists of absolute power.' He swiftly adds that three kinds of law limit the sovereign power. These are the laws of God and nature, as well as the fundamental laws of the state (which guaranteed the royal succession, the royal domain and the life, liberty and property of the people). In the middle of the century a certain Doctor Bernier rejoiced that God had not made French monarchs proprietors of their subjects' lands. Had they sought to be more absolute than the laws of God and nature permitted, they would soon have found themselves 'kings of desert and solitude, of beggars and savages'. The consensus is evident. Regal raids on subjects' property were short-sighted. In the long run they killed the goose that laid the golden egg. The same opinion was common a century later, when Moreau asserted that there was no legitimate government without the protection of liberty and property. 'Property has been precarious whenever our kings have ceased to be powerful and absolute . . . those who under the feudal regime oppressed the people were the same tyrants who divided among themselves the debris of royal authority . . . the crown had to regain its rights for slavery to disappear.'[16]

The crucial issue was taxation. The absolute authority of the English king did not extend to appropriating his people's property. He required their consent. So did the French king. The permanent *taille* was theoretically levied by extension of the consent of the Estates-General of 1439. Until the Revolution no new taxes could be imposed without the consent of the *parlements* – and of the Estates in the provinces which retained them.[17] Historians refer airily to the right of French monarchs to levy taxes without consent,[18] but when cross-examined the usual authorities do not yield what is required of them. Far from advocating taxation without consent, Bodin denounced it. He was adamant that property rights were not subject to the ruler's will. It is usually argued that he had dozed into inconsistency. Far from it. It is the crux of his distinction between monarchy and despotism. Subjects who could be robbed of their property were not subjects but slaves. Rulers who could do it were not monarchs but thieves.

Some seventeenth-century writers distorted Bodin by suggesting that subjects' property rights could be invaded, but none of them was the official spokesman of the king. Bossuet, however, was. As the tutor of Louis XIV's grandson and most regular preacher in the royal chapel, he was an oracle on 'absolutism'. His defence of the rights of the individual was unambiguous and consistent with the fundamental laws of the realm. These forbade tinkering with the axioms of royalty. The royal domain could not be alienated nor the succession altered. Divine and natural law (common to Christians and all humanity respectively) must be obeyed. The property and person of the individual must be respected.[19] Any encroachment was arbitrary despotism, which Bossuet passionately denounced.

He distinguished four characteristics of this sinister mutation of monarchy. 'First, subjects are born slaves, truly serfs; and among them are no free persons. Second, nothing is owned as property: everything belongs to the prince. Third, the prince has the right to dispose at will of the lives as well as the goods of his subjects, as would be done with slaves. Finally there is no law but his will.' Here the alleged protagonist of 'absolutism' is uncannily close to Locke. The champion of 'limited' monarchy fulminated against a ruler with 'Absolute, Arbitrary, Unlimited and Unlimitable Power over the Lives, Liberties and Estates of his Subjects; so that he may take or alienate their Estates, sell, castrate or use their Persons as he pleases, they being all his Slaves, and he Lord or Proprietor of every Thing, and his Unbounded Will their law'. The difference is that Locke created the semantic tradition of identifying both arbitrary and absolute power as tyranny: Bossuet was true to the older European tradition of sharply distinguishing them. Arbitrary power was hell-bent on destroying men's rights. Absolute power, far from menacing them, was ordained to protect them. If an inspiring invocation of 'absolutism' as usually understood cannot be had from its high priest, there is little point in looking elsewhere.[20]

So subjects' rights, individual and corporate, were respected by the theory of an allegedly 'absolutist' French monarchy. It is equally true that the theory of the allegedly limited monarchy in England stressed the absolute power of the crown. Under Tudors and Stuarts the royal prerogative was invariably described as 'absolute' in the sense that it was subject to restriction or control by no other power. In 1565 Sir Thomas Smith listed the areas where the monarch 'useth absolute power'. They included war and peace, appointment of counsellors and officers, coinage and pardons. According to the Speaker of the House of Commons in 1571, the queen had absolute power over religion – a statement which merely confirmed the Reformation Parliament's attribution of the supremacy over the Church to the king rather than itself. The list was repeated by Justice Fleming in Bate's Case. Nor was he especially partisan, since Coke could champion the common law and still speak of the king's 'prerogative indisputable, as to make war and peace'. Whitelocke stated in the Impositions debate in 1610: '. . . in the king is a twofold power – the one in Parliament as he is assisted with the consent of the whole state; the other out of Parliament as he is sole and singular, guided merely by his own will'. The former includes the power to make laws, while the latter recognises his prerogative in matters of coinage and war, showing that Whitelocke refers to the same 'absolute' authority as Smith and Fleming, though without using the word. At his trial in 1641 Strafford defined royal prerogatives in the same terms as Pym, his accuser. Their only difference was whether those prerogatives had been abused.

So did subjects of Tudor and Stuart monarchs agree about the boundaries of royal power? Not according to an influential recent work by Sommerville. He argues that they quarrelled over the extent to which the crown could legitimately invade subjects' rights. A group of 'absolutists' is identified, notably among churchmen. They shared the notion that, though rights and liberties were protected by law, the king made the law and was therefore above it. In emergencies he could ignore the law and suppress the rights. This is a restatement of the classic Whig view of the causes of the Great Rebellion. Charles and James suffered from a surfeit of 'absolutist' ideas, mainly of French extraction. They paid the price of trying to force down the throats of politically mature Englishmen (and Scotsmen) an ideology designed for unsophisticated Continentals.[21] The real problem with this has gone unnoticed. The spokesmen of the allegedly 'absolutist' Continental rulers repudiated the 'absolutist' ideas detected in Stuart England.

Historians know Bossuet more by repute than acquaintance. When actually read he proves a grave disappointment as the species of 'absolutist' for which Sommerville is looking. English 'absolutists' placed subjects' rights and liberties at the disposal of the monarch and permitted encroachment. Bossuet places them beyond him and forbade it. As seen above, that is precisely the point of his distinction between absolute and despotic monarchy. Elsewhere he is anxious to establish that the monarch is subject to no superior: consequently there is no appeal against his decisions. 'The prince is accountable to none for what he commands. . . When the prince has pronounced a decision, no other decision can stand. . . No other power can challenge that of the prince.' The sense in which his authority is absolute is carefully defined. It is 'absolute in relation to constraint: there being no power capable of coercing the sovereign, who in this sense is independent of all human authority'. Unfortunately for the presumed theory of 'absolutism', Bossuet also defines the sense in which it is *not* absolute. 'But it does not follow from this that the government is arbitrary since, besides everything being subject to the will of God, there are laws in states and anything done contrary to them is legally null.' Sommerville's 'absolutists' postulate a monarch who is above the law. Bossuet's monarch is emphatically under it.

This vital concept of absolute authority in a limited sphere was maintained in identical terms in the eighteenth century. A clutch of quotations gives the gist.

> '. . . in the exertion of lawful prerogative the king is and ought to be absolute; that is so far absolute that there is no legal authority which can delay or resist him.'

[He is] 'inferior to no man on earth, dependent upon no man, accountable to no man.'

> In the king, therefore, as in a centre, all the rays of his people are united, and form by that union a consistency, splendour and power that make him feared and respected by foreign potentates; who would scruple to enter into any engagement, that must afterwards be revised and ratified by a popular assembly?'

The problem is that this is no theorist of French 'absolutism'. It is Blackstone – the greatest authority on the constitution of eighteenth-century England.[22]

Once one has recovered from the shock, it becomes apparent that Bossuet and Blackstone are speaking of the same thing – a royal power of policy-making to which there is no legitimate challenge. This Blackstone elaborates in the same terms as Sir Thomas Smith. From the sixteenth to the eighteenth centuries it was as much a part of the theory of English monarchy as of French. Blackstone is neatly echoed by a recent guide to the *ancien régime* monarchy. 'French kings were absolute rulers, which meant that they were not limited in the execution of their powers by any other individuals, groups or institutions . . . they were not accountable to their subjects for the manner in which they ruled.'[23] But the author clearly thinks he is distinguishing the French monarchy from the English, not equating them.

ABSOLUTIST LEGISLATIVE AND EMERGENCY POWER?

The theory that law embodied the will of the monarch rather than the consent of the people has been hailed as the essence of 'absolutism'.[24] Bodin explicitly defines law thus, and divorced from his qualifications his statements can engender 'absolutist' conclusions. The same is true of the extreme theorists who followed him, including Hobbes. To establish an indefeasible hereditary title to the awesome authority he described, some added an updated version of the divine right of kings. But this proves little about 'absolutism' since law as royal will dates from the medieval coronation orders. Ullmann has demonstrated that they bristle with statements of the king's legislative sovereignty.[25] At that rate 'absolutism' dates from the ninth century at the latest. Legislative sovereignty is clearly *not* the key to the problem.

Monarchs have always been theoretically the source of law in the sense that their authority gives it life and force. This was no less true in England than in France. From Tudors to Hanoverians the formula for statutes was the same: 'Be it enacted by the king's most excellent Majesty, by and with the advice and consent of the lords spiritual and temporal and commons, in parliament assembled.' By the eighteenth century this was an empty form of words. So, in much the same way, was the endless repetition of the Bourbons' legislative sovereignty, 'sans dépendance et sans partage' – 'independent and undivided'. While dismissing the English formula as quaint archaism, historians have billed the French as an accurate description of the constitution.

Parker has shown that historians of 'absolutism' may have miscalculated in placing so much weight on the king's legislative sovereignty. It occupied a less prominent position in legal theory (and practice) than previously supposed. The reforming codes and the treatises of theorists like Le Bret and Domat portray the monarch as provider of justice rather than as lawmaker. The concentration of power at the centre of the legal system owed little to theories of the omnipotence of the king's legislative will. It owed most to the need to arbitrate between competing factional claims. Sovereignty implies something imposed, but this was a response to demand. The judicial machinery, like the whole administrative system, was enmeshed in patronage and riven by the feuds of rival clans. We assume anachronistically that decisions were determined by impersonal legal rules. Far more crucial, in the highest courts of the realm, was personal influence. Most disputes were about judicial and financial office — who should occupy them and what should be the extent of their authority. In 1681 succession to one office was disputed by twenty four claimants. The courts spent much of their time settling their own affairs. The image of the sovereign Louis XIV giving orders to everyone is therefore wide of the mark. His government devoted much energy to solving disputes about itself.[26]

The influence of Roman law on legislative 'absolutism' has also been exaggerated. As shown above, Ulpian's famous passage certainly kicks off with a claim flattering to 'absolutists' as usually understood: 'What the prince has decided has the force of law.' Historians rarely read the rest of it. 'By a special enactment concerning his government the people has conferred to him and upon him the whole of its government and power.' Seventeenth-century jurists did read it and realised that it was just as flattering to the concept of popular sovereignty. They also knew that the impact of Roman law was mainly on private law, which regulated relations between individuals, rather than on public or constitutional law. It now seems that French and German lawyers and officials not only failed to welcome Roman law: they opposed it. Some have claimed a Roman influence on the developing notion of *raison d'état* — the monarch's right to overrule law and liberties in emergencies. It is now clear that such incursions had medieval origins, were stated to be temporary and invariably turned out to be. Provisional modifications did not effect permanent change. Taxation without consent, like the Capitation of the 1690s, was the subject of agonised soul-searching between the king and his judges, was confined to the stated emergency and was lifted as soon as it ended. *Raison d'état* was a temporary and abnormal expedient. It was never the Trojan Horse by which a new 'absolutist' system was insinuated.[27]

Traditional Whig views, recently reiterated by Sommerville, identify the defeat of the 'absolutist' Stuarts with the termination in England of the argument from 'necessity'. On the contrary, if Charles I's invasion of liberties in its name constituted 'absolutism', there has been a lot of it about subsequently. Not until 1965 was compensation awarded for property seized under the war prerogative of the crown.[28] In 1982 the British government requisitioned ships for the Falklands War by virtue of the crown's emergency prerogative, though it made no attempt to deny compensation. Though the royal prerogative is now delegated to leaders of the majority party in parliament, that does not alter the principle at stake. The emergency power remains a shadowy area. Like most royal powers governed by an unwritten constitution, it was and is progressively defined by being tested in the courts. Their continued intervention underlines the problem of drawing boundaries between royal power and subjects' rights, whether under Louis XIV or Elizabeth II. The argument from vestigial organs may be transferred from biological to constitutional evolution. That this part of the royal armoury is still a lively issue makes it unlikely to have been negligible in early modern England.[29]

Historians usually identify a late medieval/early modern trend from shared legislative power to the royal monopoly which is 'absolutism'. The reverse is true. As monarchs became more powerful they increasingly acknowledged the need for *parlementaire* approval for their most important laws.[30] This is no paradox. The more responsibilities they undertook, the more they required the backing of their leading subjects – their influence to bind the realm to their policies and their purses to foot the bill. The mistake is to assume that stronger monarchy meant weaker representative bodies. Mightier monarchs needed grander *parlements* and Estates. Louis XIV never claimed to make law at will, without reference to any other authority. His prerogative extended to *initiating* legislation; but the crown's lawyers were clear that 'laws have no validity unless made public', that is, registered by the *parlements*. By their scrutiny of royal legislation, and their confirmation of its consistency with existing law, the judges restrained the monarchy and regularised it.[31] Unregistered laws were not well observed and they died with the ruler. The doubtful validity of laws promulgated by French kings without the consent of the *parlements* can be compared with the dubious status of English royal proclamations, also made without parliamentary consent, if they departed too far from existing law or touched life or property. Two spheres of law survived the reign of Louis XIV – public, governing relations between the individual and the state, and private, governing personal and property rights. Jurists like Domat emphasised the independence of each from the other more sharply than before. The latter was beyond the monarch's legitimate authority.[32]

Historians have not bothered to ask exactly what fell inside the field of 'legislation'. The answer is surprising. Isambert's *Recueil général des anciennes lois françaises* reveals the *parlements* perusing edicts, ordinances and letters patent declaring war, granting privileges, and incorporating companies. English monarchs from Henry VII to George III would have considered them matters for the royal prerogative and not parliament – not 'legislation' at all. The Bourbon output makes poor reading. Much of it is parochial and lacks the sweep and significance of legislation by England's king-in-parliament. In no sense is it the equivalent of England's statute law. It made little contribution to French legal history, except in the 1660s and 1730s – and those peaks of activity were occupied merely with codifications. French kings were not necessarily more generous in laying their laws before an assembly, since they wanted the *parlements*' seal of approval and repeatedly reminded them that matters of state brooked no opposition. But it remains true that much Bourbon law-making would have been regarded as policy-making by English monarchs, and that much of it was submitted to the judgement of bodies who would never have got near it in England.

In legislative terms England was a mixed monarchy. This had been the official theory for centuries and was totally compatible with the absolute power of the crown.[33] In the fifteenth century Fortescue stressed England's mixed polity and simultaneously conceded absolute power to the king. Hooker advocated strong absolute power in the crown combined with laws made in consultation with parliament. Smith gave the mixture new ingredients; yet his 'aristocracy' and 'democracy' were regarded as consistent with absolute royal authority. The 1688 Revolution made little difference, in spite of repeated statements that sovereignty was henceforth deemed to lie with king-in-parliament. This could have been true only of legislative sovereignty, as it had arguably been for centuries – and more convincingly since the break with Rome when parliamentary statute determined the constitution of the Church. Even here there were doubts, especially among Jacobites and Tories, while others surrounded it with so many qualifications as to make it a legal fiction. A further hue now restored to the eighteenth-century picture is the robust survival of divine right ideas: Clark has persuasively discredited reports of their death in 1688. Below the academic level, the secular and contractual speculations of Locke were a minority taste. Until the 1780s or 1790s the agenda of political debate, as well as the paradigms and metaphors which articulated it, revolved round God-given rights and duties. Under these influences there were many who still saw the king as the divine law-giver, with parliament in the role of consenting spectator. This was appropriate for an age in which the clerical schoolmaster and the clerical magistrate welded ecclesiastical perspectives firmly to the established order.[34]

If England's legislative sovereignty was located more clearly in a mixed body than in France, political sovereignty in a broader sense remained with the king alone. The 1689 Settlement left the royal prerogatives intact, limited only by the dispersal of the fog enveloping the dispensing power. Otherwise the old powers remained to limit the scope of parliamentary sovereignty.[35] The king continued to appoint ministers, make war and peace, grant pardons, issue charters, incorporate companies, coin money and wield all the other powers subsequently listed by Blackstone. Legislation in the English sense was rarely needed. Some Georgian statesmen believed a time would come when there were no laws left to be made. In France 'legislation' was more continuous, since it embraced most government policy. Its activities were constantly scrutinised by the *parlements*; only foreign policy was excepted and even there the Paris *parlement* registered peace treaties and declarations of war. 'Absolutism' is an odd theory in relation to a French royal prerogative which was dwarfed by the English equivalent.

ABSOLUTIST VERSUS CONSTITUTIONAL IDEOLOGIES?

Much of the political debate in early modern France and England has been interpreted as the struggle of two irreconcilable ideologies. On one side was that of 'absolutism'. Power descended from above and was monopolised by the monarch. The divine right king was answerable only to God and to no human law or institution. His people were subjects, in his care but not consulted, and unable to resist his authority. On the other side was 'constitutionalism'. Power ascended from below and was shared. The king negotiated with institutions possessing authority of their own. His people were citizens, participating in the government process and legitimating it by their consent. Political obligation was contractual: if the interests of ruler and ruled diverged, loyalty was withdrawn. The crudest and most popular view identifies these as the official ideologies of France and England respectively – though whether England qualifies as 'constitutional' before 1688 as well as after has not been decided. This is encountered in school textbooks but also in more reputable histories – especially Whig productions inspired by pride in the antiquity of English liberty. A more subtle rendering casts them as rival ideologies *within* each country – in France royalists and Huguenots, royalists and *parlementaires*, *thèse royale* and *thèse nobiliaire*, in England royalists and parliamentarians, Tories and Whigs. This at least has the advantage of not crediting contentious peoples with unanimity.

By the eighteenth century it is easy to conclude that there were two official ideologies in France – the crown's and the *parlement*'s. According to some authorities the *parlement* never accepted the 'absolutist' ideology of the court and was hell-bent for the last three decades of the *ancien régime* on breaking it down.[36] It was nearer to the *thèse nobiliaire or parlementaire* of pamphleteers who divided sovereignty between king and nobles. This owes much to hindsight. The temptation to view the *ancien régime* as programmed to self-destruct has extended to its ideology as well as its politics. Yet it seems improbable that the crown's highest court of appeal would dissent from royal views of the constitution. We now know that court factions pervaded it and that most of the crown's ministers and officials were drawn from it. It encroached upon the crown's prerogative on occasions, but these were confined to wartime crisis, government incompetence or royal minority. It is true that the *parlement* never accepted the ideology of 'absolutism'. There was no such ideology. But Shennan and Rogister argue that the *parlement* was consistent to the end in defending absolute monarchy and attacking despotism. Its struggles with the crown represented resistance to what it perceived as increasingly arbitrary government, without respect for liberties or the laws and institutions which embodied them. It sought to implement the constitution, not to destroy it.

Rival theories of the French constitution derive from the tendency of both sides to make extreme statements in the heat of confrontation.[37] Historians pick these up as definitive constitutional utterances. A case in point is Louis XV's speech to the *parlement* in 1766, when he shredded its recent claims to veto royal legislation. 'It is in my person alone that sovereign power resides . . . it is from myself alone that my courts hold their existence and their authority; the plenitude of this authority, which they exercise only in my name, remains always in me; it is to myself alone that the legislative power belongs, independent and undivided.' Though he did not write it himself, he lent his authority to an oversimplification. The intention was to safeguard royal authority against further opposition with an uncompromisingly clear pronouncement. At the end of a long wrangle, it was to be the punch line.[38] This precluded a careful analysis of the subtle inflexions of the French constitution – if, indeed, anything so nebulous was capable of being precisely stated. The resulting announcement reiterated the king's monopoly of legislative power. This was purely academic, since though he alone could initiate laws they were not valid until registered. But since the disputed edicts were mainly matters of state, it is clear that the *parlement* was as extreme in insisting on a right of veto as the king in claiming a monopoly of power. Neither was the whole truth.

Yet the encroachments of which the *parlements* were guilty have been exaggerated. Their position was well characterised by Montesquieu in his influential *De l'esprit des lois* of 1748. Though often presented as the greatest upholder of the *thèse nobiliaire*, he never denied that the crown was the source of all power. But he also insisted that powerful 'intermediate bodies' in the shape of nobility and *parlements* were vital as liberty's barrier against despotism. They were cast in the same role as Blackstone's House of Lords – shade for the people against royal authority. *Parlementaires* naturally found his argument acceptable, but it implied no derogation of royal authority. In normal mood they accepted the implications of absolute power and indignantly denied the innovations of which they were accused. Echeverria and Van Kley have recently stressed the subversive notion of national sovereignty, in the name of which they opposed the crown. The king regarded himself as the sole embodiment of the French nation and recriminations followed. But it has already been suggested that the spectre of the *parlements'* revolutionary intentions was propaganda. Historians have accepted too readily an impression which the government and its pamphleteers sought to create, and which the *parlements* repudiated.[39] Ideas of national sovereignty were undeveloped: the nation had little constitutional role except as represented by the monarch.[40]

The most accurate way to depict 'rival' viewpoints is as two sides of the same coin. Both were held in solution by the political systems of the two countries. The classical republican values of liberty and political participation were excavated by Renaissance humanists. The work of Pocock has made us aware that they survived during the succeeding age of princes. There was no need to revive them in the age of Rousseau. They never died. Instead they had been deftly coupled to monarchical values in the guise of representative institutions.[41] Thus Hume's essay *Of Civil Liberty* could praise absolute monarchy. 'It may now be affirmed of civilized monarchies what was formerly said in praise of republics alone, that they are a government of laws, not of men. . . . Property is there secure.'

Hence the early modern obsession with harmony and balance within the body politic or commonwealth. This in turn reflected the macrocosmic harmonies of the celestial bodies and the microcosmic humours of the well-ordered man. It was the monarch's duty to maintain a balanced constitution. The concept of harmony is an essential context for interpretations of early modern attitudes to power. Here the fashionable interest in iconography is helpful. Models of order were more suited to visual media than to verbal discourse. Throughout the Renaissance and Baroque periods monarchs addressed their subjects in progresses, processions and festivals as well as in speeches and proclamations. The harmonious proportions of royal palaces and portraits announced a king's Olympian self-control as well as demonstrating his power.[42] Even personal behaviour was part of the performance: in a reign of seventy-three years Louis XIV was never seen to lose his temper. Passion ordered is a theme of Van Loo's depiction of Louis XV with his regalia, calm, glacial and remote – though the spectacle might tax the credulity of those aware of the royal taste for nymphets. It contrasts with David's celebration forty years later of the Romantic ruler-hero: Bonaparte rampaging over the Alps on a demented stallion. Equally eloquent were royal entries.[43] When a ruler visited a town he performed a ritualistic enactment of the reciprocal duties of state, society and institutions. Civic representatives first demonstrated their fealty as subjects by dramatically surrendering the city's keys. Gifts were then exchanged to emphasise mutual obligation. Finally the prince guaranteed the rights and privileges of the inhabitants as citizens. Onlookers beheld the mysteries of their political universe reduced – but not diminished – to the palatable level of local soap opera.

This cohabitation of apparently opposed ideologies led to tensions within a consensus of shared beliefs rather than between rival value systems. The common coin of political discourse had the same parentage. It also throws up some surprising correspondences. The Patriot opposition to Louis XV adopted as its slogan *Vie, Liberté, Propriété*. This was intended as a protest against the abolition of the *parlements* in 1771. Yet it is significant that they turned on one absolute monarch the artillery forged by Bossuet, spokesman of another. Another Patriot writer, Morizot, denounced the regime in the exact words of Bossuet.[44] The people were slaves, their lives and property were at the disposal of the ruler, and there was no law other than his will. Clearly their target was despotism, not absolute monarchy. Once it is realised that most people are speaking the same language, it is less odd to hear praise for French absolute monarchy from the lips of a critic of the early Stuarts. 'The Kings of England', announced Henry Shervile, 'have a monarchical state, not a seigniorial. The first makes freedom, the second slavery.'[45] The reference was to the French distinction between sovereign princes, who wielded a public power which could not threaten private rights, and seigniorial princes, whose power intruded into the private sphere and could. Its most celebrated exponent was Loyseau, a leading apologist for absolute power. He praised the first and condemned the second.

Absolute and mixed elements coexisted in French constitutional theory – as in English. This refutes the usual assumption that absolute power was incompatible with active Estates. For to respect subjects' liberties was to will the means of their defence and modification by consent. Consent should not be viewed merely as a limitation to royal power: it extended it into a wider context. Without Estates representing élites (who in turn represented their subordinates), monarchs were confined to their prerogatives. Anywhere else was a no-go area. As rulers justly expected their own prerogatives to be inviolate, so they should not invade their subjects' rights. They would otherwise flout cosmic harmonies and be branded as despots. Some contemporary theorists found this inconsistent – as have most historians subsequently. When they say 'absolute', they mean it. This oversimplification flows from the usual misunderstanding of the scope of absolute power, namely that it precluded consultation in *any* sphere.

Nor was this blend of mixed and absolute theory confined to France and England. Each of the Hapsburg provinces was a *Ständestaat*, in which an absolute ruler had to share power with Estates. Maria Therese stressed her objection to the abuse of power by the Estates, not to the power itself.[46] Frederick II publicly proclaimed not only his subordination to the law but also the extent to which his people participated as citizens in government and shared in sovereignty.[47] Prussian schoolboys in the 1790s regarded theirs as a free country.[48] Sweden's written constitution of 1789 has the reputation of restoring outright 'absolutism'. It actually awarded the king power to declare war, make treaties, grant pardons and appoint ministers, while the Estates had the right to consent to taxation – which makes it not unlike Blackstone's account of the constitution of England.

DIVINE RIGHT ABSOLUTISM?

Much confusion has been created by discussion of divine right theories. It is often argued that the divine right claim inaugurated a new concept of monarchy. Yet such ideas were as old as the institution itself. From the eighth century the monarch was God's vicar on earth and medieval coronation ceremonies stressed that he ruled by the grace of God. French rulers were descended from the Merovingian priest kings, who were almost credited with divinity themselves.

Before them, monarchs emerged from a shadowy world of magic, with the monarch as miraculous talisman. Stress on obedience and non-resistance was constant throughout the period. Only an ungodly ruler could be disobeyed and the culprit then had to submit meekly to punishment: hence the additional obligation of passive obedience. An English congregation was informed in 1547 of the perils of resisting God's lieutenant, while Bossuet's famous injunctions to submission are echoed irrespective of party in eighteenth-century English sermons.

The only novel element in early modern ideas of divine right was arguably hereditary succession. The two most notable medieval monarchies, making the most sweeping claims to power – the papacy and the Holy Roman Empire – were elective.[49] Yet too many subjects were attempting to exchange their monarch for one of their own religious persuasion, and indefeasible hereditary succession gave divine right tighter definition. Title to rule was deemed to adhere inseparably to one family rather than to anyone who happened to wear the crown. But the chief result was to reduce the number of candidates rather than alter the duties owed to those wearing it. The older opinion of the matter enabled most Englishmen to take a relaxed view of the change of dynasty in 1688. Divine right was consistent with a variety of regimes and in the Dutch Republic it was deployed to defend the provincial Estates.

Too much has been made of the polarity between 'absolutism', divine right and non-resistance on the one hand and limited monarchy, contract and resistance theory on the other. We now know that divine right survived the 1688 Revolution. Though Hanoverian England was certainly a limited monarchy, few, Whigs or Tories, believed it was based on contract or the legitimacy of subjects' resistance.[50] By then it was the so-called 'absolutist' regimes which were soft-pedalling divine right. In the 1760s the Enlightenment was bringing the concept into disrepute and in his supposedly classic exposition of the subject in 1766 Louis XV hardly mentioned it. Prussia had no time at all for such theories. Frederick II regarded himself as a craftsman fulfilling a contract to promote his people's happiness rather than a priest-king requiring their worship. Rulers were beginning to be seen as managers rather than gods. Royal robes were shunned, military uniforms adopted and religious coronation ceremonies viewed as a waste of a working day. Frederick pronounced his crown a hat that let the rain in.

Divine right raises the issue of accountability. In all its forms the doctrine specifically denied that a monarch was accountable to his subjects. This was as true of English theory as of French, before the 1688 Revolution and after. Apart from an extreme clique of Lockean Whigs, most agreed with Blackstone that no court or other agency could control or correct him: '. . . no suit or action can be brought against the king, even in civil matters, because no court can have jurisdiction over him . . . no jurisdiction upon earth has power to try him in a criminal way; much less to condemn him to punishment.' It is widely believed that eighteenth-century ministers were responsible to parliament. So in a sense they were, but not in the manner imagined. They were not answerable to parliament as a political assembly. Hanoverian ministers regarded themselves as the king's servants and responsible to parliament only as a court of law which could indict or impeach them for their actions.[51] That was seen as giving parliament no more competence to call the king to order than did the same right of impeachment in the fourteenth century. If subjects of so-called 'absolutist' monarchs were without theoretical means of making them fulfil their obligations, so were the subjects of 'non-absolutist' monarchs. Again 'absolutist' is a misnomer.

CONCLUSIONS

An unchanging and 'non-absolutist' ideology dominated the period from the late Middle Ages to the French Revolution. This is under-standable since continuity was highly prized. It was unthinkable for any government deliberately to change the basis of its power. The Enlightenment enabled eighteenth-century theorists to contemplate innovation; but even then Montesquieu could deplore a monarch who changed the order of things rather than preserving it.[52] The notion of 'absolutism' as something more modern than consultative monarchy is anachronistic. The political order reflected the divine order and the state's main function was the preservation of the status quo. The appeal to history and precedent was an automatic reflex. Though it could form a smoke screen for originality in practice, novelty in theory was out of the question. No writer on absolute power hints at innovation. Absolute monarchs saw themselves as triumphing over those who had tried to usurp their authority, not as establishing a new system of government.[53] Shifts of authority from feudal nobles to Bourbon kings, and from popes to Tudors, were presented as restoration of what was originally owed to monarchs. Political discourse was wedged in a time-warp. In 1789 a manifesto renounced the allegiance of the Austrian Netherlands to Joseph II. The preamble was based on the 1581 renunciation of allegiance to Philip II.[54]

'Absolutist' and 'constitutional' are nineteenth-century terms which create nothing but confusion when related to early modern political ideas. 'Absolutism' was the product of the unique period of reaction after 1815. 'Constitutional monarchy' suggests contrary arrangements which began at the same time, by which ministers were answerable for their power to a representative assembly rather than a monarch. But if we talk of absolute and limited authority, they are seen as located side by side in the same constitution. Some commentators, near to the truth but ruining everything in their excitement, refer to a royal power which was absolute and limited at the same time – an intriguing thought of little value outside metaphysics.[55] Royal power was absolute and limited in the entirely logical sense of relating to different areas of a king's activities. His people were 'subjects' in relation to his prerogative: he commanded and they obeyed. As members of Estates and corporations they were 'citizens', upholding their rights and participating in affairs: the epithet was popular in France long before Rousseau and the Revolution. The two elements were held in balance – and sometimes in tension. If absolute power left its proper sphere and got the upper hand over subjects' rights and liberties, the result was naked despotism. If institutions charged with the defence of subjects' rights triumphed, the result was outright republicanism.

There was thus one type of legitimate kingship: monarchy; and two negations of it: despotism and republicanism. According to Montesquieu this was the political vocabulary of ordinary people: he accepts it as the starting point of his great treatise. Monarchy degenerated into despotism when it monopolised the powers it was supposed to share and veered towards republicanism when it shared the powers it was supposed to monopolise. The question at the start can now be answered. 'Absolutism' is an alien term which does not fit readily into an early modern theoretical framework. With an effort it can be forced in somewhere between monarchy and despotism. Not the least of its contributions to confusion is to blur a distinction which is vital to any understanding of the *ancien régime's* theoretical perspectives.

So the existence of a theory of 'absolutism' is doubtful on two counts. The first is the failure of French monarchical ideas to add up to anything of the sort. The features usually associated with it are missing – overemphasis on state power and neglect of the people's rights and privileges. The second is its failure to distinguish itself at significant points from the theory of England – which by universal consent was never 'absolutist'. The crucial distinction was then between limited and despotic monarchies, which took opposite views of the rights of their subjects. It was not between limited and absolute monarchies, which were two aspects of the same thing. The ideology of 'absolutism' is merely the ideology of monarchy, which taught that for some purposes power was most effective if concentrated in one pair of hands. It has often been remarked that the practice of 'absolutism' falls short of the theory. More accurately, the theory falls short of what is usually taken to be the practice.

REFERENCES

1   Langford P 1989 *A Polite and Commercial People*. Oxford University Press, p. 320
2   Burns JH 1990 The Idea of Absolutism. In Miller J (ed.) *Absolutism in Seventeenth-Century Europe*. Macmillan, pp. 37–42; Skinner Q 1978 *The Foundations of Modern Political Thought*. Cambridge University Press, vol.1, pp. x–xi
3   d'Entrèves AP 1967 *The Notion of the State*. Oxford University Press, pp. 82–99
4   Skinner Q 1978, vol. 2, pp. 263–4
5   Koenigsberger HG, Mosse GL and Bowler GQ 1989 *Europe in the Sixteenth Century*. Longman, p. 276
6   Hartung F and Mousnier R 1955 Quelques problèmes concernant la monarchie absolue. *Relazioni*, **4**, pp. 14–15
7   Kamen H 1983 *Spain 1469–1714*. Longman, pp. 14, 32, 147–51
8   Sabine GH 1963 *A History of Political Theory*. Harrap, p. 278
9   Burns JH 1990, pp. 27–30
10 Salmon JH 1987, *Renaissance and Revolt*. Cambridge University Press, pp. 123–35
11 Sharpe K 1989 *Politics and Ideas in Early Stuart England*. Pinter, p. 16
12 Salmon JH 1987, p. 178; d'Entrèves AP 1967, pp. 118–121
13 Dickinson HT 1979 *Liberty and Property*. Methuen, p. 44
14 Foster ER (ed.) 1966 *Proceedings in Parliament 1610*. New Haven, pp. 191, 195
15 Dickenson HT 1979, p. 44
16 Echeverria D 1985 *The Maupeou Revolution*. Baton Rouge, Louisiana, p. 128
17 Behrens CBA 1962 Nobles, Privileges and Taxes in France at the end of the *Ancien Régime*. *Economic History Review*, xv, p. 462
18 Koenigsberger HG 1987 *Early Modern Europe 1500–1789*. Longman, p. 182
19 Bluche F 1990 *Louis XIV*. Basil Blackwell, pp. 128–9
20 Le Brun (ed.) 1967 *Politique tirée des propres paroles de l'Ecriture Sainte*.

Droz, pp. 292–3; Laslett P (ed.) 1965 *Two Treatises of Government*. Mentor, p. 182

21 Sommerville JP 1986 *Politics and Ideology in England 1603–1640*. Longman, pp. 46–7

22 Blackstone W 1765 *Commentaries on the Laws of England*. Oxford University Press, pp. 284, 292–4

23 Shennan JH 1983 *France before the Revolution*. Methuen, p. 2

24 Treasure G 1985 *The Making of Modern Europe 1648–1780*. Methuen, p. 182

25 Ullmann W 1965 *A History of Political Thought: the Middle Ages*. Penguin, pp. 57, 89–90, 133

26 Parker D 1989 Sovereignty, Absolutism and the Function of the Law in Seventeenth-Century France. *Past and Present*, **122**, pp. 36–74

27 Shennan JH 1968 *The Parlement of Paris*. Eyre and Spottiswoode, pp. 283–4, 297; Mettam R 1990 France. In Miller J (ed.) *Absolutism in Seventeenth-Century Europe*. Macmillan, p. 49; Gagliardo J 1991 *Germany under the Old Regime*. Longman, pp. 94–5

28 Turpin C 1985 *British Government and the Constitution*. Weidenfeld and Nicolson, p. 56

29 Turpin C 1985, pp. 320–3

30 Myers AR 1975 *Parliaments and Estates in Europe to 1789*. Thames and Hudson, p. 30

31 Bluche F 1990, p. 130; Mettam R 1990, pp. 48–9

32 Church WF 1969 Louis XIV and Reason of State. In Rule J (ed.) *Louis XIV and the Craft of Kingship*. Columbus, pp. 371, 401; Bluche F 1990, pp. 128–9

33 Harriss GL 1985 Medieval Doctrines in the Debates on Supply 1610–1629. In Sharpe K (ed.) *Faction and Parliament*. Methuen, pp. 73–103

34 Dickinson HT 1976 The Eighteenth-Century Debate on the Sovereignty of Parliament. *Transactions of the Royal Historical Society*, xxvi, pp. 193, 209; Clark CD 1985 *English Society 1688–1832*. Cambridge University Press, pp. 134–6, 174–9; Hole R 1989 *Pulpits, Politics and Public Order in England 1760–1832*. Cambridge University Press, pp. 248–51

35 Ogg D 1969 *England in the Reigns of James II and William III*. Oxford University Press, pp. 486–8

36 Behrens CBA 1985 *Society, Government and the Enlightenment*. Thames & Hudson, p. 48

37 Shennan JH 1968, pp. 327–8

38 Antoine M 1989 *Louis XV*. Fayard, p. 854

39 Rogister J 1986 *Parlementaires*, Sovereignty and Legal Opposition in France under Louis XV. *Parlements, Estates and Representation*, **6**, no. 1

40 Black J 1990 *Eighteenth-Century Europe*. Macmillan, p. 386

41 Pocock JGA 1975 *The Machiavellian Moment*. Princeton University Press; Koenigsberger HG, Mosse GL and Bowler GQ 1989, p. 99

42 Sharpe K 1989 *Politics and Ideas in Early Stuart England*. Pinter, pp. 13–14, 44–7

43 Strong R 1984 *Art and Power*. Boydell, p. 7

44 Echeverria D 1985 *The Maupeou Revolution*. Baton Rouge, Louisiana, pp. 105–7

45 Judson M 1949 *The Crisis of the Constitution*. Rutgers University Press, New Brunswick, pp. 248–9

46 Macartney CA 1970 *The Hapsburg and Hohenzollern Dynasties in the Seventeenth and Eighteenth Centuries.* Macmillan, p. 124
47 Lentin A 1985 *Enlightened Absolutism.* Avero, p. 25
48 Behrens CBA 1985, p. 182
49 Burns JH 1990, pp. 30–1
50 Clark JCD 1985, pp. 119–98
51 Ehrman J 1984 *The Younger Pitt: the Years of Acclaim.* Constable, p. 182
52 Goldschmidt V (ed.) 1979 *De l'esprit des lois.* Garnier–Flammarion, vol. 1, p. 248
53 Behrens CBA 1967 *The Ancien Régime.* Thames & Hudson, p. 95
54 Black J 1990 *Eighteenth-Century Europe.* Macmillan, p. 402
55 Antoine M 1970 *Le Conseil du Roi sous le Règne de Louis XV.* Droz, p. 33

CHAPTER SEVEN
Royal Prerogatives and their Context

Monarchy is absolute by definition. As has been said, that was the point of it. It means 'rule of one' – not rule of a committee. Yet it is compatible with several managerial styles. A king may rely on ministers to give him advice or to implement his decisions. He may even allow them to make decisions on his behalf, when he is lazy or prevented by the complexity of government from keeping tabs on everything. He may delegate successfully, as did Henry VIII, and be able to stand back from the action. Or he may insist on seeing everything and disappear under mountains of paper like Philip II. It makes not the smallest difference to the number of those who rule, for the warrant for their action is royal authority. All the way down the line humble parish constables make arrests 'in the King's name'. Because the authority is the crown's and not their own, it cannot legitimately be resisted. Armies take oaths of allegiance to His Majesty, not to representative assemblies or to abstractions like 'the state'. The crown, mythic and potent, was the ultimate logo of power. No early modern monarch after about 1650 sat for a portrait without it gleaming officiously at his side. In England, where subjects are supposed to have been the least awestruck, the nomenclature of some 5,000 inn signs testifies to its abiding charisma.

PERSONAL MONARCHY

For centuries historians have worried about the role of individuals in history. Do they personally affect the course of events or are they merely the instruments of forces greater than themselves – productive, demographic or ideological? The institution of monarchy provides an answer. Because it focused power on one man, it made the unpredictable accidents of birth and heredity crucial to the fate of nations. The laws of succession imparted epic significance to royal matrimonial and reproductive activities. National and international politics in the late seventeenth century were dominated by English and Spanish monarchs' lack of an acceptable heir. Most eighteenth-century wars before 1792 were succession disputes. Peripheral regions in rebellion often sponsored rival branches of the royal family against the crown. Brittany in 1718 invoked the assistance of Philip V, Bourbon king of Spain, against the regent Orléans. Monarchs themselves could be anything from a genius like Frederick the Great to an infant or a half-wit. It made no difference whether they were active or withdrawn, vigorous or diffident. They stamped their personality just the same on the character and style of government.

Some continuity between reigns might be achieved by the retention of ministers. But if they occasionally continued to serve it was only through royal support. And since new rulers had their own ideas, or at least their own associates, swift ejection of previous incumbents was normal procedure – under England's system of supposedly parliamentary monarchy after 1688 as much as on the Continent. In 1727 a London newspaper published a letter warning overweening politicians that:

> . . . as their power only depends on the breath of their sovereigns, an angry blast of that flings them at once from the summit of their glory, and height of their ambition; or, at most, their authority generally determines with the life of their Prince, it being very rarely found that the most expert statesman can continue a favourite to two Princes successively.[1]

Walpole's attraction in the eyes of Hanoverian monarchs is conventionally supposed to have been his command of the House of Commons. Nevertheless he did not expect to survive the death of George I. Sometimes the old monarch was dramatically repudiated by his successor. The destruction of Henry VII's ministers in 1509, and of Louis XV's in 1774, partly reflected their discredited policies and the attraction of easy popularity. The health of a reigning monarch was, unsurprisingly, an object of universal interest.

Of the personal importance of monarchs there is no doubt. Though policy was subjected to endless discussion in court circles, action adopted needed at least tacit royal approval. Even when they relied on chief ministers and favourites, royal support for both men and measures was indispensable. And many of the larger-than-life mon-

archs of the early modern period effectively constituted themselves as
the primary impulse in politics. Peter I of Russia, Frederick II of
Prussia and Joseph II of Austria were so decisive that debate over
policy was minimised. Where less forceful personalities enlarged the
role of advisers, royal mood and temper were scrutinised feverishly
by experienced king-watchers. They eagerly noted the most appropriate times to make requests, as well as any new directions in which
royal affections were running.

The monarch's own personality was not the only fortuitous ingredient which kept the political classes guessing. Another was his
relations with the rest of his family. Bourbon, Romanov and Hanoverian monarchs were seriously weakened by disputes with their own
kin. In extreme cases family hostilities could shatter the integrity of a
regime. Richard III's usurpation irretrievably destabilised Yorkist
kingship and created an opening for the Tudors. Few kings could
wisely trust their nearest and dearest. A focus for political discontent
within the royal family was manna to the disaffected, since it
legitimised opposition. Sons could be a serious threat unless they
succeeded their fathers before they were mature enough to threaten
them. To succeed when they were immature made them a worse, if
inadvertent, threat. A minority signalled at best a power struggle and
at worst an orchestrated asssault on royal prerogatives which had
fallen into unacceptable hands. Strains were placed upon crown–élite
relationships in France by royal minorities in the 1550s, the 1610s, the
1640s, the 1710s and the 1720s. Brothers and princes of the blood
were the gravest menace. Some, like Louis XIII's brother Gaston,
repeatedly dabbled in treason to secure the throne. Strong rulers like
Louis XIV managed to turn them into dignified items of scenery and
strove to divert them into a suitable role. They could usefully be
deployed as spare candidates for elective or vacant thrones which
came on the market. Nor were wives and mothers beyond suspicion.
Catherine of Anhalt Zerbst would never have made her name as
Catherine the Great had she not condoned the butchering of her
husband, Peter III of Russia.

PREROGATIVES AND THEIR JUSTIFICATION

Behind a monarch's influence lay his prerogatives. They were invoked
every time an unpopular order was challenged. When an official was
asked by what title he acted, the answer was 'on royal authority'. Up

to a point royal prerogative powers were clearly defined, but not without leaving areas of ambiguity and flexibility. Prerogatives were not static. They withered if not wielded wisely and confidently. Prerogatives were potential dynamite, since their deployment was likely to offend more aspirants than they pleased. Louis XIV remarked that for every post he bestowed he made ninety-nine enemies. Yet monarchs who were afraid of exerting their powers soon lost them. So did those who stretched them too far.

The prerogatives in which royal power was embodied had two sources for most of the early modern period. The first was the belief (derived mainly from Bodin) that in every state there must be one authority which is sovereign or supreme, rather than the division of authority between monarch and feudal fiefs was typical of the Middle Ages. The second was belief in the king's appointment by God as His representative on earth, an office hereditary in the ruling family. Since Bodin did not specify who actually should wield sovereignty, the two fused neatly together to produce the divine right of kings. However evil, kings could not be opposed (the duty of non-resistance). Evil commands could be disobeyed but subjects must meekly accept the consequences (the duty of passive obedience). Kings were answerable to God, who would deal with bad ones in His own good time; meanwhile their subjects must put up with them. This ideology replaced the medieval notion of the feudal contract, according to which leading subjects could withdraw their allegiance if the king failed to fulfil his obligations to them. But in the eighteenth century the contractual idea returned in a different form. The monarch ruled according to a 'social contract' by which he pledged himself to promote the welfare of his people and they undertook to obey. The consequences of consumer dissatisfaction were never spelt out.

But royal prerogatives were not a recipe for kings doing as they liked. A monarch's authority derived mainly from his status as the source and upholder of law: he therefore had to be lawful or he would undermine that authority. Nor was law mainly legislation he himself decreed. The 'fundamental law', which he swore to uphold in his coronation oath, subjected him to divine and natural law (which was conveniently vague), but also to the customary laws of his country (in which the rights of his people were embodied).[2]

THE MAIN PREROGATIVES

It seems appropriate to enquire exactly what an early modern monarch was entitled to do. Since monarchy was almost universal in the early modern period, we should expect comparative surveys of royal prerogatives. Historians' neglect of royal powers is astonishing. Presumably in England the Whig tradition has emphasised the elements of the constitution which promoted liberty rather than authority. On the Continent the powers of monarchs have been assumed rather than examined. Belief in an 'absolutist' offensive there has induced historians to overlook the inherent powers which monarchs had always enjoyed, *jure maiestatis*.

Contemporaries did not share their indifference. Royal prerogatives were listed in dozens of treatises and in remorseless detail, but they have not been systematically studied. In the present state of ignorance, it seems that the ancient powers of royalty were similar, though not identical, in most states. Variations were created by the periodic success of aristocratic councils and Estates in appropriating some or all royal prerogatives. Monarchs normally controlled foreign policy and the armed forces, appointed ministers and officials, summoned Estates of the realm, initiated legislation, collected feudal and regalian revenues, issued ordinances and proclamations, created new courts and administrative bodies, regulated trade, industry and coinage, granted charters, controlled the highways, pardoned deserving convicts and were the fount of honour and patronage.

These powers were recognised as absolute – subject to no one save the king. Within the area they staked out he could do what he liked, without anyone's let or hindrance. The crown had no superior within or without the realm. In an age when not everyone automatically regarded the royal word as final, it was vital to establish that kings could not legitimately be challenged. As Louis XIV's spokesman Bossuet put it, the king was independent of all human authority: there was no lawful means of controlling or correcting him if he did wrong. Bossuet stated four propositions. The king was answerable to no one for his actions; when he had made a decision no other was valid; no other power might challenge him; but he was not exempt from the law.[3] This has been offered as a definition of 'absolutism' but was as true of the English crown as of Continental equivalents – and under Hanoverians as much as Tudors. The *Oxford English Dictionary* defines the king's prerogatives as 'theoretically subject to no restriction'. Ministers could be impeached by the English parliament but the king was inviolable – unlike the Spanish monarch who could be sued like any subject.[4]

Preogatives could be made to sound more all-embracing than they were – at which point they clashed with subjects' rights. This usually occurred in confrontations, when monarchs were provoked into exaggerated and one-sided assertions. Such was Louis XV's contribution to political theory in 1766, when he claimed to be the sole source of power and law. Usually treated as a classic statement of 'absolutism', it omitted any reference to the rights of his subjects – or of the *parlements* which embodied them. Since the French constitution was vague and held various components in balance, it was always possible to mislead by being selective.

French treatises listed a royal prerogative of legislation. The confusion caused by this has already been discussed. A monarch's right to make what laws he liked, which 'absolutist' historians believe he possessed, must have included subjects' rights and liberties, which were *excluded* by his obligation to respect them. French monarchs helped to create the same impression by trumpeting their claim to legislative power without dividing or sharing it. It is important to distinguish between the rhetoric and the reality. French kings were *not* able to make what laws they liked.[5] Their legislative prerogative was an unlimited right to *initiate* law. The right to *register* laws as consistent with established principles of equity belonged to the *parlement*: without registration they were invalid. English monarchs, in contrast, had no sole right to initiate law: their prerogative was to veto it. French kings complicated matters further by submitting to the *parlement* what the English considered to be policy matters, such as wills and declarations of war. If they chose to do so, the *parlement* was expected to register them without question.

In this area Montesquieu's theory of the separation of powers has wrought historiographical havoc. He ruled that well-regulated monarchies left executive and legislative power in different hands as a guarantee of liberty. This was as untrue of England as of France. In both, the executive was the monarch and he made law with the consent of the legislature, whether parliament or *parlement*.

Kings also claimed a prerogative of control over their subjects' religion. This was disputed in England by parliament and in France, Spain and Austria by the pope. Most prerogative lists also included a vaguely defined emergency power, entitling the monarch to act with despatch in times of crisis. This argument from *raison d'état* enabled him to encroach on his subjects' normally sacrosanct rights. Richelieu and Olivares are notorious for these activities and some historians assume that they shifted the state on to an 'absolutist' basis. Yet there is no justification for treating these emergency powers as permanent norms.

They remained exceptional and the French monarchy retained its legal status.[6] England is simultaneously shunted to the opposite end of the spectrum by treating normal prerogative powers as exceptional. Some have suggested that after 1688 the royal prerogative was used very little.[7] Certainly it helps to promote England as a special case if the basic powers of monarchy are presented as normally non-existent.

The prerogative of patronage

The royal prerogative made the king's court the centre of politics. It was precisely because he was in crucial respects absolute that he was the centre of attention. This in turn enabled him to use the court to *impose* his prerogatives and bind together his heterogeneous territories. The greatest prerogative was the appointment of officials and the distribution of patronage, which included titles and honours, letters patent and royal charters. The king's pleasure was honour and his wrath was death – usually figuratively and sometimes literally. Few waited on parliaments and Estates, though lobbying became an expert activity during the period and especially in England. The pole-star in England and on the Continent was the monarch. Decisions on patronage were his alone and all courtiers dreamed of influencing his choice: then they would be esteemed for the favours they could pass on to their own clients. Petitions for favour could reach the ruler only via those who had access to him. The *entrée* to the royal presence was therefore crucial and the king's household was the key to it. This was as true of kingdoms with powerful representative assemblies like England as of those with weak ones like France. Because monarchical states concentrated executive authority in an individual, power was where the king was. Those who attended to his physical and social needs were in a position to seek favours and advise on policy. Under an athletic monarch like Henry VIII much policy was formulated in the equivalent of the men's locker room. This had advantages. Since a monarch's major problem was deciding whom he could trust, to make political confidants of his intimate friends was good sense.

No one who nurtured ambitions could be absent from court for long: competition was universal and rivals moved fast. Courtiers competed for royal attention on the dance floor and on the hunting field, in the masque and in the council chamber, in office and in bed. Jealousies were fierce, disputes bitter and duels frequent: court intrigue was a high-risk activity. At ministerial level the stakes rose, so that professional politicians often played for each other's heads. This was due less to bloodthirsty monarchs than to faction leaders' reluctance to allow fallen rivals to live and fight another day. Recent events have confirmed that enemies with scores to settle can be fatal to the most firmly entrenched statespersons, nowadays deprived of the axe and the block.

To strengthen their hand courtiers played as part of a team or faction – a group cemented by common purpose or kinship or both. Yet faction was not the crucial determinant of politics. The royal response to it was. Monarchs had to avoid two opposite perils. Those like Louis XV who failed to stick to ministers they appointed merely advertised their lack of confidence in their own judgement. They had no peace once other factions were convinced their support for ministers could be shaken. Mistresses manipulated Louis XV as much as politicians: Louis XIV never listened to them but his successor's pillow talk was political. Rulers who allowed a faction permanently to monopolise power, as George II did with Walpole, saw the others write against it. Louis XVI managed to make *both* mistakes. The ideal was a stable balance of different groups. Determind monarchs such as George III and Louis XIV played factions off against each other to maximise their own freedom of action.

Factions sought power and patronage. They originated in kinship and clientage, rarely in issues of policy. When they did, coalitions of factions resulted; such were the political groupings which took sides over Henry VIII's break with Rome in the 1530s. Though opinions opposed to those of rivals were often adopted for political convenience, views on policy were rarely the real nub of political conflict. The vital consideration was who held them. In 1730 the Russian Empress Anna was confronted with the demand that her prerogatives of making war and peace, granting titles and deciding appointments should be subject to the consent of her Privy Council. This can be interpreted as an attempt to turn Russia into a constitutional monarchy based on noble oligarchy. It was more probably a power struggle. The opposition to the Privy Council's demands came from prominent nobles excluded from office.[8]

All central governments lacked comprehensive systems for ruling the localities. A comfortable old cliché assures us that English monarchs could not be 'absolutists' since they lacked an effective local bureaucracy. This has been exploded by the discovery that French rulers suffered from the same deprivation. Most early modern monarchs faced the age-old task of persuading provincial nobility to govern in the crown's interests. They needed the co-operation of those who wielded local power in their own right. All administrative policies and reforms attempted by rulers were made with this in mind and should be assessed in this light. Monarchs squatted like spiders at the centre of a nationwide web of patron–client relationships. They tweaked threads and peripheral agents scuttled. The mechanism is becoming clear for France, though much work remains to be done on states such as Austria, Prussia and Russia, where a more serious attempt was made to extend state control – if only by officially enrolling local nobility in state service.

The local impact of royal power depended on the availability of patronage at the centre. The court was the central switchboard for management of the ruling élite: a malfunction spelled disaster. The courts of Charles I, Joseph II and Louis XVI ceased to earth the localities to the centre: instead they became the resort of royal cliques and those excluded revolted. The problem was tricky for the Enlightened rulers of the later eighteenth century, since court ceremonial bored them. One of the reasons that Catherine II was more successful than her Austrian counterpart is now emerging. Though she preferred informality in private, the public figure dominated a court of legendary brilliance.[9] The third of the Enlightened trio, Frederick II, remains an enigma. If the silence of his biographers is to be believed, he had no court. It is probably truer to say that it awaits its historian.

The financial prerogative

The financial prerogative was the most controversial. It endowed the crown with certain regalian revenues in its own right. These included royal lands, profits of justice and royal claims on the nobility by the king as feudal overlord. Some lawyers argued for a prerogative of taxation. Since this implied the king's right to take the property of his subjects and denied their rights, it was highly contentious. Alert students are as baffled as contemporaries: some eminent historians endorse it and others deny it.[10] Confusion has partly sprung from the ability of several early modern monarchs to gain financial independence *without* direct taxation. They did so by spectacular exploitation of prerogative revenues which were by definition beyond the control of Estates. In the case of Henry VII and his Council Learned royal rights were pursued in a manner clearly contrary to the spirit of the law. More artfully, the lawyers of James I of England could claim that his unparliamentary customs duties, excluded from the prerogative, were really an attempt to regulate trade, which it encompassed. More legitimately, the exceptional extent of their royal lands made Prussian monarchs far less dependent than other rulers on tax granted by Estates.

Also muddying the water is the power of emergency taxation claimed by Continental rulers on the grounds of wartime *raison d'état*. It has already been argued that French monarchs failed to make this a permanent right to tax without consent. The principle was clearly invoked in 1695 and 1710 when the Capitation and the Tenth taxed all regardless of social status. Louis XIV secured the agreement of the lawyers of the Sorbonne only by his assurance that the taxes were indeed a temporary wartime measure. So they proved to be. Even the Sun King's monarchy with its relative administrative strength was unable to tax subjects' property at will or make *raison d'état* effective on a long-term basis.[11] Though historians talk loosely of the ability of 'absolutists' to tax without consent, this prerogative dwindles on inspection.

The prerogative of administrative, economic and social regulation

Early modern governments felt an urge to regulate. This appears to be one of their few innovations. Though it had roots in the Middle Ages, Raeff argues that the impulse to order and systematize stems from a key feature of the Renaissance: the search for a rational order. The Enlightenment was ambiguous, still seeking a rational order but increasingly believing that in economic affairs it was imposed better by nature than by governments. Many areas of life where we take regulation for granted and some where we do not – the duties of officials, the discipline of armed forces, the status of social and professional groups, the clothes they wore, the labour of wage-earners and the pricing policies of producers – all felt the hand of government planners for the first time. Previous regulation had been the responsibility of town corporations, churches and Estates: central control now gave it wider scope. But 'absolutism' was not enhanced since no centralised machinery was provided. Enforcement remained in the hands of corporate bodies. Nor was this hyperactivity confined to states traditionally deemed 'absolutist'. Everywhere, regulation was felt to be preferable to leaving things to chance, market forces, the whim of individuals or the haphazard inheritance of the past.

All early modern governments regulated social and economic life. This was not a prerogative only of 'absolutist' states, since England and the Dutch Republic were no more prepared than France to condone the free play of market forces. Economic instinct and the profit motive were viewed as anarchic impulses which disrupted public welfare for the benefit of private greed. Everywhere the aim was to subordinate gilds, ports, provinces and other selfish interest groups to the well-being of the whole community. Only in the later eighteenth century did Enlightened Physiocrats proclaim market forces as promoters and not subverters of the common good. Many of these activities could be covered by royal prerogative or the authority of Estates and town corporations. Rulers therefore had a choice. Some, like special agents selecting their weaponry, made tactical estimates in each case of the likely opposition and the difficulties of enforcement. In England prerogative letters patent were often preferred since they enabled economic regulation to be more exact and flexible. Fine distinctions between the required imports of Spanish as opposed to American tobacco would have meant little to parliamentary legislators: it was far simpler to grant a monopoly by royal charter.[12]

This prerogative embraces the increasing emphasis on what Raeff has called 'the well-ordered police state'.[13] In an early modern context this misleading phrase means no more than 'well-regulated social welfare'. It expressed itself in a body of seventeenth-century ideas known as Cameralism, which stressed the identity of interest between government and people, and required professionally trained officials to regulate the lives of subjects in the interest of the community. Higher education in Cameralist political science was prescribed for German administrative élites. Health, hygiene, morals and education were subjected to searching scrutiny. French and German town councils were compelled to clean streets, remove refuse, regulate traffic, impose safe building standards and superintend corpse disposal. After the convulsions of the Reformation the church's provision of poor relief declined, creating a new role for state intervention in the management of social casualties and misfits. The effectiveness of all these regulations remains unexplored. As usual in early modern government, plans were probably more impressive than performance. But their existence refutes the persistent belief that early modern governments were primarily out to strengthen themselves rather than improve the material and cultural life of their subjects. This is to travesty the Enlightened rulers after 1750 and to libel many of their predecessors.

The foreign and military prerogative

Another vital royal prerogative was control of foreign affairs – most spectacularly, the making of war. Partly because they marked out an area where where co-operation between crown and élites was least necessary, diplomacy and treaty-making, war and control of the armed forces were areas where royal prerogative was least disputed. The crucial determinants were therefore the personal views of the monarch or those who could influence him: policy reflected court politics and factional pressures. It was therefore volatile and unpredictable.

Yet the dominance of foreign policy by royal personalities and priorities has been disputed. The academic study of diplomacy began in the late nineteenth century and reflected the assumptions of that period. The result has been as misleading as that century's treatment of other aspects of 'absolutism'. The subordination of grave international matters to the trivia of royal whim and court intrigue so distressed nineteenth-century historians that they felt obliged to look deeper. In seeking more they perceived less. Attempts were made to show that international relations in this period were based on a rational estimation of national interest. The error was compounded by the dominant role allocated to official diplomatic sources, which tended to rationalise decisions. Traditional historiography severed foreign relations from their roots in the fortuitous preferences of monarchs and their courtiers. Yet the random quality of international events was a common contemporary theme. Remarking that the smallest court disputes could lead to war, a French lawyer claimed in the 1730s that 'most great events pompously transmitted by history had only frivolous causes'. A decade earlier the French ambassador in Vienna reflected on the terrifying dominion of chance: 'at a time when we are in a situation to give the law to Europe the smallest event could make us the weakest state in Europe'.[14]

Most monarchs ruled territories lacking in ethnic, linguistic, religious or cultural unity. A sense of shared interests in the present or heritage in the past was often absent. In countries as apparently unified as France, as well as hotchpotches like the Hapsburg inheritance, the only reliable bonding agent was loyalty to the ruling dynasty. Nationalist ideologies were unavailable, though they were an identifiable force against outsiders. Instead monarchs depended on the reputation of their dynasty: they devoted their resources to enhancing its glory and pursuing its inherited claims. Historians of international relations are now stressing their consistently dynastic emphasis in the context of court culture, which presented war as heroic.[15] Eighteenth-century monarchs continued to expose themselves on the battlefield, however decoratively. When their arms were victorious they claimed the credit. Handel's *Dettingen Te Deum* celebrated George II's prowess. The royal hero as victor was part of a long tradition of exalting Majesty in its most impressive role – at war. Voltaire, the peace-loving *philosophe*, performed the same service for Louis XV after his exploits at Fontenoy in 1745. His opera, with music by Rameau, saluted his victory by comparing him to the Emperor Trajan at the moment of his admission to the Temple of Glory. It failed to mention the incidental presence of Marshal Saxe on the same battlefield.

The dynastic perspective was evident in other ways. Monarchs referred frankly to wars and treaties as personal arrangements between themselves. Even a less dynastically-minded ruler such as Frederick the Great, amid much talk of being 'the servant of the state', spoke of Maria Theresa as *his* enemy and of *his* decision to go to war. Most wars were struggles about succession and most ruling dynasties intermarried with several others: claims and counter-claims proliferated. Many international conflicts were therefore family quarrels.

Further attempts have recently been made to elevate early modern foreign policy into something more. It has been suggested that Russian expansion on the Black Sea under Catherine II should be 'depersonalised' as a permanent dynamic of Russian history rather than an initiative of the empress. While this was possibly an element in Russia's war effort, it is doubtful if it represented her main motivation. As an insecure German usurper of the Romanov crown, she was unlikely to be pushed into war by anything so vague as a dynamic. Her priority was survival and spectacular conquests increased her chances. Arguments have also been advanced for the birth of the idea of the modern impersonal state – with, by implication, impersonal foreign priorities.[16] Medieval monarchs identified the state with their dynasty. Shennan claims that increasing numbers of eighteenth-century rulers and their propagandists embraced an idea of the state which identified it with the combined interest of ruler and ruled, to which both were subordinated. This is convincing in that it corresponds to the contempt for their own relatives of monarchs like Peter I and Frederick II – and to their readiness to sacrifice self or kin to a higher cause.

The theorists on which Shennan's thesis relies are less persuasive. Most are eminent but unrepresentative philosophers such as Hobbes, who are now discredited as guides to the political thought of informed people. And whatever the merits of Shennan's argument, it does not apply to foreign policy. There any notion of state interest as something separate from the monarch's was so nebulous as to be unworkable. Nor do increasing appeals to *raison d'état* provide evidence for it. On the lips of Frederick and Catherine they merely furnished a less disreputable justification for dynastic ambition. What was selfish if pursued for their own ends sounded morally more uplifting if undertaken for the higher good of the state where all interests miraculously fused. Similarly, the partition of Poland was old-style dynastic aggrandisement smartly packaged under a bright new trade-name – the balance of power. Too much has perhaps been made of Louis XIV's willingness in the Partition Treaties of 1699–1700 to waive his dynastic claims in deference to this principle. Prudence had always affected the extent to which such claims could be pushed, and in 1699 France was exhausted.

Thus, in spite of the usual assumption that foreign policy became less obsessively dynastic in the eighteenth century, most innovations were new names for old habits.

AGENTS OF THE PREROGATIVE

Max Weber defined two types of authority: patriarchal and bureaucratic.[17] The first is personal and partial. The boss has power in his own right and is obeyed by those who already owe him the loyalty of client to patron. Officials are therefore amateurs with little training, procedures are informal and much business is oral. The second is impersonal and impartial. The boss owes his power to the post he occupies and is obeyed by subordinates because he occupies it. Officials are trained professionals, operating programmed routines and keeping written records.

Weber was, however, formulating two models and not suggesting they could be found in the early modern period. Most of its government agents were a mixture of both types. Though it somehow became famous for efficiency, the Prussian bureaucracy was impossible to disentangle from the hereditary noble dynasties who colonised its offices like parasites. They were trained in formal routines but in a context of clientage totally alien to the meritocratic nineteenth century. The anxiety of that century's historians to predate origins has again hindered understanding.

Yet the concept of 'absolutism' depends heavily on the alleged existence of a programmed bureaucracy, which could transmit royal orders to society because it was independent of the potentially obstructive power structures of that society. That is not how the royal prerogative seems to have worked in practice. Early modern bureaucracy could be less misleadingly labelled 'officialdom'. Most royal officials owned their offices and viewed them as personal possessions to be exploited in the interest of themselves and their connections rather than of the state. The ubiquity of personal ties of kinship and clientage blurred divisions between administrators and those they administered. Social historians emphasise the amateurish concept of public office engendered by early modern society. An official's function was determined more by who he was than by the office he occupied. His ability to command obedience depended less on his official authority than on the rank and number of his friends. Institutional historians stress instead the bureaucratic features of the so-called 'administrative monarchy' in later Bourbon France and the German states – codes of procedure and job descriptions, professional training and high standards of public service.[18] In truth, bureaucratic and patronage mechanisms were found side by side in the period: they intermeshed in a manner which defies precise analysis.

Equally erroneous is the widespread misconception about the 'new men' raised by 'absolutist' rulers of the seventeenth century as the instrument of royal prerogative and its absolute power. New men there were, in the sense that they came from families previously outside the ruling élite. New men there were not, in the sense that 'absolutist' monarchs were turning to a class ignored by their ancestors. The alleged originality of the policy is based on ignorance of medieval history. The existence of similar theories about the so-called 'new monarchy' of rulers such as Henry VII of England, Louis XI of France and Ferdinand of Aragon should put us on our guard. For it had long been the practice of medieval monarchs to choose their officials, at the policy-making as much as the administrative level (the two were far from distinct), from the fringes of the nobility or lower. Their loyalty to the crown was thus increased. They were rapidly awarded title and status commensurate with their new position, if they had not obtained these already through the purchase of office. Alternatively, upstarts like Wolsey and Fleury received a cardinal's hat. A degree of social tension between 'old' and 'new' nobles was therefore a permanent feature at any time. It was not unique to the era of 'absolutism'.

As we have seen, there is general acceptance of the concept of a 'crisis of the aristocracy' in this period. According to this speculation, a hereditary 'feudal' nobility of princes of the blood, grandees and nobles of the sword, already reeling under the impact of seventeenth-century economic depression, was displaced in government service by the bourgeois lawyers and bureaucrats of the robe nobility. Important work on the nobility of Normandy has seriously undermined this thesis, though we still do not know how typical the province was. Few were in economic decline, prevailing conditions notwithstanding. The key discovery, still too little known, is that most officials swiftly abandoned their offices when they became noble and merged as discreetly as possible with the existing nobility. They married the scions of established families and adopted their life-style. Though individuals in one particular generation might be distinct, fusion was rapid and it prevented the development of separate nobilities, one effete and the other effective. Two-thirds of the eighteenth-century nobility at whose expense their bourgeois rivals were rising had risen the same way a century or less before. Since at least the fourteenth century the nobilities of eastern and western Europe had originated in and renewed themselves through service to the crown. Aristocracies have always deluded their contemporaries with legends of their antiquity – and, it seems, historians too.

It is thirty years since Hexter's witty reminder that the middle classes are *always* rising. Evidently myths are not so easily derailed. Historians of each European century from the twelfth to the twentieth still proclaim bourgeois ascent as the unique feature of their own period. The only new factor in the early modern period was that the old traffic was given a new highway code. Increasingly in Western Europe the crown profited from the ambitions of the upwardly mobile by selling them offices; in Eastern Europe old realities were institutionalised by tables of rank which formally graded and evaluated the nobility in terms of their service to the monarch. The aim was to ease the old tension. The new framework could continue to be dominated by old noble families, while a recognised route was charted for someone of non-noble origins whose money or services the ruler wished to use. 'Absolutism' as an alien imposition on society is also refuted by the nature of royal armies. Officered by nobles who often commanded their own tenants and equipped them at their own expense, they neatly fused crown and élite interests. [19]

The consequences of this discussion are vital for 'absolutism'. Doubt is thrown on the notion that the nobility was remodelled in conformity with the wishes of a new kind of regime. It seems more accurate to claim that governments had to accommodate themselves to a prevailing noble regime. We are also warned against the facile assumption that nobles opposed the growth of royal authority. Doubtless some did, especially if they had happily tyrannised over towns or villages where their style was now cramped. But not all nobles fit the cliché of confrontation with absolute authority. Some, if they could benefit from it, promoted it. For agencies of the prerogative were not merely a mechanism of government: the rich opportunities they offered were one of its prime attractions.

Only a bureaucracy purged of all partiality towards the influential could have freed monarchs from the need to flatter élite preferences. The existence of such a bureaucracy has been inferred as a conceptual consequence of 'absolutism' rather than demonstrated from the evidence. To have dispensed with the needs of the 'old' nobility would have required a social revolution which never happened. It follows that royal prerogative, however absolute, was constrained in practice by the need for co-operation with the landed élite.

PREROGATIVE ENTHRONED

Modern tourists shuffle round Versailles, Schönbrunn and Caserta with their jaws on the floor. They cannot believe such ostentation was for one family. It was, but the purpose was far from decorative self-indulgence. Concentrating enormous prerogative powers in the hands of one man raised awkward questions. The republican tradition was far from dead and provided an alternative model of government. The Dutch Republic was a tacit challenge to kings everywhere (as Louis XIV perceived in 1672), and in the 1640s and 1650s militant republicanism reared its head in France and England. If it was hard to defend rationally, monarchy had to be buttressed by stressing its spiritual mystique. Sovereign majesty could not be seen to be outraged with impunity: traitors were executed in effigy if their actual person was unavailable. In 1661 a Danish nobleman's wax look-alike was ceremonially beheaded in the King's presence. There was exploitation, partly deliberate and partly instinctive, of atavistic impulses as old as the human species. The world known to us in Frazer's *Golden Bough* was evoked, with its echoes of priest kings and supernatural powers, of royal sacrifices and taboos. In France and England, though not in Spain, the cure for certain ailments lay in the royal touch. The 1688 Revolution failed to dent the crown's therapeutic influence, and the gullible queued for treatment until Queen Anne's reign – though William III was reputed to mutter during the laying on of hands: 'God give you better health and more sense'.

Varying degrees of remoteness were imposed: majesty was sacrosanct and remained inviolate. In all courts menial tasks associated with washing and dressing the monarch were performed, actually or symbolically, by the highest household officers, nobles or members of the royal family. Glimpses of royalty were rationed by confining access to its private moments to a privileged few. Admission to the public intimacies of Versailles was skilfully exploited by Louis XIV to establish differences of rank and favour.[20] The remoteness of monarchy was thus paradoxically accentuated by making it semi-public: this had the advantage of investing the most trivial activities of the monarch with cosmic dignity and significance. Precision and punctuality were essential for a ruler whose biorhythms were explicitly compared with those of the heavenly bodies. Courtiers were reputed to set their watches by the movements of Louis XIV. They were also expected to bow to the dishes bearing his food and to the cupboard in which his underwear reposed. In most courts mealtimes were a focus of ritual. Only royalty ate: everyone else watched. Each dish was presented by a nobleman on bended knee. Every time the king drank, the air was rent by a trumpet blast or a cannon salvo.

Nor was the Versailles of Louis XIV the ultimate development of courtly refinement for which it is often mistaken. The Spanish court protected and isolated the sacred person of the king by meticulous protocol which made the Sun King's arrangements look casual. Commoners were forbidden, on pain of death, to touch the royal person. By the mid-seventeenth century house rules permitted the hundred grandees to wear hats in the royal presence. That was merely the start. There were three categories of grandee – those who could put on their hats before speaking to the king, those who remained bareheaded until they had finished speaking and those who began speaking and then put on their hats.[21] In other ways the Spanish court was austere. There was no coronation ritual and royal portraits depicted the king not in the robes of majesty but in a plain black suit. The *lever* and *coucher* were not public, as in France. Philip IV was invisible and inaccessible, shielded from the public gaze in the depths of his palace and surrounded always by the same few faces. He dined silent and alone.

Contrary to popular assumptions, the French monarchy was one of the most easygoing in Europe. The celebrated rituals of Versailles effected no major change in this respect. No one knelt before Louis XIV or walked backwards in front of him, as in London, Madrid or Vienna. A Frenchman merely bowed to his king, as he did to any other gentleman. The English monarch opened parliament seated on his throne and equipped with robes, crown, orb and sceptre. The king of France wore his regalia only twice – at his coronation and at his effigy's lying in state after his death. He spoke from the throne only when impressing important embassies or putting his *parlement* in their place. The Sun King, though always guarded, lived in public. Peered at night and day, private only when *entre les draps* with one of his mistresses, he was merely maintaining the tradition of his ancestors. Henry III had been assassinated while giving an audience on his chamber-pot.

The interior planning of palaces, viewed in relation to the social and political life that went on in them, has attracted historians' attention in the last two decades. The result is a new form of historical evidence. It illuminates the preoccupation which was at once the chief purpose and central problem of court organisation – the regulation of access to the monarch. Somehow he had to distance himself from increasing numbers of importunate courtiers. Courtiers' access to the monarch had to be regulated. His status, or his minister's, was defined by how long he made supplicants wait. Wolsey allegedly kept one petitioner dangling in an ante-room for years. In England the solution was to multiply rooms of progressively restricted access which had to be traversed before gaining admission to the royal presence. The courts of Austria, Spain, Saxony, Brandenburg and Bavaria were organised on similar lines. Versailles operated on totally different principles. There the royal bedchamber was at some stage open to all sorts of riff-raff. What mattered was the exact point in the royal *lever* when spectators were admitted: it was more prestigious to see the king in his dressing-gown than in his waistcoat, in his stubble than shaven (every other day), in the small wig he wore in bed than in the large one he donned out of it. *Entrées* occurred in three waves. Courtiers waited in the antechamber until the moment in the proceedings when they were entitled to be called to the state bedchamber. They soon had to give way to their less privileged successors but took care to stay long enough to be seen.[22]

Little of this was new. Kings had been surrounded by ceremonial rituals since the early Middle Ages. Two changes gave them fresh significance. One was the tendency of the royal court to settle in the capital city rather than itinerantly sponging off the nobility. The establishment of a permanent residence like Versailles enabled monarchs to develop and perfect the arts of presentation on an unprecedented scale. The other development, neatly fusing with the first, was baroque art, which swiftly exposed the inadequacy for royal propaganda purposes of all previous styles. Guides at the Prussian palace of Charlottenburg still explain how portraits of the Great Elector executed in the 1660s were required to be overpainted in the 1700s. The addition of flamboyant gestures and swirling draperies deftly waved a magic wand over an originally boring depiction of a fat little man. Cunning designers crafted sculpture and fountains, grass and trees, glass and marble, paint and stucco into the supreme statement of monarchy that is Versailles. For mastery of visual media and command of audience response baroque artists were unrivalled. Not a string was left untwanged. Le Brun and le Nôtre were the Steven Spielbergs of the Bourbon monarchy.

Behind everything lay the desire to impress. Monarchs needed *maiestas*, an imposing and magnificent display. The weaker the actual means of coercive power at their disposal, the more they sought to reinforce the ideology of obedience by enveloping subjects in lavish spectacle. And because grandees in their châteaux and *Schlossen* shared the same intention, the royal entourage had to strike a uniquely awesome note. Monarchs addressed their subjects in symbols, of which language was only one. Only now, with help from experts in the literary and visual arts, are historians beginning to decode them. The announcement was not merely one of power. The monarch's virtue, justice, piety and military prowess jostled for a place on his propagandists' agenda. Festivals and processions were drenched in biblical and classical allusions, all deftly evoking mythic expectations.

These continued from the Renaissance until the late eighteenth century, when monarchs are frequently supposed to have been converted to repentant austerities. The Hapsburgs are often deemed one of the more economical ruling dynasties – and certainly one of the most poverty-stricken. Like their English counterparts, they came late to the pleasures of monumental palace construction. In 1705 a Frenchman smugly reported the Hofburg at Vienna to be insignificant, its stairs devoid of ornament and its state rooms of petty-bourgeois proportions.[23] But at Schönbrunn in the 1760s the dynasty completed the last of the great rococo palaces, walls frothy with gilded stucco and ceilings wriggling with rosy-cheeked cherubs. The Hapsburgs were also partial to mobile display. In 1760 Isabella of Parma arrived in Vienna to marry the future Joseph II in a line of nearly a hundred coaches-and-six which stretched for miles. Marie Antoinette reached Versailles for her own wedding in 1770 with comparably extravagant transport. Maria Theresa herself was more abstemious. A retinue of a mere seventeen coaches marked her visit to Prince Esterhazy in 1773. But then she had come only to see an opera.

PREROGATIVE DETHRONED

What prompted this unprecedented emphasis on the prerogatives and prestige of monarchs? Most specifically, the 'general crisis' of the 1640s and 1650s. The hypothesis of the 1960s has been discredited by recent research, which has blasted to bits the suggestion that revolts in France, Spain, England, Sweden, Holland and Russia could have similar causes – if only because in some of these areas there was not one confrontation but several. But it would be a pity to lose sight of what *was* common. In each case war-induced financial exhaustion and European-wide harvest failures combined with royal minorities, government incompetence and loss of nerve to produce rebellion at roughly the same time in different places.[24] As monarchs in these states re-established their prerogatives, the illusion of an 'age of absolutism' was created. But this was not the creation of autocracy –

merely the restoration of normal monarchy. Rulers had done the same before and would do it again. This time, however, there was a new and seductive accompaniment – baroque propaganda. The novelty was not absolute authority but its media coverage.

The 'general crisis' was only the most severe challenge to the prerogatives of monarchy in the period. The clue to the 'absolutist' state is what precedes it. In each one so labelled, Estates or councils of nobles had previously been unusually powerful or assertive. In the early seventeenth century the Estates of Brandenburg Prussia intervened in all foreign and military matters. The French Estates-General in 1484 and the *parlement* in 1597 claimed to appoint the royal council, and from 1634 and again from 1718 the Swedish *Riksdag* did so. In 1641 the *parlement* of Paris was reprimanded for meddling in matters of state or prerogative, as were the parliaments of Elizabeth I throughout her reign. In 1642 the English parliament claimed to control the armed forces, though in 1661 Charles II recovered unequivocal control of them. In 1661 Louis XIV was more alarmed at the *parlement*'s disposition to usurp his prerogatives than to usurp theirs. Most states saw attempts to dismantle the royal prerogative at some time during the early modern period: many rulers were faced with the task of restoring it. But these absolute monarchs sought to restore and maximise their authority within an existing order, not to construct a new one.

Charles XI and Gustavus III of Sweden are traditionally associated with dramatic shifts towards 'absolutism'. But in the context of what came before this is illusory. In 1634 a clique of grandees seized the opportunity of Gustavus Adolphus's sudden death. By the Form of Government the royal prerogative was permanently subordinated to the consent of an aristocratic council. Since he was hamstrung by these arrangements, Charles XI's celebrated move to 'absolutism' in 1680 can with more justification be interpreted as a return to normal prerogative kingship. This is supported by the declaration of the Estates (*Riksdag*) that the Form of Government applied only during royal minorities and that the council's powers were merely advisory. The right of the Estates to consent to extraordinary taxation survived intact. A recent attempt to save the Vasas for 'absolutism' argues that Charles XI's subjects had no legal remedy against him. He was supposed to respect their life, liberty and property; but if he did not they had no recourse to law against him. Their sole redress was to petition the king for relief and abide by his decision.[25] A comparative perspective is appropriate. Until 1947 the English king could legally do no wrong and could not be sued in his own courts. The only procedure against him was by petition of right, requesting a trial by the king's grace. Spot the difference.

In 1720 the experiment of 1634 was repeated, with the Estates instead of an aristocratic council directing government policy. It was against this erosion of his prerogatives that Gustavus III acted in 1772. The constitution of that year has the reputation of re-establishing 'absolutism': again it shrivels under close scrutiny. It allocated to the monarch prerogatives in foreign policy and patronage. It also divided power over legislation and taxation between the king and the Estates and prohibited offensive war without their consent. This left Gustavus with marginally less sweeping prerogatives than George III of England.

'Absolutism' in Savoy and Denmark has attracted recent attention, partly owing to new studies endorsing the concept.[26] They do not succeed in eliminating the suspicion that too much is still being made of too little and that reputation again exceeds reality. Once more the previous distribution of power explains much. The reign of Victor Amadeus II of Savoy was inaugurated by a nine-year Regency. He began to rule in person in 1684 and extended central control over the localities with a degree of success not improbable in a minor state. His 'absolutism' amounts to little more than the retrieval of highly personal power over a small kingdom in which it was viable. In Denmark earlier Danish kings had been puppets and the strongest of them failed to direct the government without constant interference from Estates and councils dominated by nobles. The Danish monarchy had been elective. Even though the succession was not in practice disputed, this enabled the grandees to impose restrictive charters on the rulers. These vested sovereignty jointly in the king and the aristocratic council of state (*rigsråad*), the consent of which was required for declarations of war and to some extent for appointments to high offices of state. In 1660 these arrangements were terminated by the disasters of war and the council's blatant failure to provide an alternative to royal authority. The monarchy was declared hereditary in the line of Frederick III and was granted absolute prerogatives. To this extent Denmark followed the pattern of many early modern states which tried to rule by committee and found the system wanting.

CONCLUSIONS

Absolute rulers did not aspire to unchallenged power over everything they could think of, in the manner vaguely defined by the concept of 'absolutism'. The connotation of absolute power was more specific. It first repudiated any rights of resistance or conditional loyalty, such as those claimed by the French nobility before the sixteenth century and by the Hungarian nobility before 1687. Absolute power required obedience. It secondly indicated that matters of state were the monarch's prerogative and not at the disposal of aristocratic councils and Estates. It rejected the kind of constitutional arrangements imposed on Anna of Russia in 1730 and Frederick I of Sweden in 1720. These delegated the royal policy-making prerogative to aristocratic committees of which the monarch was merely chairperson. Absolute monarchs, by contrast, sought advice from their ministers, but their decision was final. It was republics which entrusted to committees matters such as foreign policy and control of the armed forces, or which vested in Estates decision-making powers. A monarchy which submitted to such indignities was nothing more than a quasi-republic. The meaning and distinguishing characteristic of monarchy was not hereditary succession (kings could be elected) but control of policy by one man or those whom he appointed. Other kinds of monarch were unworthy of the name. 'The king governs by himself' was one of Louis XIV's many mottoes. These simple criteria reveal the point of monarchy. They explain why there were so many contests for crowns and such keen competition to influence those who wore them.

In this sense Hanoverian monarchs claimed powers as absolute as any enjoyed by Bourbons and Hapsburgs. The English monarchy had long been the strongest in Europe. As they became more absolute, Continental monarchies became more like the English model – and not, as usually supposed, less. The wider concept of 'absolutism', in which regal power embraced taxation and law-making at will, admittedly eliminates England from consideration. It also eliminates all early modern states apart from Russia, none of which subscribed to such despotic arrangements. This throws new light on the revolutionary constitutions of 1788 in America and 1791 in France. Their originality lay not in their recognition of the right of representatives to assent to taxation: that merely defined what absolute rulers had vaguely accepted for centuries, though the concept of representation was broadened. It lay above all in their attack on monarchical prerogative. The executive was expressly denied absolute control over foreign policy, the American president's right to declare war being subordinated to Congress and the French king's to the National Assembly. Nor were such anti-monarchical fetters forged only by revolution. A few rulers proved capable of self-immolation. The constitution proposed in 1782 by Leopold of Tuscany, though never implemented, would have shared with an elected assembly the former royal prerogatives of making treaties, declaring war and raising troops. Significantly, he owned and had studied a copy of the constitution of Pennsylvania.[27]

These measures were not unprecedented but had never before been glorified by a written constitution and held aloft as a model for mankind. They terminated the era in which absolute power was on the whole the admired form of government – though not in the way commonly understood. It was because no such impetus caught the imagination of the English that they preserved the awesome power of the royal prerogative even after transferring it to ministers commanding a majority of the House of Commons. While Roosevelt had to await the meeting of Congress before declaring war on Japan after Pearl Harbour, Churchill took a quicker way. He and George VI declared war and confronted parliament with a *fait accompli*.

Light is also shed on the vexed question of relations between absolute monarchs and nobles. There is truth in the old belief that they were anti-aristocratic, but again not in the sense usually claimed. With landed nobles wielding their own power in the localities rulers had no option but to seek their co-operation. Though they might enrol alternative royal clients to prevent dangerous reliance on only one regional boss, there was no species of bureaucrat who could free them from dependence on one component or another of the local power structure. Nobles dominated local government in two ways – by getting themselves appointed to official or semi-official posts and by undertaking judicial and fiscal responsibilities in their capacity as lords of manors. In appointing to offices in central government Louis XIV can be considered anti-noble only if the nobility is equated with a handful of grandees. Secretaries of state, ministers, councillors and administrators were recruited from the lesser nobility, most of whom were originally neither rich nor powerful and therefore most likely to be tied to royal interests. Dudley and Cecil, los Cobos and Campomanes, Richelieu and Phélypeaux started humbly and ended festooned in the ribbons of high nobility. Royal officials who belonged originally to the bourgeoisie did not do so for long, since royal service was at all times the chief mode of noble recruitment. French Bourbons in the seventeenth century and Spanish Bourbons in the eighteenth used them to break the grandees' stranglehold on the central councils. But even grandees were not entirely omitted. All monarchs awarded them the posts for which the highest social status was vital – at court and in the army, as viceroys, provincial governors and ambassadors. An absolute monarch was resolutely anti-noble in one sense only. He declined to be reduced to the chairmanship of a self-appointed committee of aristocrats. They could advise and administer but the king appointed them and his decision was final. Nothing less was true monarchy.

Another issue to benefit from this perspective is the alleged ambition of noble-dominated Estates to take over government – an odd aspiration since they did not regard it as their concern. For too long historians have depicted relations between crown and Estates as a tug of war. There has been little cross-fertilisation from the contention of Tudor and Stuart experts that English parliaments had no wish to extend their power at the expense of monarchs. But royal prerogatives were quickly lost unless confidently deployed: kingly power, though arousing certain expectations, was what a ruler could effectively claim. Feeble rulers provoked Estates to claim more power, of which energetic ones subsequently deprived them. Despotic action, fiscal mismanagement, royal minorities or ministerial incompetence usually resulted in encroachment on royal prerogatives by Estates or the nobles who ran them. In this respect the early modern period re-ran the battles of the Middle Ages, when appointment to office had been a major constitutional issue contested between crown and parliament. Policy issues were viewed through the prism of patronage and faction. Opposition to royal prerogatives from an institution meant that royal ministers had temporarily offended more of its members than they had conciliated, not that they all considered constitutional principle to be at stake. Since management of élite groups and distribution of patronage was the prime responsibility of monarchy, challenge to royal prerogatives was the chief symptom of royal incapacity.

Nimbler monarchs had subsequently to retrieve their position. Their objection to Estates which had usurped royal powers does not make them 'absolutist' – any more than it reduced to insignificance Estates which were cut down to a normal supporting role. This challenges the Whig parliamentary myth that control of government by Estates was a desired norm. It was not. They were no keener to eliminate the prerogatives of competent kings than were kings to liquidate the function of Estates. Yet European historians tend to view Estates as debilitated unless they shared the ruler's prerogative[28] – by which token England's parliament was one of the weakest in early modern Europe. Once the tug-of-war model is abandoned, we can see that strong monarchy did not have to be accompanied by weak Estates. If the ruler did his job properly, consultative organs would work for him and not against him: therefore the stronger the better.

Accentuation of royal prerogatives was a refrain in European history after periods when they were challenged. Royal authority, within broad parameters, was a matter of what individual monarchs could make of it. Yet many historians have assiduously asked the wrong questions. They have investigated the socio-economic basis of 'absolutism' when they should have explored the vagaries of high politics and personalities. Poland had the same socio-economic basis as Prussia – a dominant nobility, a weak peasantry and an economy based on the production of grain for Western Europe. Yet that basis sustained neatly contrasting forms of monarchy in the two countries. Sweden's monarchy oscillated between absolute and non-absolute power. Yet there is no evidence that its Marxist fundamentals experienced metamorphosis between 1680 and 1720 – only to undergo a further transformation before 1772. Historians have also explored the official machinery of 'absolutism' when their antennae should have been intercepting the signals which animated it. Finally they have been obsessed with the conflicts provoked by absolute rulers rather than the powers which they wielded. No attempts have been made to compare kingly prerogatives in early modern states, to estimate their relative extent and to identify areas in dispute. Yet successful exploitation of prerogatives distinguished able monarchs from incapable ones – and the ability to push out the boundaries while minimising opposition signified a great one. Adroit lawyers found ways to extend monarchs' prerogatives without flouting the rules too ostentatiously. To study an early modern reign armed with vague notions of prerogative is like watching a tennis match on a court without lines.

REFERENCES

1 Black J 1990 *Robert Walpole and the Nature of Politics in Early Eighteenth-Century England*. Macmillan, p. 37
2 Bluche F 1990 *Louis XIV*. Basil Blackwell, p. 128

3 Le Brun (ed.) 1967 *Politique tirée des propres paroles de l'Ecriture Sainte.* Droz, pp. 92–7

4 Kamen H 1983 *Spain 1469–1714.* Longman, p. 148

5 Bluche F 1990, p. 130

6 Shennan JH 1968 *The Parlement of Paris.* Eyre and Spottiswoode, p. 252

7 Miller J 1987 *Bourbon and Stuart.* George Philip, p. 34; Wilson C 1988 King William – a 1988 Assessment. In Butler M, Price B and Bland S (eds) *William and Mary.* William and Mary Tercentenary Trust, p. 23

8 Black J 1990 *Eighteenth-Century Europe.* Macmillan, p. 411

9 De Madariaga 1990 Catherine the Great. In Scott HM (ed.) *Enlightened Absolutism.* Macmillan, pp. 310–11

10 Koenigsberger HG 1987 *Early Modern Europe 1500–1789.* Longman, p. 182; Zagorin P 1982 *Rebels and Rulers 1500–1660.* Cambridge University Press, p. 91; Behrens CBA 1962/3 Nobles, Privileges and Taxes in France at the end of the *Ancien Régime. Economic History Review*, xv, p. 462; Munck T 1990 *Seventeenth-Century Europe.* Macmillan, p. 35

11 Church WF 1969 Louis XIV and Reason of State. In Rule J (ed.) *Louis XIV and the Craft of Kingship.* Columbus, p. 375

12 Hinton RWK 1957 The Decline of Parliamentary Government under Elizabeth I and the early Stuarts. *Cambridge Historical Journal*, XIII, 2, p. 126

13 Raeff M 1983 *The Well-ordered Police State.* Yale University

14 Black J 1990 *The Rise of the European Powers.* Arnold, pp. 149–54

15 Black J 1987 *The Origins of War in Early Modern Europe.* John Donald, pp. 7–8

16 Hufton O 1980 *Privilege and Protest.* Fontana, pp. 233–5; Shennan JH 1974 *The Origins of the Modern European State 1450–1725.* Hutchinson, p. 9

17 Weber M 1968 *Economy and Society.* New York, Part 2, Chapters 10–14

18 Behrens CBA 1985 *Society, Government and the Enlightenment.* Thames and Hudson, p. 41; Campbell PR 1988 *The Ancien Régime in France.* Basil Blackwell, pp. 54–60; Gagliardo JG 1991 *Germany under the Old Regime 1600–1790.* Longman, pp. 118–20; Shennan JH 1986 *Louis XIV.* Methuen, pp. 14–16

19 Bitton D 1969 *The French Nobility in Crisis.* Stanford; Wood JB 1980 *The Nobility of the Election of Bayeux 1463–1666.* Princeton University, pp. 69–98; Lander JR 1973 *Ancient and Medieval England.* Harcourt Brace Jovanovich, pp. 159–63; Hexter JH 1961 *Reappraisals in History.* Longman, pp. 71–116

20 Elias N 1983 *The Court Society.* Basil Blackwell, pp. 84–5

21 Elliott JH 1977 Philip IV of Spain. In Dickens AG (ed.) *The Courts of Europe.* Thames and Hudson, pp. 173–5

22 Baillie HM 1967 Etiquette and the Planning of the State Apartments in Baroque Palaces. *Archaeologia*, **101**

23 Evans RJW 1977 *The Austrian Hapsburgs.* In Dickens AG (ed.) *The Courts of Europe.* Thames and Hudson, p. 138

24 Munck T 1990 *Seventeenth-Century Europe.* Macmillan, pp. 235–6; Symcox G 1983 *Victor Amadeus II. Absolutism in the Savoyard State 1675–1730.* Thames and Hudson

25 Upton A 1988 Absolutism and the Rule of Law: the Case of Karl XI of Sweden. *Parliaments, Estates and Representation*, **8**, no. 1, pp. 43–6

26 Munck T 1979 *The Peasantry and the Early Absolute Monarchy in Denmark.* Landbohistorisk Selskab, Copenhagen
27 Anderson MS 1990 The Italian Reformers. In Scott HM (ed.) *Enlightened Absolutism.* Macmillan, pp. 67–8
28 Carsten FL 1959 *Princes and Parliaments in Germany.* Oxford University Press, p. 189

CHAPTER EIGHT
Liberties and Consent

The absolute power of rulers ended where subjects' rights began. That is why they were also called liberties, since they staked out an area of immunity from the monarch's power. In the Middle Ages the concept was almost geographical. Kings granted charters to thriving towns which permitted a degree of self-government, a market and the building of a fortified wall, enabling the community to defend its patch of independence – physically if necessary. By the early modern period this almost tangible insistence on barriers which the monarch could not cross was turning into the abstract concept of liberty.

Monarchs did not enjoy a monopoly of power. This is proved by the care with which jurists in every state defined and refined the royal prerogative. Had it extended to everything this would have been unnecessary. Even in matters of justice, royal authority was commonly restricted to particular crimes (such as treason) and particular places (such as the King's Highway). Most courts of law were not royal but civic or seigneurial, though there was a right of appeal to the crown. In particular the fundamental laws of every state except Russia stressed that the royal prerogative did not extend to the life, liberty and property of subjects. These were the birthright of free men.

In the nineteenth century 'patriotism' meant the promotion of national greatness against foreign enemies. A century earlier it referred to the defence of rights and liberties against native tyrants.[1] It is often asserted that the rights in question were corporate rights – that a concept of individual rights was unknown before the French Revolution. A glance at popular imagery shows that this is untrue. A motif which haunted the imagination of early modern Europe was the Phrygian cap of liberty. It was displayed by crowds exercising themselves over matters more plebeian than corporate rights. In the

Ancient World the cap was awarded to a slave on his release as a symbol that his life, liberty and property had been placed in his own hands. There was no ambiguity. For two millenia this has been one of the deepest and simplest convictions of Western man. Those whose life, liberty and property were at the disposal of another were slaves. Those who stripped them of their human dignity were despots

MONARCHS AND DESPOTS

Bossuet, official spokesman of Louis XIV's regime, echoed the convictions of most of his subjects when he declared that individual rights were securely embedded in the fundamental law of the regime. His exposition excludes ambiguity. He defines arbitrary or despotic government as one in which the prince disposes at whim of the life, liberty and property of his subjects, who are indistinguishable from slaves. 'There are peoples and great empires who are satisfied with it; and it is not for us to make them uneasy about their form of government. It is enough for us to say that it is barbarous and odious. These four conditions are far removed from our customs: thus arbitrary government has no place amongst us.'[2] That seems clear enough. Despotism is incompatible with law and liberty.

Students may therefore expect a clear statement from historians on the attitude of 'absolutism' to rights and liberties. If so, they are doomed to disappointment. Some authorities even deny their *theoretical* existence. One of the most recent studies of the dynasty portrays Louis XIV as working hard to sustain the doctrine that the lives, liberties and properties of his subjects were at his disposal.[3] Others still refuse to acknowledge any *practical* difference between absolute power and despotism: distinctions based on the former's subordination to divine and natural law were vague and amounted to no definable limitation. They seem to have suffered from a surfeit of Hobbes, whose ruthless logic dismissed the possibility of limitations on an absolute power. Either it is absolute, in which case nothing can limit it. Or it is limited, in which case it is not absolute. Rights were therefore negligible and Bourbon deference was merely lip-service.[4] A final mode of confusion is totally to ignore the 'absolutism'/ despotism distinction and delineate 'absolutist' Bourbons riding roughshod over the rights and privileges of provinces and people.[5] The jury is still out.

To blur the distinction between absolute and despotic power is disastrous for historical understanding. It imposes on early modern monarchy a despotic model which was usually condemned. The crucial mistake is to assert that absolute power extended to everything, that so-called 'absolutist' kings had a monopoly. This makes absolute monarchs and limited monarchs different species. It is totally anachronistic for the early modern period, when a limited monarch *was* absolute except in certain spheres defined by law and custom.[6] Royal power was absolute within a specific area staked out by the royal prerogative – mainly foreign, military and religious matters of state. Beyond that lay subjects' rights which were inviolable (except in what the ruler judged to be emergencies and in most states even that was disputed). The right to life, liberty and property was protected by the rule of law. Subjects were not supposed to be deprived of them without due legal process and if the law was changed it was supposedly with the consent of those whose rights were affected. English arrangements have always been much admired as the guarantor of rights, while French administrative law (the infamous *droit administratif*) was until recently pilloried as hostile to them. We now know that it has been misunderstood, that French administrative courts have always acted independently of government and that they pose no threat to popular rights. For similar reasons the attempt to present 'absolutism' as an earlier version of the Fascist corporative state is wide of the mark. In Mussolini's Italy corporations lost their rights; in Louis XIV's France they kept them.[7]

The actual interpretation of rights to life, liberty and property varied. Of the three property was probably the most obsessively defended everywhere. It has to be seen in the context of a society based on kinship and lineage and drenched in conceptions of honour. A gentleman's self-respect was founded on the deference paid by law and custom to his property.[8] Freedom of expression was respected in 'absolutist' states as much as in republics – and sometimes more so. The Spanish Hapsburgs were tolerant and frequently encouraged public discussion of politics, while in 1746 the Venetian Senate banned it. In the early part of the period the press was severely censored by most governments, irrespective of whether they have been considered 'absolutist' or 'limited'. France enjoyed *de facto* freedom of the press by the later eighteenth century, especially when Malesherbes was censor from the 1750s. Later in the century in Austria, Prussia and Russia censorship was abolished or curtailed by royal decree. Simultaneously the Genevan Republic was busy condemning Rousseau. In 1762 it ordered his books to be burned and the author to be arrested if he set foot in the city.

Rights were enshrined in law and guarded by Estates and parliaments. There has been little comparative investigation of their powers and composition, though work is now beginning – notably in the new periodical *Parliaments, Estates and Representation*. Modern research is discovering teeming forms of representative life where they had been pronounced extinct. Bush's study of the European nobility and its privileges is also valuable in the context of representation.[9] The structure of Estates was diverse. Peasant membership was unusual: it was assumed that nobles represented their tenants. The only non-noble element was composed, in some assemblies, of delegates from towns or peasant freeholders. The English national variant had Lords and Commons, the French and Danish had clergy, nobles and commoners, the Swedish had clergy, nobles, town-dwellers and peasants, while the Polish had only nobles and the Castilian only town-dwellers. Provincial Estates were equally multicoloured, ranging from the French with the normal three estates to the Dutch with eighteen town votes and one noble. Local assemblies were usually confined to one estate while those at national and provincial level consisted of several. Rights of membership also varied. In local assemblies nobles enjoyed rights of personal attendance, while provincial assemblies in Normandy, Brandenburg, Saxony and East Prussia required the election of deputies. The same applied to national assemblies in England, France and the Dutch Republic. Even at the higher levels some states permitted noble rights of personal attendance, modified only by restrictive property qualifications or other strategems for excluding social climbers by insisting on four generations of nobility. In Sweden all persons technically of noble status were allowed to attend the national assembly. The oratorical log jam thus created was solved by the provision in 1626 that only one member of each family was allowed to speak.

THE RITUALS OF CONSENT

Though some historians of 'absolutism' now accept the presence of rights and privileges which the ruler had to respect, they stress that they were corporate and not individual in character[10] and that they did not prevent taxation without consent. This modifies only slightly the crude equation of absolute power with its despotic opposite. They miss an essential component of regimes which have been called 'absolutist' – their habit of consulting their subjects. Indeed, this is usually taken as the antithesis of 'absolutism'.[11] To insist on an element of consent is to say something new about these states.[12] The traditional view is that absolute monarchy was intrinsically despotic and that by the eighteenth century bodies like the French *parlements* were rejecting it. But, as has been shown, rights, representation and consent did not reach the agenda for the first time in the Enlightened eighteenth century. They were part of the heritage of civic republicanism, which survived throughout the early modern period and was built into the theory and practice of every monarchy. The Enlightenment merely sought to give them clearer definition.

The obsessive defence of traditional rights in the face of every appeal to reason is part of the myth of the *ancien régime*. It fixes in lurid tones the image of a crown which was progressive and public-spirited and an opposition which was backward-looking and selfish. Throughout the early modern period historians have overplayed the theme of monarchs attacking rights and privileges and consultative bodies defending them. Exciting drama is not always good history. Monarchs knew as well as Estates that their own duty was to defend law and the rights it protected. Few deliberately set out to subvert them if their ends could be achieved without such provocation. The alternative options were less spectacular and have been overlooked. Most reforms of law and property rights (including taxation) were achieved with the agreement and co-operation of consultative bodies. Governments could not have survived had their subjects proved permanently unwilling to modify their privileges in the face of persuasion. Such a static posture would have created an impasse every time taxation was considered, leaving no legitimate way to alter property rights without precipitating revolt. Legitimation was bestowed by consent, which was inseparable from rights and liberties. Consultative and representative mechanisms were essential to so-called 'absolutist' rulers, not least because without them legal taxation was impossible. Absolute power ignored consent only in matters where it was inappropriate.

It is often stated that Estates existed to defend rights and liberties. They did, but not in the negative sense usually assumed. They existed to give the consent of community or corporation to government acts which affected their rights. They were in effect a republican component in an otherwise monarchical system. They embodied an ideology which looked to ancient custom, prescriptive privileges, contracts and charters. Their rhetoric was freedom and its sanction was the past. Their business was to negotiate over the intervention of government in an area of immunity. By so doing they in one sense provided a limitation on royal power, since they restricted the activities which it could encompass by itself. But this was a limitation only if it is assumed that monarchs wanted power that was unlimited. Clearly they did not, since most respected the law. More significant was the sense in which Estates enhanced royal authority. They increased its range by extending it into areas which the ruler's prerogative could not reach. Yet even when historians are aware of the importance of rights and privileges under absolute monarchy, they treat them, and those who defended them, as immovable.[13] The negative fashion in which Estates have been depicted confirms the general misunderstanding of their true function. They existed not to obstruct the extension of royal power but to legitimate it.

'Absolutist' historians have overlooked these activities. They have fallen victim to their own circular argument, identifying Estates with the post-1688 English model of frequent and national parliaments. They define the absence of organs of consultation as the nub of 'absolutism' and exclude such institutions from France on the grounds of their non-resemblance to England's. On that basis it is not hard to prove that France was 'absolutist'. Yet even by this arbitrary touchstone England was not alone. We now know that annual meetings were not peculiar to the Westminster Parliament after 1688. Frequency of assembly varied, but in the German-speaking states it was unflattering to comfortable notions of England's uniqueness. And there is no reason anyway why consultation should rely for its validity on its approximation to English arrangements. National Estates were less common outside England and Poland, but this is unsurprising since united national states were exceptional. Once the national perspective is abandoned, a myriad of consultative devices comes into focus. Occasionally Estates spoke for the whole of a ruler's territory: more usually they represented regions and provinces, or corporate groups like clergy and nobility. Most rulers sought consent over matters touching their subjects' rights, but they institutionalised it in many ways – not all of them subscribing to an alleged English monopoly of constitutional wisdom. English scholarship now approximates less to a historiographical equivalent of the old headline: 'Fog in Channel – Continent cut off'.

Only in rare circumstances did rulers ignore these conventions. One was rebellion, after which a province might justifiably be deprived of its privileges. Another was conquest, which entitled a victor to treat new territories with less respect than old ones. On this basis Philip V abolished the privileges of his new Spanish kingdom after 1707. But in absolute monarchies loss of rights was deemed a disgrace, not a norm. Here Louis XIV's France proved orthodox, all his territorial conquests retaining their traditional rights. So far were some rulers from pursuing allegedly 'absolutist' ends that they created privileged bodies where they had not existed before. Estates were introduced in Galicia on its annexation by the Hapsburgs in 1772 and in Corsica on its conquest by France in 1769.

ESTATES: CRUSHED OR CO-OPERATING?

Throughout the early modern period most Estates, central or local, quietly co-operated in the business of administration. They also helped to plan and implement changes in law and taxation. Reforms which affected rights and privileges were not automatically opposed: more usual was negotiation, compromise and action. The agenda of many 'absolutist' historians omits this working relationship between monarchs and their Estates. If there are rows, 'absolutism' is attacking Estates' powers and privileges. If there is calm, 'absolutism' has crushed them into apathy and insignificance. 'Absolutist' historiography wins both ways.

All historians accept a significant role for Estates in the late Middle Ages. But in the early modern age they are conventionally supposed to have fallen into irretrievable decline. A reduced role for them has always been seen as central to 'absolutism'.[14] And a reduced role they had in the regimes which have been called 'absolutist' – but not in the way usually implied. A vital distinction has not been made. Absolute power excluded representative bodies from areas traditionally subject to the royal prerogative. It was entirely compatible with consent in others. We have noted that monarchs as diverse as Isabella of Castile and George III of England were approvingly described as 'absolute' while working with powerful parliaments. When the Sun King's apologists stressed his independence from human authority, they referred to areas traditionally the prerogative of the monarch – not to all aspects of government activity, as is usually assumed. The despotic connotations of 'absolutism' are inappropriate to rulers who were merely retrieving their prerogative. But if Estates were eliminated from areas touching subjects' rights and traditionally subject to their consent, such connotations are appropriate – for that was the meaning of despotism in the early modern period. Everything depends on what the monarch was trying to do independently – be a king or usurp his people's rights.

When monarchs talked of absolute power, they consequently did not suggest that they could dispense with the services of Estates and help themselves to taxation. Yet it is precisely the assumption that absolute power extended to everything which has induced historians to overlook the methods by which rulers came to terms with the fact that it did not. They have assumed that Estates and 'absolutist' regimes are incompatible – organs of consent had to be adversarial, weak or non-existent. The confrontational model assumes inverse proportions: the stronger the crown the weaker the assemblies. Adoption of a co-operative perspective reverses it: stronger Estates meant stronger monarchs. But the presence of vigorous consultative institutions was missed since it was not expected. Historians are bad at finding what they are not looking for.

There is another sense in which Estates seemed to decline during the age of 'absolutism'. Many disappeared. A comment by the political theorist Harrington makes the point: 'Where are the Estates, or the power of the people in France? Blown up. Where is that of the people in Aragon, and the rest of the Spanish kingdoms? Blown up. On the other side, where is the king of Spain's power in Holland? Blown up. . . .' The obituary for monarchs is less familiar than the lament for the people's Estates. It balances the picture and suggests Harrington was not indicating a general trend. Nevertheless early modern textbooks make much of the dramatic disappearance in state after state of the traditional organs of consent. The Spanish cortes, the French Estates-General, the Danish *rigsråd* and the Brandenburg diet vanished from the scene in the later seventeenth century. The temptation to insert such shocking events into an 'absolutist' scenario proved irresistible. Yet closer scrutiny of each episode reveals that nothing is quite what it seems. In every case historical reality was less sensational.

Activity 'behind the scenes' in Bourbon France shows that appearances (or lack of them) can deceive. The 175 years during which the Estates-General was dormant are a well-publicised feature of French 'absolutism'. That it met only twice between 1460 and 1560 is less celebrated. It is at least arguable that its bluntness rather than its cutting edge as a consultative body may be to blame for its final demise, and that far from hating Estates rulers preferred effective ones. The Bourbons continued to consult assemblies in provinces and *sénéchaussées* which had a significant fiscal and administrative role. Consultative procedures were merely displaced to a lower level. Did similar movement occur elsewhere? The vanishing act performed by the big assemblies has hardly been studied and the reasons are a matter of guesswork. What, if anything, replaced them is even more obscure. But a few pointers are beginning to emerge.

Most recent studies of Austrian government in the seventeenth and eighteenth centuries emphasise the continuing importance of Estates. Like the Hanoverians, Leopold I had to summon his Estates every year. His prerogative revenues accounted for less than a fifth of the total required and land tax voted by the diet was essential to make ends meet. Joseph I is supposed to have wanted to limit the powers of the Estates. Yet he deferred to their rights, abandoned plans for an excise collected by royal officials and established commissions drawn from the Estates to codify the laws of Bohemia and Moravia. The Hungarian diet is traditionally considered a victim of Hapsburg 'absolutism' between 1765 and 1780, when it never met. But the county assemblies, which appointed all local officials, continued without interruption. Recent work on Austria confirms a crucial administrative and consultative role for the Estates, long after Haugwitz's reforms of 1748–9 are supposed to have phased them out.[15] He negotiated important new tax deals with each of the Estates in an impeccably constitutional manner, personally visiting each province and arguing the government's case. This has usually been interpreted as a crucial step in the development of Austrian 'absolutism' and the end of their effective power. In fact it confirmed their status.

Maria Theresa's *Political Testament* of 1750 makes it abundantly clear that her objection was not to the Estates as such but to their links with court intrigue: ministers stirred up opposition among provincial Estates as a means of torpedoing the plans of their rivals. They lost some of their administrative functions but retained others. Crown and Estates were partners rather than opponents in the great Hapsburg reform programme of 1740–80. Much of it was discussed and implemented jointly by royal officials and the Estates' permanent committees.[16] Government policy at grass-roots level was partly in the hands of agents of the provincial assemblies: the Styrian Estates office was bigger than a French intendant's. The best evidence for their continued authority is Joseph II's implacable determination to be rid of them.

Sweden has always enjoyed a high profile in 'absolutist' historiography. Yet on closer inspection Charles XI's 'absolutism' proves something of a non-event. In 1686 the Swedish Estates, far from dormant, authorised a commission which began to codify the mainly medieval laws. The result remains the basis of the modern Swedish legal system.[17] In recent years Denmark has been presented as a laboratory specimen of 'absolutism'. The demise of the Danish Estates was sudden and final. But a local study of Schleswig and Holstein suggests that political participation did not end in 1665.[18] At the lowest level of corporate organisation (*Landschaft*) it increased. Representatives negotiated directly with the king about the amount of taxation and accepted responsibility for collecting it. These provinces stood in a special relation to the Danish crown, but arrangements are unlikely to have been totally different elsewhere.

The diet of Brandenburg has suffered the same fate at the hands of historians as the French Estates-General. Consigned to oblivion after 1652, its destruction plays a key role in the demonology of 'absolutism'. Again the truth is more prosaic. The full diet of Brandenburg rarely met *before* 1652.[19] Its disappearance merely increased the importance of the local assemblies (*Kreistage*) by making them the tax-consenting bodies for rural areas. In 1769 they acquired the right to nominate candidates for the office of *Landrat*, the chief local official. Full diets were costly and unwieldy: all over Germany princes increasingly consulted the smaller committees which were empowered to act for them.[20] Nor did the Great Elector expel the Estates from areas where they were useful and constitutionally legitimate – only from activities which rendered them a menace, such as claiming to consent to his sovereignty and negotiate with foreign powers. His Recess of 1653 is usually hailed as one of the founding charters of 'absolutism'. This is odd, since it confirmed all the Estates' ancient rights, privileges and liberties, control of taxation and right to be consulted over foreign policy (the latter being a role which his contemporary, Charles II of England, explicitly denied to his own Estates).[21] Emergencies apart, he taxed with their consent, refrained from levies to which they refused agreement (namely the imposition of excise on nobles) and abandoned all attempts to introduce the excise in the face of opposition from the Estates of Cleves-Mark. Yet this is not the picture of the Great Elector which is given in the textbooks.

We now know more about the cortes of Castile, which met for the last time in 1664. The traditional view is of a long-declining institution to which the crown gladly delivered the *coup de grâce*.[22] Yet it had been more active in preceding decades than ever before. Prerogative matters were frequently put before it and ministers sat as deputies, Olivares himself representing Madrid. There was a need for careful management and copious bribery. In the cortes the crown had centralised the mechanisms of consent, but it had to go back to the cities represented if its requests went beyond the assembly's competence. Consequently, in the 1640s the decision was taken to return to direct negotiation with the cities – a possibility since there were only twenty-three constituencies. If this is 'absolutism' in action, it is an odd performance. Consultation was not terminated: it continued at a lower level. Authority was not centralised but devolved. And the cortes was destroyed, not by the power of the crown, but by the power of the cities.[23]

CONFLICT

If royal co-operation with some form of consultative body was the norm, it could not be permanently guaranteed. Changes in the form of government sounded the most serious alarm. If the constitutional pendulum oscillated violently one way, it frequently swung back to the other extreme. Monarchy degenerated into despotism when it monopolised the powers it was supposed to share: despotism provoked retaliation against misused prerogatives, which rulers thereupon schemed to reinstate. In the eighteenth century the Swedish monarchy went through this routine. At his coronation in 1697 Charles XII swore no oath and crowned himself. He never summoned the Estates and his policies flouted the law. Reacting against his despotism, the establishment of a parliamentary regime in 1720 placed policy-making prerogatives in the hands of the Estates, from which Gustavus III retrieved them in 1772. Every stage was accompanied by institutional conflict over these political issues, even if it reflected factional rather than institutional initiatives.

Several Estates gained control, temporarily or permanently, of aspects of government normally under the royal prerogative. Some German Estates controlled foreign policy between the fifteenth and the seventeenth centuries. They also had permanent committees which were consulted on aspects of policy and allocated and collected taxes, as well as appropriating them to specific purposes. So did the French provincial Estates and the national Estates of Portugal, Aragon, Sicily, Bohemia, Austria and Sweden. Ennoblement was controlled in the sixteenth century by the Bohemian Estates and in the eighteenth by the Swedish. In Denmark, Aragon, Austria, Bohemia, Sicily, East Prussia, Brandenburg, Mark and Cleves, as well as the French *pays d'état*, Estates enjoyed the right to appoint public officials. Nor was the ultimate royal prerogative of appointing ministers and court officials immune. A battlefield between crown and parliament in medieval England, this issue precipitated the Civil War in 1642 when the opposition demanded control of the militia and the composition of the king's council. The Polish Estates were unique in the early modern period for possessing all these powers and more.[24] Hence the travesty of monarchy exhibited by its unhappy king in the eyes of his fellow practitioners.

Early modern Estates did not usually control legislation – or taxation which was logically a part of it. Even in England, where a parliament got nearest to doing so, its legislative sovereignty won general acceptance only in the later eighteenth century – and in the later seventeenth century the accepted constitutional doctrine placed it firmly in the hands of the king. Initiation of legislation and taxation was among the oldest rights of monarchy and few early modern Estates apart from England's gained that right. Law was made by the king and he imposed taxes on his people.

But law and taxation were not a straightforward part of the prerogative. It made nonsense of conventional abhorrence of despotism, as well as of fundamental law which monarchs swore to respect, if monarchs could make what laws they liked at the expense of life, liberty and property. This has caused immense confusion, deriving from modern conceptions of law as the will of a legislator. But it has been argued that the laws of the Bourbons were codifications of existing law or government orders which in England would have been classified as policy. And both were usually subject to the consent of the *parlement*: law was the guardian of rights and the possessors of those rights should be consulted if it was altered. There was consequently a conviction even in 'absolutist' monarchies that consent to law was desirable. French kings were the acknowledged source of law, but decrees affecting their subjects' rights (and much else) were submitted to the *parlements*. In the right of proclamation English monarchs possessed quasi-legislative power, but permanent alterations in the law or infliction of penalties touching life or property required the intervention of parliament. This acceptance of participation was partly practical necessity. Since *parlements* and Estates were themselves vital administrative agencies, monarchs found it prudent to secure their co-operation. A deliberate policy of phasing out bodies with power in their own right would also have dismantled the administrative underpinning of much government policy. At national level they were also an effective device for binding the whole realm to a new law. The alternative was separate contracts with local communities – like the twenty-three Castilian towns. But above all the participation of the community's representatives reflected a deep-seated conviction that consent bestowed legitimacy.

Taxation marked out a similar danger zone into which most

monarchs would not venture on their own authority.[25] Adroit monarchs in Prussia and Russia exploited war emergencies to enlarge their authority. But in most states war limited rulers' powers by making them reliant on Estates for the extra funds to which their prerogative did not entitle them. This in turn imposed the need for co-operation and concessions. This is the reason for the annual meeting during the seventeenth and eighteenth centuries of Estates in Austria, Bohemia and Germany, and for the biennial or triennial meetings in Naples and Sicily. English governments were not alone after 1688 in calling annual parliaments to meet the money-gobbling demands of international rivalry. Provincial Estates in France assembled between once a year and once every three years. In all these states the crown was unable or unwilling to impose new taxes without the Estates' consent. Historians of 'absolutism' disagree. Along with the existence of bureaucracy, the ability to levy tax without the consent of a representative assembly is seen as a crucial litmus test for 'absolutist' rulers.[26] Yet with this facility eighteenth-century French monarchs would have had no financial problem. Where the tax-granting powers of Estates were not displayed prominently, this was often because the major part of royal revenue was beyond their clutches. Royal prerogative accounted for the crown's income from its monopoly of mining and salt production in Hungary, from colonial empires in Portugal and Castile, from extensive crown lands in Prussia and from indirect taxes in Naples, Sicily and Hungary. In France, Prussia, Castile and Sicily once indirect taxes had been granted they could be levied, unless altered, without further application to the Estates.[27] None of these sources of income were available to the English crown by the eighteenth century – which is the sole reason why it was more dependent on parliament than most European monarchies. But nor do any of these revenues indicate 'absolutist' contempt for Estates' consent. They were taxation for which their consent was unnecessary.

Taxation was one of the issues which frequently provoked conflict between rulers and their Estates. So did accompanying attempts to smooth out administrative anomalies and promote uniformity. Another was the drive for religious conformity. Conflict has attracted more historical attention than agreement and produced a double misunderstanding. First, conflict has been seen as the essence of relationships between monarchs and Estates. Consequently Estates are regarded as satisfactory from the ruler's point of view if weak, in abeyance or non-existent.[28] This reflects the traditional view that they were incompatible with absolute power: they could coexist with it only if marginalised or moribund. There has been little cross-fertilisation from the discovery, already mentioned, in Tudor and Stuart England that their essence was co-operation. Yet on the Continent the argument applies more strongly, since Estates and their officials were the executants as well as in some sense the financiers of government policy. Instead consultative assemblies are persistently presented as a check on monarchical power. When examiners ask students about the 'limitations to absolutism', they want to be told that by guarding traditional privileges diets and Estates set boundaries to the absolute powers of the crown. As indeed they did. But in depicting them as brakes on the great flywheel of monarchy, this historiography neglects the real sense in which Estates also added to its momentum. They were part of government rather than its rival – though this is harder to grasp in the twentieth century when government policy is carried out mainly by government officials. It is precisely because they were an intrinsic component of government that Estates and *parlements* could be obstructive: issues involving them usually divided the personnel of central government. Consultative bodies, linked to them by ties of patronage and clientage, consequently took sides in their turn.

Second, conflict itself has been misunderstood. The temptation is always to read it as impending collapse, if not incipient revolution, in a failing system – as rumblings of approaching storms or symptoms of terminal illness. No period in history has suffered from these clichés more than eighteenth-century France, where understanding has been wrecked by an excess of medical and meteorological metaphors. For conflict is a healthy condition which early modern constitutional mechanisms were designed to absorb. It prevents the ossification of social and political systems by exerting pressure for innovation, as vested interests are challenged by new demands for wealth, power and status. Constitutional arrangements are instruments for managing conflict.[29]

Some conflicts could not be managed. The most dangerous were invariably inspired by attempts to impose change on a conservative society, in which the privileges of individuals, corporations and communities were deeply embedded. Anyone who sought to eradicate them was attempting perilous surgery in which the growth was part of the living tissue. Though yet another medical metaphor, this one has the virtue of highlighting the true nature of the issue of privilege – potentially deadly. In every realm privileges were a permanent refrain. They were ceremonially reiterated when kings were crowned, mayors elected or lowly officials installed. Their sanction was the past and their beneficiaries were universal. Even peasant villages enjoyed their collective rights of harvest and pasture. Since all were convinced that the main purpose of civil society and secular rule was the maintenance and defence of their liberties, rulers who tampered with them in anything more than an absent-minded and deferential manner were courting revolt.[30] Despotic inroads on privilege swiftly undermined respect for the monarch as the defender of law.

Yet in the early modern period this bedrock of continuity clashed with an equally profound force for change, which has lately aroused historical interest.[31] This was the rise of the 'imperial' monarchies of the Spanish and Austrian Hapsburgs and the French Bourbons – 'imperial' in that, despite the theoretical equality reflected in their monarchs' multiple titles, one central territory containing the royal court and the burgeoning administrative capital assumed dominance over the rest. This usually presaged the attempt to impose its laws and customs on the provinces. It was this type of imperial programme which destroyed Philip II in the Netherlands, Olivares in Catalonia, Charles I in Scotland and Joseph II in Belgium and Hungary. Equally dangerous in multiple kingdoms was permitting in one realm a religion forbidden in another. This Charles I discovered in Scotland, as did Philip II in the Netherlands.[32] By the seventeenth century monarchs no longer conceded the contractual basis of their subjects' obedience, conditional on maintenance of their rights. But that did not prevent subjects from withdrawing their allegiance in practice if they felt that law was flouted and rights or privileges imperilled.

Liberal historians of the nineteenth century liked to portray the *ancien régime* as a stuffy repository of outworn ideas and institutions, resisting the revitalising influence of the Enlightenment which alone could have saved it. In fact change was promoted by early modern government from the sixteenth century, and with the rise of Cameralist ideas in the later seventeenth it took off. Itself building on earlier notions of the 'well-ordered police state', Cameralist thinking stressed the interdependence of a monarch's revenue and the prosperity of his subjects. The perceived need for administrative and economic reform was hardly novel by the eighteenth century, and most change originated with governments – just as most political crises were the result of attempts by offended interests to resist it. Only a few policies wrought serious havoc during the period, since most rulers were cautious and knew when to stop. The most dangerous periods were during and after wars, as governments strove to respond to unprecedented financial demands. The so-called General Crisis of the mid-seventeenth century followed the Thirty Years War, and the great reform initiative of 1763–89 was in part the result of the wars of the mid-eighteenth century. Many of these initiatives were taken with the consent and co-operation of bodies which defended rights and privileges. But whereas Olivares did at least try to persuade suspicious provinces of the advantages of a closer union with Castile, a century later there was a new mood of contempt for the old techniques of management and negotiation.

ENLIGHTENED DESPOTISM

The traditional organs of consent were increasingly perceived as the spokesmen least likely to agree to anything innovative. They were denounced as bastions of class and regional privilege, as archaic obstacles to effective government and state power. In spite of their status as the guardians of liberty, they were often in the forefront of those who sought to suppress Enlightened ideas. In spite of their reputation for defending the rights of the people, they were often seen as protecting selfish sectional interests. The issue has been tossed around by historians of every shade of political opinion. Though post-Marxist observers can spot the class basis of *parlements* and Estates, they seem to have done a creditable job in standing up for the wider interests of people and province. In the last years of the *ancien régime* it did them little good. The notion of 'legal despotism' was first announced by Mercier de la Rivière in the 1760s. It was inspired by the need for a strong ruler who could bulldoze his way through the clutter of privilege and particularism in the name of a higher law of nature deemed valid whether recognised by Estates and *parlements* or not. It called for a short cut.

The intellectual weaponry for this was furnished by the Enlightenment. This bristles with difficulties for the historian. Was it one movement or many? Who were its adherents and how new were its beliefs? At one level much of its thinking was the traditional rhetoric of liberty. Its originality has been exaggerated, though it had more to say about freedom of expression than was usual in sixteenth and seventeenth discussions of life, liberty and property. It emphasised human welfare and rational scientific method as the means to promote it. Deriving from the Cameralist ideals of the central European 'well-ordered police-state', these objectives were also less original than often supposed.[33] Since the sixteenth century, government regulation had been seen as an orderly answer to the haphazard arrangements inherited from the past. Only the accent on equal rights was completely new, and that was soft-pedalled as it clashed with the privileges which *ancien régime* society equated with liberty. Enlightened thinkers were hopelessly divided over the issue of privilege, some wanting an end of it whatever the cost in despotism and others seeing it as one of the rights which constituted liberty – a contradiction at the heart of their programme which they never resolved.

The most influential political thinker of the Enlightenment was Montesquieu. Much of his condemnation of despotism merely enlarges on Bossuet. But he was original in demanding the separation in different hands of the executive, legislative and judicial functions of government. This system of checks and balances would prevent abuse of power and preserve liberty. He institutionalised the defence of rights and liberty in 'intermediate bodies', whose overthrow would spell the end of legitimate monarchy. Most of the *philosophes* agreed with him and viewed privileged and powerful consultative bodies as a vital check on royal despotism. But not all. An important minority dismissed all privileged bodies as selfish, reactionary and illiberal. Their dilemma has been insufficiently emphasised: the defence of liberty depended on the forces of reaction. Aristocratic, clerical and judicial assemblies were of all bodies the least likely to rationalise law and administration, equalise tax, free serfs, promote economic growth, enlarge toleration, curb the power of priests and spread education. Voltaire was less agitated about who should govern than about what government should do: if it did the right things, restraints on its power were unnecessary. Forced to choose between despotism and privileged bodies clinging to their unequal rights, he preferred monarchs who could clear a path through the rubble.

So too did the physiocrats. They were convinced that only a despotic ruler would be capable of upholding the free market forces in which they believed against the entrenched vested interests of industrial gilds and peasant communities. He had to intervene to prevent intervention. It was a view shared by the thinkers of the German Enlightenment, the heirs of Cameralism and the 'well-ordered police-state'. They aimed to increase government resources and raise standards of public welfare – objectives perceived as interdependent, comprehended in the state as union of ruler and ruled. They needed strong monarchs: the desired improvement could be effected only by the minute regulation of health and morals, poverty and education, industry and trade.

Only Rousseau arrived at a different conclusion. He despised parliaments and assemblies but refused to embrace monarchs. Instead he gave a new twist to an idea on which Enlightened pundits were united – the social contract. The divine right of kings was rejected: monarchs could scarcely be appointed by a Christian God in whom the *philosophes* disbelieved. Instead they pictured ruler and people as partners to a contract of mutual advantage, with the ruler in Frederick II's phrase as first servant of the state. The implication was that sovereignty lay originally with the people, who consented by contract to transfer it to a ruler. Rousseau's *Social Contract* of 1762 changed the terms of debate. He left sovereignty with the people and embodied it in their 'general will', activated when they forgot their selfish wills and opened their hearts to republican *virtu* – the public spirit which seeks the good of the community as a whole. For those disillusioned with élitist assemblies but unwilling to place sovereignty in the hands of the people, there was a final option. This was the German Enlightenment's solution of embodying subjects' rights in a clearly defined body of law.[34]

Enlightened Despotism was based on the first group of ideas, advocating deliberate despotism. For too long historians have dismissed them as vapid theorising with little discernible impact. They have concluded that Enlightened 'absolutism', with its more constitutional reverberations, was a better name for what went on. Rousseau commented at the time that 'legal despotism' was a contradiction in terms. So it is. But logic never ruled men's minds, even in the Age of Reason, and the programme made converts. Despite the revulsion evoked by the word 'despotic' (which the prefix 'Enlightened' or 'legal' was intended to counter), its adherents so described it at the time – and meant it.[35] The recent rediscovery of Joseph II's juvenile jotting known as the *Rêveries* affords the clearest example of its influence on the thinking of a young ruler.[36] In it he contemplates the size of the problem confronting the Hapsburg Empire and concludes that drastic action is required. He wants to be able to do all the good against which the provinces' rules, statutes and oaths erect barriers, to their own loss. 'I believe we must strive to convert the provinces and make them feel how useful the short-term despotism, which I propose, would be to them. For this purpose I should want to make an agreement with the provinces requesting full power for ten years to do everything for their good without consulting them.'

This is illuminating confirmation of the need to gain the consent of the provincial Estates *before* Joseph's projected deal – a necessity doubted by conventional views of late eighteenth-century Austrian 'absolutism'. Even more significant is the accurate pre-echo of his icy remark to the Estates of Brabant in 1789: 'I do not need your consent to do good.' What he spotted more clearly than most was the need to attack corporate rights in order to safeguard individual rights. He was enlarging freedom: the question was whose. Like Turgot, he saw that a despotic attack on the liberty of the guilds (embodied in their privileges) would promote the liberty and equality of individual craftsmen. Clearly despotism was a consistent theme of his professional life. And it was premeditated, planned and practical – not airy philosophy for the likes of Rousseau.

The consequences were catastrophic. Revolts in Belgium and Hungary finally undid most of his reforms and left Joseph perplexed at his rejection by those he had sought to help. This explains the impossibility of finding one title or formula which embraces Joseph II, Frederick II and Catherine II – not to mention the rulers of smaller states such as Tuscany and Baden. Their innovations, most of which modern societies take for granted, deserve more recognition than they have received. They all promoted liberty in the modern sense of rights of free speech, press and person. They all defined the rights of their subjects by incorporating them in clearly stated constitutional law. They all believed to some extent in equal rights. Even the cynical Frederick the Great considered a peasant's life, liberty and property as significant as a noble's – and he demonstrated his belief in the case of Miller Arnold, when an entire bench of judges whom the king suspected of social discrimination was marched off to Spandau. They all dismissed doctrines of divine right and saw themselves as managers fulfilling a contract to maximise their people's happiness – a commitment which took tangible forms. Historians have dismissed it as merely the obverse of state power: institutions for the poor kept orphans and paupers off the streets and set them on useful work. It is difficult, though, to explain along these lines the theatres and museums founded after 1750 by rulers for their people. In 1769 Frederick II of Hesse began a museum at Kassel which was freely open to the public from the start.[37]

If tax rights were to be equal in the name of Enlightened equality, tax privilege and exemption must be abolished. But though equality was an Enlightened virtue, so was liberty. It consisted of rights and embraced the right to privilege. The early modern word 'liberties' *meant* privileges. Even Enlightened *philosophes* did not distinguish the privileged rights claimed by some from the basic rights claimed by all. After the dissolution of the *parlements* in 1771 Diderot fretted: 'Farewell to every privilege of the various Estates constituting a corrective principle which prevents the monarchy from degenerating into despotism.' Joseph II's problem was that he approved of equality and detested privilege, which was its opposite; but he also loved liberty and privilege was part of it. If he wished to eradicate privilege, it must be at the expense of liberty. This meant despotism unless he could win the consent of those whose rights were affected, and that contingency he dismissed. Instead he took the view that seeking agreement was a waste of time since most people were unaware of their own true interests. Reforms would therefore have to be carried out despotically, without consultation. Providing they promoted happiness and equality, he believed they would be accepted in the end. It is a mistake to see Joseph as in some sense despotic in spite of his Enlightenment, as though in the light of his principles he should have known better. It was *because* he was desperate to promote Enlightened policies that he had to be despotic.

The same dilemma confronted Louis XVI. Like Joseph he wanted rational uniformity, equal taxes and religious liberty; in 1788 he demanded 'one king, one law'. But faced with intransigent consultative organs his solution was force – *lits de justice* and *lettres de cachet*. He is rarely presented as practitioner and victim of Enlightened Despotism. Yet impulse and outcome were the same as Joseph's.

To understand Enlightened Despotism its two paradoxical strands must be grasped. Its ends were libertarian: hence the emphasis on freedom of expression, definition of rights, economic derestriction and alleviation of serfdom. But the means were autocratic. The benighted outlook of the organs of consent and an authoritarian strain in the Enlightenment itself made it reform from the top. For those who adopted it, the point was to eliminate the element of consent inherent in what are known as 'absolutist' regimes. Enlightened Despotism is valuable evidence for the non-existence of autocratic 'absolutism'.

The alternative solution was attempted by the more patient Maria Theresa. Rejecting the defeatism of her grandfather Leopold I, who had conscientiously deferred to the hotch-potch of local rights which hamstrung his monarchy, she resolved on a fundamental change in the basis of the Hapsburg state. The end of noble and clerical tax exemption and a decennial tax deal were the prerequisites. In 1748 she despatched Haugwitz to each province in turn to try every persuasive art on the Estates. Only in Carinthia did she despair of agreement and fall back on the despotic solution of what she called her *jure regio*, by which she presumably meant her supreme emergency power. Many explanations have been offered for the mother's greater success in promoting a comprehensive reform programme. They rarely include the fact that she confined herself to what were seen as legitimate methods while her son was denounced as unconstitutional.

If Joseph's ideal was Enlightened Despotism, Catherine II's was

Enlightened monarchy. Russia is notoriously hard to discuss, not least because of the difficulty of translating precisely the Russian equivalents for 'autocrat', 'sovereign' and 'absolute'. There is growing dissatisfaction with the belief among Western historians that Russia was an Asian despotism alien to the traditions of European monarchy.[38] This misconception, if such it proves to be, was shared by early modern observers. Acutely conscious that the Russian monarchy was *already* considered despotic by the refined sensibilities of Western Europe, Catherine determined to transform it into the absolute monarchy with intermediate powers praised by Montesquieu. Plans were therefore laid to make good the lack of organs of consent and consultation which were present in the West. The Empress made over 700 pages of notes on Blackstone's *Commentaries on the Laws of England*. The earliest progeny was her *Nakaz* or discussion document of 1767, in which she argued for absolute power in the monarch and intermediate corporations to embody the rights of the people. She subsequently attempted to establish the rule of law where there was none before: citizens should not be deprived of life, liberty or property without judicial formalities. An equity court was established to safeguard individual rights, including a modified version of habeas corpus.[39] Like Joseph she defined the rights of her people, in the Town Charter of 1775 and the Nobles' Charter of 1785. Unlike Joseph, she planned a high court endowed with the legislative and judicial powers of the English parliament. One of the chambers of the court was to be elected by nobles, townspeople and state peasants. This associated elected representatives with the machinery of central government in a way never contemplated in Russia previously – or again before the reign of Alexander II.[40]

Thus at the end of the *ancien régime* two rulers took opposite views of the traditional organs of consent. The would-be despotic monarch inherited elaborate consultative apparatus and strove to bypass it. The would-be limited monarch inherited no such apparatus and sought to create it. Their cases may stand as testimony to the continuing vitality of representative institutions, the idea of the liberty they embodied and the barrier they presented to a despotic ruler. Most rulers were *not* despotic and the nineteenth-century Whig obsession with Estates as a check on regal power is inappropriate. They existed to give it legitimate extension. If absolute monarchs had no monopoly of power, they needed them. And if they were compatible with absolute monarchical power, representative assemblies can be regarded not as marginal to 'absolutist' states but as central. Rather than downgrading them as dispensable we can recognise them as essential.

REFERENCES

1   Dietz MG 1989 Patriotism. In Ball T, Farr J and Hanson RL (eds) *Political Innovation and Conceptual Change*, Cambridge University Press, pp. 182–91
2   Hartung F and Mousnier R 1955 Quelques problèmes concernant la monarchie absolue. *Relazioni*, **4**, pp. 7–8; Le Brun J (ed.) 1967 *Politique tirée des propres paroles de l'Ecriture Sainte*. Droz, pp. 291–2
3   Miller J 1987 *Bourbon and Stuart*. George Philip, p. 14
4   Hartung F and Mousnier R 1955, p. 4; Behrens CBA 1967 *The Ancien Régime*. Thames and Hudson, p. 107
5   Durand G 1976 What is Absolutism? In Hatton R (ed.) *Louis XIV and Absolutism*, Macmillan, p. 23; Knecht RJ 1982 *Francis I*. Cambridge University Press, p. 429
6   Chrimes SB 1936 *English Constitutional Ideas in the Fifteenth Century*. Cambridge University Press, p. 339, n. 68
7   Wade HWR 1988 *Administrative Law*. Oxford University Press, pp. 26–7; Olivier-Martin JM 1938 *L'organisation corporative de la France d'ancien régime*. Librarie du Recueil Cirey
8   Kiernan WG 1989 *The Duel in European History*. Oxford University Press, p. 162
9   Bush M 1983 *Noble Privilege*. Manchester University, pp. 93–97
10 Shennan JH 1983 *France before the Revolution*. Methuen, pp. 2–4
11 Behrens CBA 1967, p. 117; Upton AF 1990 Sweden. In Miller J (ed.) *Absolutism in Seventeenth-Century Europe*. Macmillan, p. 104
12 Black J 1990 *Eighteenth-Century Europe*. Macmillan, pp. 369–77
13 Behrens CBA 1967, p. 117; Campbell PR 1988 *The Ancien Régime in France*. Basil Blackwell, p. 55
14 Behrens CBA 1985 *Society, Government and the Enlightenment*. Thames and Hudson, pp. 24–5
15 Dickson PGM 1987 *Finance and Government under Maria Theresa*. Oxford University Press, pp. 257–96
16 Scott HM 1990 *Enlightened Absolutism*. Macmillan, pp. 157–8
17 Black J 1990, p. 335
18 Kruger K 1987 Regional Representation in Schleswig and Holstein. *Parliaments, Estates and Representation*, **7**, no. 1, 33–7
19 Macartney CA 1970 *The Hapsburg and Hohenzollern Dynasties in the Seventeenth and Eighteenth Centuries*. Macmillan, p. 229
20 Bush M 1983, p. 107; Gagliardo JG 1991 *Germany under the Old Regime*. Longman, p. 104
21 Macartney CA 1970, pp. 230, 234
22 Myers AR 1975 *Parliaments and Estates in Europe*. Thames and Hudson, p. 98
23 Thompson IAA 1984 Crown and Cortes in Castile, 1590–1665. *Parliaments, Estates and Representation*, **4**, no. 2, pp. 125–33
24 Bush M 1983, pp. 105–6
25 Munck T 1990 *Seventeenth-Century Europe*. Macmillan, p. 34; Gagliardo JG 1991, p. 100; Black J 1991 *A System of Ambition: British Foreign Policy 1660–1793*. Longman, p. 17
26 Koenigsberger HG 1987 *Early Modern Europe 1500–1789*. Longman, p. 182

27 Bush M 1983, pp. 103–4

28 Black J 1990. pp. 369–70

29 Metcalf MM 1988 Conflict as Catalyst: Parliamentary Innovation in Eighteenth-Century Sweden. *Parliaments, Estates and Representation*, **8**, no. 1, pp. 63–4

30 Lossky A 1984 The Absolutism of Louis XIV: Reality or Myth? *Canadian Journal of History*, XIX, pp. 5–6

31 Robertson J 1989 *Union, State and Empire: the Britain of 1707 in its European Setting*. Unpublished paper delivered to the Centre for Historical Studies at Princeton; Russell CSR 1982 Monarchies, Wars and Estates in England, France and Spain. *Legislative Studies Quarterly*, VII, pp. 215–16; Russell CSR 1987 The British Problem and the English Civil War. *History*, 72, pp. 395–415

32 Russell C 1990 *The Causes of the English Civil War*. Oxford University Press, p. 29

33 Raeff M 1983 *The Well-Ordered Police State*. Yale University, p. 252

34 Strakosch HE 1967 *State Absolutism and the Rule of Law*. Sydney University, pp. 44–9, 219–33

35 Beales D *Was Joseph II an Enlightened Despot?* Unpublished paper, pp. 3–9

36 Beales D 1980 Joseph II's *Rêveries*. *Mitteilungen des Österreichischen Staatsarchivs*, **33**, pp. 155–6

37 Summerson J 1986 *The Architecture of the Eighteenth Century*. Thames and Hudson, pp. 124–5

38 De Madariaga I 1982 Autocracy and Sovereignty. *Canadian–American Slavic Studies*, **16**, nos 3–4, pp. 369–87; Longworth P 1990 The Emergence of Absolutism in Russia. In Miller J (ed.), *Absolutism in Seventeenth-Century Europe*, Macmillan, pp. 175–93, 232, 254, n. 37

39 De Madariaga 1981 *Russia in the Age of Catherine the Great*. Weidenfeld and Nicolson, p. 283

40 De Madariaga I 1990 *Catherine the Great*. Yale University, pp. 207–8

CHAPTER NINE
Life Cycle of a Myth

One of the few statements which can be confidently made about 'absolutism' is that it was never English. Much definition has proceeded along the lines of what 'absolutism' is *not*. Whatever it *was*, it never took root north of the Channel. There is no reason to revise this traditional verdict: no one is suggesting that England was 'absolutist'. It remains appropriate to ask if the Continent was.

The myth of English limited monarchy and Continental 'absolutism' is so strongly entrenched that some exaggeration is essential to its correction. If both have been depicted here as essentially static, this reflects the growing conviction of several historians that for much of the early modern period continuity triumphed over change – that the eighteenth century refought many of the battles of the sixteenth and the seventeenth centuries, if not of the Middle Ages. If differences between England and the Continent have not been emphasised, that is because few are in danger of overlooking them. It is not suggested here that England and France had identical systems of government: the issue is whether the similarities were greater than the contrasts. It is clear that the parliament with which English monarchs had to deal was more prominent and powerful than any comparable body in France. It met annually, spoke for the entire realm and had a stranglehold on royal finance. French organs of consultation were more amorphous and untidy than England's and were commonly treated more impatiently. They were no less real. The difference is of degree and not kind: they were clearly the same species. A chihuahua is a very small dog but to call it a rodent would hinder biological understanding.

Nor do the splendours of England's parliamentary heritage detract from the similarity between the powers of the two monarchs and the function of their courts. Though 'absolutism' cannot sensibly be related to England, in some respects it displayed more of the features commonly associated with it than France itself. The monarch monopolised the standard royal prerogatives at an earlier date, and by the sixteenth century they included absolute control of the Church. Both before and after the 1688 Revolution he was developing a huge fiscal bureaucracy free of the private enterprise element dominant in France, which deployed a range of quasi-legislative instruments independent of parliament. Significantly, there was never a 'state' in English constitutional tradition, only 'the crown'.[1]

Nor does a weaker parliamentary system in France establish the existence of French 'absolutism', for a national parliament made Henry VIII and George II mightier monarchs than their French rivals. As long as representative institutions were subordinate to the crown and not to the electorate they were an instrument of royal government, and the English institution was a heavyweight. The powers of the Scottish clan chiefs were coolly eliminated after 1745 in a manner which would have been impossible in France. An adversarial perspective makes little sense of relations between assemblies which embodied rights and monarchs normally reluctant to infringe them.

The practical limitations within which 'absolutism' functioned are well known. Financial necessity involved compromises with private contractors and government officials who had bought their posts; reliance on patronage mechanisms dictated prudent handling of power groups and vested interests; geographical distance and diversity precluded ruling any state as a united entity. The theoretical limitations are less celebrated but more crucial. No monarchs west of Russia were conceptually absolute to the extent of justly overriding their subjects' rights or taxing them without consent. It has also been shown that blanket description of certain regimes as 'absolutist' is impossible. First, no monarch's authority was uniform throughout his territories but varied according to their laws and customs. Second, governments were directed by ministers who did not have the same constitutional views. How then did the French monarchy, and after it the other Continental monarchies, come to be regarded as 'absolutist'?

BIRTH

The myth began with Sir John Fortescue, writing during the 1460s. He was responsible for the ever-popular legend that there was something specially English about parliaments. The claim was ludicrous when he made it. Financial necessity had prompted rulers to establish consultative assemblies all over Europe. Many had already developed permanent officials and standing committees who could speak in the Estates' name between meetings; they voted and collected taxes and paid their own officials. The English parliament enjoyed no such advantages.[2] Yet Fortescue announced that while English kings had a royal prerogative (*dominium regale*) they were unique in needing the consent of parliament to legislation and taxation (*dominium politicum*). By contrast French monarchs could help themselves to their subjects' property. Had he troubled to consult the contemporary memoirs of Commines, minister to Louis XI, he would have been assured of the opposite. We now know that *dominium politicum et regale* was the European norm, not the exception.[3] But it is clear from the context that Fortescue was uninterested in accurate analysis of a foreign constitution, since he attributed the contrast to the craven unwillingness of the French to rebel against their rulers. His intention was to score points off the national enemy.

Throughout the sixteenth and early seventeeth centuries Englishmen continued to congratulate themselves on their good fortune. Their parliament was seen as unique protection for rights to life, liberty and property. A ruler who enjoyed his people's love had no need to take their property by force: they would freely grant it for his legitimate needs. At the same time there was cheerful willingness to acknowledge the crown's absolute power in its own sphere. Though the constitution was partly mixed, the royal component entailed an absolute monarch, who was seen not to threaten but to secure the rights of his subjects. Before the conviction grew that Continental monarchs were exceeding their powers, MPs could be found admitting that the authority of their own ruler was in some respects stronger than theirs. In 1610 Dudley Carleton contrasted the wide powers of James I with the more circumscribed prerogatives of the king of Spain.[4]

CHILDHOOD

But as Continental Estates apparently wobbled, and their own rights were threatened at home by the despotism of Charles I, Englishmen's pride became less complacent and more strident. An important shift took place in their use of the word 'absolute'. It acquired pejorative overtones during the Civil War: instead of praising absolute monarchs men came to blame them. Absolute power began to be equated with despotism.[5] It also began mysteriously to suffer from English detestation for all things popish. In the early decades of the seventeenth century, papists had been criticised for attacking the legitimately absolute authority of monarchs. But by the middle of the century a link was forged in English minds between popery and absolute power. Charles I was linked with the Catholic religion: his authority was partly damned by association with it.

The clue to the crucial development is provided by a study of propaganda in the 1670s, when Charles II employed his prerogative power to dispense papists from the Penal Laws. This touched Protestants on two raw nerves: their monopoly of power and their anti-popery. The royal Declaration of Indulgence of 1672 explicitly connected absolute power with toleration for Catholics.[6] He simultaneously allied with Catholic France to attack the Protestant Dutch, whose propaganda fastened the link between 'France, Popery and Absolute Power'. French kingship had wrongly been thought arbitrary since Fortescue, and it was easy to equate Charles's aims with its Catholic despotism. During the Exclusion Crisis, identification of 'Absolute Power and Tyranny' was given the authority of Locke, an exaggerated critic of French 'slavery'.[7] James II's similar policy, paired with Louis XIV's Revocation of the Edict of Nantes, delivered the *coup de grâce*. Henceforth in English ears absolute power was tyrannical, papist and French.

For the next thirty years France posed a mortal threat to England's commercial and dynastic priorities, as Louis XIV annexed the trade of the Spanish empire and sponsored the Jacobites. It was desirable to accuse him of as much as possible. Despotism dovetailed snugly into the charge of 'universal monarchy', according to which he was accused of wanting to dominate the world. This helped a weak and selfish case against Louis in the Spanish Succession War. Supporters of Anne and the Hanoverians also had the strongest motives for stigmatising Jacobite ideology as despotic. Louis simultaneously continued to appear a threat to English religion. Religious affiliations have been presented as a weaker influence on international relations after 1648 than before; but they could still engender sympathy for co-religionists in other countries and determine the form in which hostility expressed itself. Common cause was proclaimed with the oppressed Huguenots as the Protestant brotherhood dedicated itself to the destruction of 'popery and arbitrary government'.[8] At the same time the theme appeared in the Huguenots' own propaganda. Attribution of despotic ambitions to Louis, 'the Christian Turk', is no more a description of political realities than were stories of Huns bayoneting babies in 1914. Religious bigotry determined political theory. The destruction of absolute power as a legitimate political concept was the work of outraged international Protestantism in fear of its life.

The earlier English disposition to refer indifferently to the mixed and absolute aspects of their government had evaporated. Henceforth England was officially a mixed or limited monarchy, and absolute power was despotism. Only Tories and embarrassingly logical lawyers like Blackstone talked of absolute power, unless the intention was to attack it. Most commentators referred delicately to the exclusively royal part of government as the prerogative. Some even forgot what the prerogative was, and identified it as an exceptional power for emergencies: that most government was still carried on in its name was overlooked. For historical understanding Protestant redefinition of terms was catastrophic. The vital distinction between a power which respected subjects' rights and one which trampled on them was blurred for all time.

This was a Whig view, and in England the Whigs had won. But in France the difference between absolute and despotic power remained official ideology. Bossuet himself complained about those who wilfully confused the two in order to make absolute monarchy 'odious and indefensible'. Throughout the next century French apologists clamoured against those seeking by cheap slurs to bring absolute monarchy into disrepute. Their fears were abundantly justified: the battle was lost. Most subsequent historians have either ignored the distinction between absolute and despotic power or failed to take it seriously.

There was an empirical element in this myth-making. Locke went abroad and pronounced the Estates of Languedoc to be a despot's rubber stamp, on the grounds that they never refused the king's demands.[9] Eighteenth-century observers interpreted rows with corporate bodies as evidence of tyranny. Hence the early appearance of those two infallible signs of 'absolutism' – agreement and conflict.

ADOLESCENCE

The propaganda worked by virtue of its antiquity. English orthodoxy in the early eighteenth century was not that France had degenerated into 'absolutism' and England escaped it by the 1688 Revolution, though some believed the French monarchy had taken a sinister turn with Richelieu and Mazarin. The official line was that little had changed in either country for 300 years. In 1701 Fortescue was republished with a smart new title: 'The Difference between a Limited and an Absolute Monarchy'. Political pamphlets quoted it exuberantly. If the contrast dated from the fifteenth century it presumably owed little to Louis XIV or William III. The interpretation of 1688 as a new beginning in England's constitutional history and liberties dates back no further than the 1730s, but it is still repeated.[10] Walpole deployed it as a retort to his opposition, who denounced the loss of liberty under the Robinocracy. In constitutional terms the Glorious Revolution was arguably a myth crafted to lull alarmist fears at the growth of the executive. Apprehensions that English liberties were vanishing were rebutted by the assertion that they had never been more secure. The older interpretation, restated by Burke, downgraded the Revolution to a mere corrective mechanism – the original meaning of the word 'revolution'. The contrast between the monarchies was attributed to genetic differences between their peoples. The English were a nation of freedom-lovers and the French a nation of slaves.

The English erred in believing the French constitution exclusively absolute as much as they did in believing their own exclusively mixed. But the French gave them good encouragement, for they had themselves shifted the theoretical emphasis. Even Bossuet talked much of the king's absolute power, less of subjects' rights. The Religious Wars and Frondes furnished compelling reason. In a divided, fragmented and particularist state the monarch's absolute power was bound to receive more publicity than its mixed capacities. Amid the chaos of conflicting claims and authorities it was vital to have one voice at the centre, commanding and irresistible, independent of factions and sectional interests. That was the point of Bodin's contribution to political debate – the indivisibility of sovereignty. Professional theorists are not the best guide to the way institutions worked, and much of their output is propaganda against those who challenged royal authority. The consultative sphere of monarchy was not abandoned, but less was heard about it.

Whig history needs a party on the side of the future. Polarities have therefore been imposed on early modern political thought for the purposes of a teleological view. In contrast, most early modern political theorists operated within a broad consensus. They could thus highlight those aspects of their ideological inheritance which served their purpose. Like organists with two keyboards they played on whichever suited their purpose, as did their medieval predecessors.[11] 'Mixed' and 'absolute' imply precisely the opposite of what they say. The absolute power of French kings was emphasised because the obstacles were so strong: it implied the weakness of the monarchy, especially during royal minorities. In England the shared power was emphasised because the barriers were weak – evidence of the monarch's strength. French and English regimes embraced mixed and absolute elements throughout the period and by the eighteenth century their constitutions, though nebulous, were still comparable. But by then the contrasting rhetoric was ingrained and French fantasies of the impotence of the English king were as wild as English notions of Bourbon despotism. When the English called a monarch absolute they meant he could do what he liked and take what he wanted. When the French used the appellation they meant that in certain matters he had the last word. Nor was understanding promoted by the tendency of each to consult the other's outcasts and critics.[12]

Political theory was subjected to other kinds of propagandist expediency. The early modern period was obsessed with the political vocabulary of the Ancient World: favoured regimes were associated with prestigious Classical norms and enemies with the reverse. Jurieu's Huguenot diatribe against Louis XIV is a slightly modified version of Plato's celebrated description of the despotic ruler.[13] More positively, the thirteenth-century revival of Aristotle and Polybius made many states anxious to claim the 'polity' or mixed government favoured by these distinguished Greeks. Fortescue repeats Aquinas's praise for Aristotle's 'polity' as the best form of government, and in the same paragraph asserts that England possessed it. Political thinkers and dabblers gave different content to the mixture. In England some favoured king, lords and commons (the blend of monarchy, aristocracy and democracy favoured by the Greeks), others clergy, lords and commons, and a few (who had read Montesquieu) executive, legislature and judiciary. Clearly political facts were being fitted to a preconceived and prestigious model, not the model to the facts. Later eighteenth-century critics saw through it. Bentham enquired whether the mixture might not combine the vices of all the components rather than the virtues and Paine ridiculed the notion of three separate bodies which promoted harmony by opposing each other. The conventional description of England's as a mixed constitution, endlessly reiterated in the seventeenth and eighteenth centuries, is lifted bodily from Cicero, the most influential classical writer from the Renaissance to the Enlightenment.[14] Yet historians solemnly repeat it as though it were based on the empirical findings of modern political science.

Early modern political labelling reflected minimal attention to political realities. Frenchmen contrasted their own legitimate monarchy with Turkish and Russian despotism: they were blissfully unaware of the limitations to which those regimes were subject. The English were equally selective. They tut-tutted about absolute (which now meant despotic) power in France and conveniently overlooked their own treatment of Catholic Irish and Jacobite Scots, who enjoyed no rights whatever. Their Prussian ally escaped the charge, as did the friendly Hapsburgs. Evaluation of representative bodies was correspondingly crass. The French *parlements* were defenders of liberty; the provincial Estates which resisted Joseph were subversive.[15]

This propaganda merely performed variations on the themes of the seventeenth century. In France it produced an original composition. A chorus of disaffected Huguenots, Jansenists, *parlementaires* and *philosophes* rejected the claims of the Bourbons to be legitimate monarchs. With a unanimity hard for government writers to refute they stigmatised them as despotic. This verdict represented the triumph in France of the English smear campaign which began in the 1670s. By accepting England's myth of itself the *philosophes* made it immortal. Voltaire's '*Lettres philosophiques*' of 1734 attacked the Bourbon regime by holding up the Hanoverian as a model. He was too crafty to describe the English as perfect. The book sniggers at members of the Stock Exchange calling infidel only those who went bankrupt and Quakers awaiting the inspiration of God with their hats on. Nevertheless he described a Never-Never Land of pluralist freedoms, innocuous churchmen, honoured merchants, tamed monarchs and parliamentary supremacy. As a stick with which to beat Louis XV and evade the censor it was highly effective.

It also determined that the Bourbon regime would never be taken seriously as an agency of Enlightenment, in spite of employing ministers of impeccably Enlightened credentials who effected some of the most spectacular reforms in eighteenth-century Europe. Why the *philosophes* disliked the regime of Louis XV and XVI so intensely when they were in some ways its beneficiaries is a good question. But to this day the 'Enlightened absolutism' chapter in the textbooks omits the Bourbons. It is easy to guess whose lethal pens disqualified them from the Enlightened Oscar awards.

A similar travesty of the French constitution was produced by the 1789 revolutionaries. They professed to be abolishing a system in which rights and consultation were unknown, and it is tempting to believe they knew what they were talking about. But the targets of summer 1789 were not those of previous months and years. The events of 1787–89 are more appropriately viewed in the context of the old order rather than of the subsequent revolution. The *cahiers* accepted the institutions of the Bourbon state and demanded reform of its abuses, while the revolutionaries of the National Assembly abolished it. The deadlock of May to July 1789 broke the political mould and transformed the terms of debate.[16] Revolutionary propaganda created a caricature of a regime in which rights and liberty were oppressed not in practice but by definition. It reflected the deadlock in the Estates-General, not experience of the old order. The polity that was attacked was a travesty of political realities. The revolutionaries defined the *ancien régime* in order to condemn it.

As yet there was no talk of 'absolutism'. No one has yet suggested when and why it appeared. Until recently most historians have been uninterested, in spite of Marc Bloch's warning that wrong labels eventually deceive us about the contents. Political labels are now arousing more interest: the history of words is firmly on the agenda.

MATURITY

Most of the great 'isms' emerged in the nineteenth century and many such words were coined in a mood of pejorative mockery. Since the sixteenth century they had been derogatory synonyms for heresy and pernicious doctrines in general – from the point of view, of course, of their opponents. One batch dates from the first age of doctrinal conflict – Protestantism, Lutheranism, Machiavellianism and so on. The second age was the early nineteenth century, which produced all the political 'isms' – nationalism, socialism, communism, capitalism, conservatism and liberalism. Metternich stated that all 'isms' were abusive. It was vital to stick a handy label on something of which one disapproved. Furthermore they all arose from a welter of prescription and prediction, as enthusiasts for political panaceas rushed to convince their readers that they could discern the unfolding pattern of history, peopled by large, impersonal, often malevolent forces. While labelling an intellectual system they also suggested an actual working system. A concept was thus reified and endowed with an operational life of its own.[17]

The Restoration period immediately after 1815 was one of icy reaction and bitter dispute over political allegiance. Witch hunts were conducted and old scores settled, in reaction to the excesses of the revolutionary period. Politics polarised with a vengeance. On the side of newly labelled 'liberalism' were the adherents of freedom of the press, a parliamentary constitution and an emasculated clergy. On the other were the devotees of divine right, hereditary monarchy and the alliance of throne and altar. Kings had been bowled over like skittles by French revolutionary armies and moved like chessmen by Napoleon. They were anxious to avoid any repetition. The result in most states was the deliberate reversal of every policy which in the late eighteenth-century had been regarded as progressive, whether promoted by monarchs or revolutions. In central Europe a blanket of censorship was imposed and civil liberties vanished. Estates were curtailed or abolished, despite the injunction of the Vienna Congress that they should be extended. Secret police proliferated and the Carlsbad Decrees of 1819 banned associations. In Austria permission had to be obtained for a dance employing an orchestra of more than two players. Under Charles X of France newspapers were confined to reporting 'facts' and weather forecasts. If there was no early modern confrontation between 'absolutist' and 'constitutional' forces, there was now. It was the supreme issue of the early and mid nineteenth century.

In 1823 Ferdinand VII of Spain overthrew the liberal constitution which he had been forced to grant and began to persecute its upholders. The result was revolt. The ministers of the restored Louis XVIII of France resolved to send an army to rescue him. French Liberals were aghast. Their feelings about their own *ancien régime* before 1789 had predetermined their attitude towards Spain. Unlike the Conservatives, they were convinced that pre-revolutionary France had lacked a constitution and that rights were at the mercy of royal whim rather than law. But they needed a way of defending the revolution of 1789 without incurring the charge that they were themselves revolutionary. The Spanish revolution was tailor-made: in Liberal eyes it was 1789 re-enacted. On it was projected all the agonies of that great dawn: for Ferdinand VII read Louis XVI.[18] The despatch of a counter-revolutionary army was the signal for Liberal uproar in the Chamber of Deputies. In March 1823 Monsieur Hyde de Neuville rose to his feet. He protested against the treatment of government supporters at Liberal hands and disowned the illiberal regime which they claimed he and his royalist allies were eager to impose on Spain. The word he used to describe it was *absolutisme*.[19]

Previous Conservative disavowals had employed the traditional phrase *un pouvoir absolu.* They were groping for the word and presumably had not discovered it. If it was used before, it had not passed into common parlance. Now it did. It represented a deliberate travesty of the Conservative position: no constitution, no parliament, no rights. That is why it is hard to define 'absolutism' without caricaturing it. It *was* a caricature – the parent of many subsequent offspring. It was coined to identify contemporary and not historical issues. But it stuck and was projected back on to the *ancien régime.* Henceforth the latter's pastel subtleties were viewed in the strident primary colours of the age of Metternich and Charles X. The crude confrontations of Ferdinand VII's realm were substituted for the sophisticated balance and compromises of Louis XIV's. Absolute and shared power which operated side by side in the same *ancien régime* now became opposed types of government, as overheated historical imaginations sought to make sense of early modern states in the light of their own exhilarating polarities. Historians looked for goodies and baddies. Bourbon ministers such as Choiseul, Malesherbes and Lamoignon had freed the press, released commerce from mercantilist regulation, granted toleration to Protestants and established consultative assemblies. The new scenario scripted them as the agents of despotism. But real absolutism did not end in 1789. It began.

By the 1850s absolutism had established itself in the books as firmly as in the palaces of central and southern Europe. At its inception it was an exaggerated mockery of the autocratic repression actually happening. And that was bad enough. All representative bodies in Austria, central, provincial and local, had been abolished and in Russia the *Nakaz* of Catherine the Great was a forbidden book. This repression bore no resemblance to anything in the previous century. There was then no bureaucratic alternative to consultative organs as administrative agencies. Nor were 'Russian tsar' and 'autocrat' viewed as interchangeable expressions. By 1850 they were.[20]

In the 1860s absolutism fused conveniently with another nineteenth-century experience – the rise of nation-states with huge armies and modern bureaucracies. Liberals rightly regarded them as the pillar of contemporary absolutism, and Liberals were prominent among nineteenth-century historians. Armies had saved the authority of tyrannical German monarchs in 1848–49; and it was to bureaucracy that monarchs turned as an alternative to aristocrats.[21] Present preoccupations again defined perspectives on the past. Epoque-making standing armies and bureaucratic devices, as they were in the 1860s and 1870s, were now detected in the France of Louis XIV and the

Brandenburg of the Great Elector. They too became part of 'absolutism'.[22]

'Absolutist' historiography was not launched on an entirely negative platform. Nationalists were enthused. They pitied early modern monarchs for their lack of liberal sensibilities; but at least they confronted the separatist forces obstructing the rise of the nation-state. For this reason nineteenth-century historians downgraded the local organs of consent – not because early modern people found them inadequate, but because they bored over-excited nationalists in the 1850s. Provincial perspectives were ignored, along with the Estates which operated at that level. The vital requirement was to provide suitable pedigrees for the new national units. Simultaneously the historical discipline was established in the European universities, with national history dominating the agenda.[23] The main themes of the early modern period were defined and for the first time 'absolutism' was among them.

At the same time Richelieu emerged as the despotic oppressor of rights and the architect of 'absolutism'.[24] The *Memoirs* of Molé, president of the seventeenth-century *parlement* which fought the Fronde, were published with their exciting bias against rampant despotism. The historiography of medieval Italy was enlivened by similar touches of Liberal make-up. It created an unhistorical contrast between republican city states like Florence and those which had installed despotic *signori*.[25] English historiography surveyed these developments complacently. Creating a parliamentary regime which was smoothly transforming itself into democracy, it could position itself at two removes from the *ancien régime* – as the official opponent of contemporary absolutism on the Continent and also of the equally 'absolutist' arrangements which were projected back into the eighteenth century.

SENILITY

The concept of 'absolutism' perpetuates an early nineteenth-century attempt to label as despotic the absolute monarchies of the early modern period. Both English and French *ancien régimes* operated in a consultative and a prerogative mode, respectively limited and absolute. But the nineteenth century experienced absolute and limited monarchy only as alternative systems of government. This perspective was fatal for understanding of a period when governments were unable to function legitimately without employing *both* modes of operation. The myth of 'absolutism' spotlit the absolute mode in France and the limited mode in England. Sophisticated early modern polities were thus reduced to a single *modus operandi* – and hence to the confrontational caricatures which have survived.

Myths are usually based on a pinch of truth. In the last days of the *ancien régime* French kings *did* act despotically – paradoxically under the influence of the liberal Enlightenment and in search of short cuts to desirable reforms for which no consent was forthcoming. But no Frenchmen equated despotism with the French constitution. The constitution was what they wanted – at least until quite late in 1789. Despotism was seen as its negation. The concept of 'absolutism' erects into an organised system what was almost unanimously recognised before 1789 as a malfunction.

In the last two decades experts have rumbled the trouble. It is the danger of imposing modern labels on a past which was either unaware of them or gave them a different connotation. The absolute monarchies of the early modern period bore little resemblance to nineteenth-century autocracy: they were more consultative, more constitutional and more patriarchal. With these insights historians of the last two decades have tried to qualify the original concept, as the discoveries of research made the old model untenable. The result is a monumental historiographical muddle. 'Absolutism' is inseparable from the confrontational politics of the period which experienced it as a system of government. It is forever too autocratic, too despotic and too bureaucratic to catch the subtle balances and compromises of the old order before 1789.

Above all, 'absolutism' is too diametrically opposed to everything English. It relegates England to a historical hold-all, along with the Dutch Republic, which it did not resemble. England's foreign policy was made by the monarch and his ministers. In the Dutch state it was formulated by the Estates-General: a deadlock sent delegates home to consult their provincial Estates and beyond them the town councils. The Dutch Estates chose the governing council; England, where the king chose it, had more in common with France. Finally, 'absolutism' pigeon-holes France alongside Russia, where corporate and individual rights were unknown. Catherine II's challenge was not to find a working relationship with the Estates. It was to invent them.

To change the metaphor, the 'absolutist' scenario is beyond repair: no amount of cutting or rewriting can save it. The plot is too sensational, the colours too strident and the setting too lurid. The time has now come to lower the curtain on the obsessions of the last century. To retain the title of 'absolutism' while removing most of the content is a hopelessly confusing half-measure. There seems little point in further extending its run. When impresarios shred the scripts and sack the cast, they commonly take off the play. With the loss of its autocrats and its bureaucrats, its theory and its practice, 'absolutism' should heed the old advice. Kindly leave the stage.

REFERENCES

1 Turpin C 1985 *British Government and the Constitution*. Weidenfeld and Nicolson, p. 107
2 Russell C 1983 The Nature of a Parliament in Early Stuart England. In Tomlinson HC *Before the English Civil War*. Macmillan, pp. 133–4
3 Commines P de 1972 *Memoirs*. Penguin, pp. 344–7; Koenigsberger HG 1975 *Dominium Regale and Dominium Politicum et Regale: Monarchies and Parliaments in Early Modern Europe*. Inaugural Lecture at King's College, London, p. 6
4 Sommerville JP 1986 *Politics and Ideology in England 1603–1640*. Longman, p. 60
5 Daly J 1978 The Idea of Absolute Monarchy in Seventeenth-Century England. *Historical Journal*, **21**, 2, p. 235
6 Haley KHD 1953 *William of Orange and the English Opposition, 1672–4*. Oxford University Press, p. 10
7 Daly J 1978, p. 245
8 Anon. 1689 *Popery and Tyranny or the Present State of France*. London
9 Lough J 1985 *France Observed in the Seventeenth Century by British Travellers*. Oriel, pp. 158–9
10 Dickinson HT 1979 *Liberty and Property*. Methuen, pp. 140–1; Speck WA 1988 *Reluctant Revolutionaries*. Oxford University Press, pp. 139–65
11 Ullmann W 1965 *A History of Political Thought: the Middle Ages*. Penguin, p. 148
12 Black J 1986 *Natural and Necessary Enemies*. Duckworth, pp. 193–4
13 Judge H 1965 *Louis XIV*. Longman, pp. 43–4; Cornford FM (ed.) 1941 *The Republic of Plato*. Oxford University Press, pp. 291–2, 307
14 Cicero 1928 *De Re Publica*. Loeb, pp. 102–4
15 Black J 1986, p. 192
16 Campbell PR 1988 *The Ancien Régime in France*. Basil Blackwell, pp. 71–3
17 Höpfl HM 1983 Isms. *British Journal of Political Science*, **13**, pp. 1–17
18 Mellon P 1958 *The Political Uses of History*. Stanford University Press, pp. 31–47
19 *Archives Parlementaires de 1787 à 1860*, vol. 28, p. 477. Librarie Administrative de Paul Dupont
20 De Madariaga I 1982 Autocracy and Sovereignty. *Canadian–American Slavic Studies*, **16**, nos 3–4, pp. 384–7
21 Macartney CA 1968 *The Hapsburg Empire 1790–1918*. Weidenfeld and Nicolson, pp. 405, 459, 520

22 Seeley JR 1878 *The Life and Times of Stein*. Cambridge University Press, pp. 231–2
23 Gilbert F 1965 The Professionalization of History in the Nineteenth Century. In Higham J (ed.) *History*. Prentice Hall
24 Knecht RJ 1991 *Richelieu*. Longman, p. 217
25 Law JE 1981 *The Lords of Renaissance Italy*. Historical Association, pp. 5–7, 30–3

Glossary of Recurrent Terms

arrêt	Administrative order on authority of *parlement*.
bailli	Medieval equivalent of intendant: royal local official without independent power in locality.
cahier	Statement of grievances and wishes drawn up by noble, clerical and third estates prior to a meeting of the Estates-General.
corporate body	Institution possessing powers and privileges in its own right.
élection	Administrative division, controlled by *élu*, of a *généralité*.
élu	Government official who collected direct and some indirect taxes in each *élection*.
Enlightenment	Body of eighteenth-century ideas emphasising individual rights and happiness, and scientific thinking rather than tradition to secure them.
Estates	(Spelled throughout with initial capital to distinguish this from more normal usage.) Consultative assembly, usually elected representatives of the three estates (legally recognised social groupings of the realm) with permanent committees for administration.
généralité	Intendancy or basic unit of fiscal administration.
intendant	Royal inspector, deriving authority solely from crown and dismissible at will, sent to supervise *généralité* with which he had no previous connection.
lit de justice	Session of *parlement* when monarch was personally present, often to enforce registration of royal edicts.

lettre de cachet	Warrant of arrest or imprisonment on sole authority of the royal prerogative.
lèse-majesté	Opposition to the royal prerogative or those who wielded it.
lettre de jussion	Royal command to *parlements* to register royal edicts.
noblesse d'épée	Nobles whose title was derived from ancient lineage and originally military function.
noblesse de robe	Nobles whose title was derived from tenure of high office (e.g. judges in the *parlement*).
officier	Purchaser of office in judicial or financial administration (hereditary if bequeathed more than forty days before owner's death).
parlement	One of sixteen law courts of appeal, combining judicial with administrative powers and participating in royal law-making.
parlementaire	Member of a *parlement*
paulette	Annual tax paid by office-holders enabling them to disregard forty-day rule, and thereby safeguard hereditary tenure of office.
pays d'élection	Province without regular meetings of Estates at provincial level.
pays d'état	Province with special rights and privileges embodied in local Estates meeting at provincial level.
philosophe	Thinker subscribing to ideas of Enlightenment
sénéchaussé	Smaller division of province, sometimes with meeting of Estates at grass-roots level.
taille	Main direct tax.
thèse nobiliaire or *parlementaire*	Argument that *parlements* should share royal sovereignty
thèse royale	Argument that monarch should monopolise sovereignty

Bibliographical Essay

The historiography of absolutism is small, though there is an immense amount of material on rulers and regimes traditionally recognised as 'absolutist'. The starting point for the former is the important recent volume in the Problems in Focus series: Miller J 1990 *Absolutism in Seventeenth-Century Europe* (Macmillan). It usefully distinguishes between varieties of 'absolutism' in the main European states, but preserves a fundamentally traditional definition of the concept. Anderson P 1984 *Lineages of the Absolutist State* (Verso) is a reissue of a much older work. Its scope is breathtaking (England to Japan) and it is full of perceptive parallels and connections; but allowance has to be made for its defiantly Marxist framework and assumptions. Also useful is the treatment of 'absolutism' in the best textbooks on the early modern period: Koenigsberger HG, Mosse GL and Bowler GQ 1989 *Europe in the Sixteenth Century* (Longman); Munck T 1990 *Seventeenth Century Europe* (Macmillan); Black J 1990 *Eighteenth-Century Europe* (Macmillan), Doyle W 1978 *The Old European Order 1660–1800* (Oxford University Press); Hufton O 1980 *Europe: Privilege and Protest 1730–1789* (Fontana); Sutherland DMG 1985 *France 1789–1815: Revolution and Counter-revolution* (Fontana).

Some of the most important insights into absolutism are found in articles, starting with the vital but neglected Mousnier R and Hartung F 1955 Quelques problèmes concernant la monarchie absolue, *Relazioni*, **4**. Also crucial is Koenigsberger HG 1975 *Dominium Regale et Dominium Politicum et Regale* : Monarchies and Parliaments in Early Modern Europe (inaugural lecture at King's College, London). Bonney R 1987 Absolutism: What's in a Name?, *French History*, I, promises more than it delivers but contains a useful review of recent writing. So does Morrill J 1978 French Absolutism as Limited

217

Monarchy, *Historical Journal*, **21**, 4, pp. 961–72. Daly J 1978 The Idea of Absolute Monarchy in Seventeenth-Century England, *Historical Journal*, XXXI, pp. 227–50, is a useful exploration of the different contemporary connations of the word 'absolute'.

There are several valuable collections of source material. Mettam R 1976 *Government and Society in Louis XIV's France* (Macmillan), and Bonney R 1988 *Society and Government in France under Richelieu and Mazarin 1624–61* (Macmillan) both stress the ramshackle foundations of French government and the fragile basis of political obligation. They are a useful antidote to the traditional picture of the all-powerful king in Judge H 1966 *Louis XIV* (Longman), and Church WF 1972 *The Greatness of Louis XIV* (Heath). Lough J 1985 *France Observed in the Seventeenth Century by British Travellers* (Oriel), provides informative eye-witness accounts from largely hostile visitors. There is no equivalent for sixteenth- and eighteenth-century France, but Hardman R 1981 *The French Revolution* (Arnold), supplies material for the period immediately before the Revolution. For the other states Macartney CA 1970 *The Hapsburg and Hohenzollern Dynasties in the Seventeenth and Eighteenth Centuries* (Macmillan), and Lentin A 1985 *Enlightened Absolutism 1760–1790* (Avero), are essential. Readers wishing to clarify the content of French 'law-making' should consult the later volumes of Isambert FA (ed.) *1822–33 Recueil général des anciennes lois françaises depuis l'an 420 jusqu'à la révolution de 1789* (Paris).

Good comparative works are few. First in the field was Miller J 1984 The Potential for Absolutism in Seventeenth-Century England, *History*, **69**, no. 26. He attempts to define absolutism on the basis of the practice of Louis XIV and usefully scans the regimes of Charles II and James II for comparisons and contrasts. This was followed by Miller J 1986 *Bourbon and Stuart* (George Philip), which fails to fulfil the promise of the earlier article. Equally significant was the appearance of Behrens CBA 1985 *Society, Government and the Enlightenment* (Thames and Hudson), which compares the administrative, economic and ideological aspects of absolutism in France and Prussia. Most recent and illuminating are Shennan JH 1986 *Liberty and Order in Early Modern Europe* (Longman), and Brewer J 1989 *The Sinews of Power* (Unwin Hyman), which relates the growth of a fiscal-military state in post-Revolution England to comparable developments in France.

Good biographies of French 'absolutists' are fewer. Knecht RJ 1982 *Francis I* (Cambridge University Press), 1991 *Richelieu* (Longman), 1984 *French Renaissance Monarchy: Francis I and Henry II* (Longman), and Greengrass M 1984 *France in the Age of Henri IV* (Longman), are the best introductions to the rulers named. Bluche F 1990 *Louis XIV* is now the best account of the Sun King, while Shennan JH 1979 *Philippe Duke of Orleans* (Thames and Hudson), provides the same service in a less competitive field. Antoine M 1989 *Louis XV* (Fayard), stands alone among serious biographies of a much-maligned monarch, but is unavailable in translation. There is no satisfactory biography of Louis XVI.

Starting points for French 'absolutism' are Hatton R (ed.) 1976 *Louis XIV and Absolutism* (Macmillan), and Goubert P *L'Ancien Régime* (2 vols), *1962 La Société and 1973 Les Pouvoirs* (Armand Colin). The two huge volumes by Mousnier R 1979 and 1984 *The Institutions of France under the Absolute Monarchy* (Chicago University Press) are surprisingly readable for so encyclopaedic a compilation; they suffer from the author's remorselessly administrative perspective which neglects the animating forces of power groups and faction lurking beneath the surface of the official machinery. Essential correctives are Parker D 1983 *The Making of French Absolutism* (Arnold), and Mettam R 1988 *Power and Faction in Louis XIV's France* (Basil Blackwell). Both of these works, the first from a subtly nuanced Marxist perspective and the second from the standpoint of court politics and manipulation, turn traditional accounts inside out. Behrens CBA 1967 *The Ancien Regime* (Thames and Hudson); Campbell P 1988 *The Ancien Régime in France* (Basil Blackwell), and Doyle W 1986 *The Ancien Régime* (Macmillan), offer crisp introductions. Goubert P 1972 *Louis XIV and Twenty Million Frenchmen* (Vintage), and Rowen H 1969 *Louis XIV and Absolutism*, in Rule JC *Louis XIV and the Craft of Kingship* (Columbus), are indispensable.

Some of the most useful insights into the working of *ancien régime* government have derived from local studies. Pre-eminent are Beik W 1985 *Absolutism and Society in Seventeenth-Century France: State Power and Provincial Aristocracy in Languedoc* (Cambridge University Press); Parker D 1980 *La Rochelle and the French Monarchy: Conflict and Order in Seventeenth-Century France* (Royal Historical Society); and Hickey D 1986 *The Coming of French Absolutism: the struggle for tax reform in the province of Dauphiné, 1540–1640* (Toronto University).

Two books are required reading for all who wish to grasp the atmosphere and centrality of the royal court in early modern states: Dickens AG (ed.) 1977 *The Courts of Europe* (Thames and Hudson), and Molesworth HD 1969 *The Princes* (Weidenfeld and Nicolson). Studies revealing the continuing importance of court patronage and aristocratic clientage are Rubin DL 1991 *Sun King: The Ascendancy of French Culture during the Reign of Louis XIV* (Associated University Presses); Kettering S, 1986 *Patrons, Clients and Brokers in Seventeenth-*

Century France (Oxford University Press), and 1978 *Judicial Politics and Urban Revolt in Seventeenth-Century France: the* Parlement *of Aix 1629–1659*; Harding RR 1978 *Anatomy of a Power Elite: the Provincial Governors of Early Modern France* (New Haven); Dessert D 1984 *Argent, pouvoir et société au grand siècle* (Paris); Bergin J 1985 *Cardinal Richelieu: Power and the Pursuit of Wealth* (Yale University Press); while Campbell PR 1985 The Conduct of Politics in France in the time of the Cardinal de Fleury 1723–43, (Ph.D. dissertation, London University), underlines the political importance of ecclesiastical patronage. Two works by Major JR stress the importance of consultative procedures in France: 1960 *Representative Institutions in Renaissance France 1421–1559* (Wisconsin) and 1980 *Representative Government in Early Modern France*, (Yale University Press). Palmer RR 1959 *The Age of the Democratic Revolution*, vol. 1: *the Challenge* (Princeton University Press), and Myers AR 1975 *Parliaments and Estates in Europe to 1789* (Thames and Hudson), underline the continuing vitality of representative institutions in most European states, as does the new periodical *Parliaments, Estates and Representation*. Carsten FL 1959 *Princes and Parliaments in Germany* (Oxford) performs the same task. Co-operation between crown and *parlements* is the theme of Hamscher AN 1976 *The* Parlement *of Paris after the Fronde 1653–1673* (Pittsburgh University Press), and 1987 The conseil privé and the *parlements* in the age of Louis XIV, *Transactions of the American Philosophical Society*, LXXVII, part II. A vital insight into the realities of royal legislative and judicial power is provided by Parker D 1989 'Sovereignty, Absolutism and the Function of the Law in Seventeenth-Century France', *Past and Present*, **122**.

Eighteenth-century France has been neglected, except by those rooting for the seeds of the French Revolution. More valuable than most in this tradition are two books by Doyle, 1980 *The Origins of the French Revolution* (Oxford University Press), and 1989 *The Oxford History of the French Revolution* (Oxford University Press), as well as Roberts JM 1978 *The French Revolution* (Oxford University Press), and Schama S 1989 *Citizens*, (Viking). Shennan JH 1983 *France before the Revolution* (Methuen), helps to fill the gap. Provocatively revisionist is Furet 1981 *Interpreting the French Revolution* (Cambridge University Press). Riley JC *The Seven Years War and the Old Regime in France* (Princeton), and Morineau M 1980 Budgets de l'Etat et Gestion des Finances Royales 18e Siècle. *Revue Historique*, pp. 289–336. Kaplan SL 1976 *Bread, Politics and Political Economy in the reign of Louis XV*, 2 vols (The Hague) deal with the financial and economic constraints on government policy. An influential group of historians sees France in the mid-eighteenth century moving towards a new political order: Echeverria D 1985 *The Maupeou Revolution: a Study in the History of Libertarianism, France 1770–1774*, (Baton Rouge); van Kley 1984 *The Damiens Affair and the Unravelling of the Ancien Regime* (Princeton); Egret J 1970 *Louis XV et l'opposition parlementaire* (Paris). In contrast, the traditional nature of much political conflict is emphasised by Campbell P 1988 (above); Shennan JH 1968 *The Parlement of Paris* (Eyre and Spottiswoode); Wick D 1980 'The Court Nobility and the French Revolution: the example of the Society of Thirty', *Eighteenth-Century Studies*, XIII; and Rogister J 1986 '*Parlementaires*, Sovereignty and Legal Opposition in France under Louis XV', *Parlements Estates and Representation*, **6**, no. 1. Doyle W 1970 'The *Parlements* of France and the breakdown of the old regime 1771–1788', *French Historical Studies*, XIII, and Antoine M 1970 *Le Conseil du Roi sous le règne de Louis XV* (Droz), take a middle view, as do two unpublished Cambridge University Ph.D. dissertations: Price M 1989 The Comte de Vergennes and the Baron de Breteuil: French Politics and Reform in the Reign of Louis XV, and Swann J 1989 Politics and the *Parlement* of Paris 1754–71. Useful studies of *ancien régime* ministers are Brierre A 1986 *Le duc de Choiseul* (Albatros), and Harris RD 1979 *Necker, Reform Statesman of the Ancien Régime* (Berkeley University Press). Political ideas at élite and popular levels are explored in Porter R 1990 *The Enlightenment* (Macmillan), and in several works by Darnton R: 1976 The High Enlightenment and the Low-Life of Literature in Pre-Revolutionary France, in Johnson D (ed.) *French Society and the Revolution* (Cambridge University Press); 1979 *The Business of Enlightenment* (Belknap, Harvard); and 1985 *The Great Cat Massacre* (Penguin).

Military aspects of the 'absolutist' state are covered in Black J 1991 *A Military Revolution? Military Change and European Society 1550–1800* (Macmillan), and Mansel P 1984 *Pillars of Monarchy: an outline of the political and social history of Royal Guards* (Quartet). Raeff M 1983 *The Well-ordered Police State* (Yale University), and Schaeper TJ 1983 *The French Council of Commerce* (Columbus), throw light on aspects of 'absolutist' economic and social policy. Zagorin P 1982 *Rebels and Rulers 1500–1660*, vol. 1 (Cambridge University Press), discusses the origins of revolt in 'absolutist' states. Strong R 1984 *Art and Power: Renaissance Festivals 1450–1650* (Boydell), Burke P 1992 The Fabrication of Louis XIV, *History Today*, vol. 42 February 1992, and Klaits J 1976 *Printed Propaganda under Louis XIV* (Princeton University Press), examine public relations techniques. Bonney R 1978 *Political Change in France under Richelieu and Mazarin, 1624–1661* (Oxford University

Press), and 1981 *The King's Debts: Finance and Politics in France, 1589–1661* (Oxford University Press), investigate change and continuity in the French regime, as does Cameron K (ed.) 1989 *From Valois to Bourbon* (Exeter University).

The relationship between 'absolutism' and society is tackled in Lloyd HA 1983 *The State, France and the Sixteenth Century* (George Allen and Unwin) and Coveney PJ 1976 *France in Crisis 1620–1675* (Macmillan). The latter includes a translation of an illuminating article by Deyon P, The French Nobility and Absolute Monarchy in the First Half of the Seventeenth Century. It reprints important articles by Porshnev and Mousnier on the Fronde, which should be supplemented by Kossman EH 1954 *La Fronde* (Leiden), and Knecht RJ 1975 *The Fronde* (Historical Association). The role and fortunes of the nobility are also discussed in Bitton D 1969 *The French Nobility in Crisis 1560–1640* (Stanford University Press). The notion of 'absolutism' rising on the ruins of the nobility is undermined in two works by Wood JB: 1976 The Decline of the Nobility in Sixteenth- and Early Seventeenth-Century France: myth or reality? *Journal of Modern History*, **48**, and 1980 *The Nobility of the Election of Bayeux 1463–1666* (Princeton University Press). The changing basis of noble power is well defined in Mertes K 1988 *The English Noble Household* (Basil Blackwell). The continuing vitality of the Tudor nobility is emphasised in Miller H 1985 *Henry VIII and the English Nobility* (Basil Blackwell) and Bernard B 1986 *The Power of the Early Tudor Nobility* (Harvester Press, Brighton). Bush M 1983 *Noble Privilege* (Manchester University), and 1984 *The English Aristocracy* (Manchester University), offer a stimulating comparative analysis of the European élite. The best studies of the nobility in eighteenth-century France and England respectively are Chaussinand-Nogaret (translated Doyle W) 1985 *The French Nobility in the Eighteenth Century* (Cambridge University Press), and Cannon J 1984 *Aristocratic Century* (Cambridge University Press). The latter challenges the comfortable notion of an open, liberal, enlightened élite – everything the Continental nobility was supposedly not. So does Stone L and Stone JCF 1986 *An Open Elité? England 1540–1880* (Oxford University Press). Rosenberg H 1958 *Bureaucracy, Aristocracy and Autocracy* (Harvard University Press) examines the Prussian bureaucratic nobility.

Starting points for the vexed question of Enlightened Despotism are Blanning TW 1970 *Joseph II and Enlightened Despotism* (Longman), and Scott HM 1990 *Enlightened Absolutism: Reform and Reformers in Later Eighteenth-Century Europe* (Macmillan). Still worth reading are Hartung F 1957 *Enlightened Despotism* (Historical Association), and

Gagliardo J 1968 *Enlightened Despotism* (Routledge & Kegan Paul). Krieger 1970 *Kings and Philosophers 1689–1789* (Norton) is vital, while his 1975 *An Essay on the Theory of Enlightened Despotism* (Chicago University Press), is the only attempt to address the vexed issue in its title. Contrasting French and Germanic views on the subject can be found in Bluche F 1968 *Le despotisme éclairé* (Paris), and KO von Aretin (ed.) 1974 *Der aufgeklärte Absolutismus* (Cologne). Porter P and Teich M 1981 *The Enlightenment in National Context* (Cambridge University Press), explores, among other issues, the Enlightenment's impact on government policy.

The essential introduction to the theory of 'absolutism' is Skinner Q 1978 *The Foundations of Modern Political Thought*, 2 vols (Cambridge University Press). With his work must be coupled that of Pocock JGA 1972 *Language, Politics and Time* (Athenaeum). Both have stressed the danger of leaving the study of language and literature to literary critics. Literature was not self-consciously aesthetic; it articulated political and religious values and the changing meaning of words is often the best indicator of shifts in those values. This approach has been developed in works such as Sharpe K and Zwicker SN 1987 *Politics of Discourse* (University of California), and Ball T, Farr J and Hanson RL 1989 *Political Innovation and Conceptual Change*, Cambridge University Press. Fundamental for recent historical thinking on political theory in general and the survival of republican ideology in particular is Pocock JGA 1975 *The Machiavellian Moment* (Princeton University). Especially useful for the theoretical background is d'Entrèves 1967 *The Notion of the State* (Oxford University Press). Church WF 1941 *Constitutional Thought in Sixteenth-Century France* (Cambridge, Mass.), and Rowan HH 1980 *The King's State – Proprietary Dynasticism in Early Modern France* (New Brunswick University Press), illuminate important sixteenth- and seventeenth-century perspectives. Marxist assumptions may be enjoyed in Macpherson CB 1962 *The Political Theory of Possessive Individualism: Hobbes to Locke* (Oxford University Press). Traditional talking points appear in Eccleshall R 1978 *Order and Reason in Politics: Theories of Absolute and Limited Monarchy in Early Modern England* (Oxford University Press) and Keohane N 1980 *Philosophy and the State in France: the Renaissance to the Enlightenment*, (Princeton University Press). Baker KM 1987 *The French Revolution and the Creation of Modern Political Culture, volume 1, The Political Culture of the Old Regime* (Pergamon), debates the controversial issue of whether eighteenth-century France produced a new 'anti-absolutist' ideology. Bossuet is available, edited by Le Brun J 1967 *Politique tirée des propres paroles l'Ecriture Sainte* (Droz), as are Locke (ed. Laslett P) 1960 *Two Treatises of Government* (Cambridge University Press), and Bodin (ed. Tooley MJ) 1962 *The Six Books of a Commonweal*, (Cambridge, Mass.). He is interpreted in the conventional 'absolutist' manner by Franklin JH 1973 *Jean Bodin and the rise of Absolutist Theory* (Cambridge University Press), and in a contrary sense by Parker D 1980 Law, society and the state in the thought of Jean Bodin, *Journal of the History of Political Thought*, **2**, pp. 253–85. Blackstone W 1765 *Commentaries on the Laws of England* (Oxford University Press), is the classic authority on England's eighteenth-century constitution. The existence of 'absolutist' theory is restated by Sommerville J 1986 *Politics and Ideology in England 1603–1640* (Longman), and Dickinson HT 1977 *Liberty and Property* (Methuen), and challenged by Sharpe K 1989 *Politics and Ideas in Early Stuart England* (Pinter), and Russell C 1990 *The Causes of the English Civil War* (Oxford University Press). Judson M 1949 *The Crisis of the Constitution: an Essay in Constitutional and Political Thought 1603–1645* (New Brunswick University Press), put the whole matter into perspective forty years ago.

It is now being recognised that discussions of 'absolutism' should extend to England, if only to establish why it was different. The essential starting point for England as an *ancien régime* is Clark JCD 1985 *English Society 1688–1832* (Cambridge University Press), and 1986 *Revolution and Rebellion* (Cambridge University Press). His argument is challenged in Langford P 1989 *A Polite and Commercial People 1727–1783* (Oxford University Press), and modified in Black J (ed.) 1991 *British Politics and Society from Walpole to Pitt 1742–1789* (Macmillan). For earlier periods Williams P 1979 *The Tudor Regime* (Oxford University Press), and Guy J 1988 *Tudor England* (Oxford University Press), make illuminating points about the capacity for English 'absolutism', to which should be added Hurstfield J 1967 Was there a Tudor Despotism after all?, *Transactions of the Royal Historical Society*, 5th series, **17**. The constitutional view of the Tudors is firmly stated in Elton GR 1977 *Reform and Reformation* (Arnold). The 'absolutism' of the early Stuarts is expounded by Sommerville JP 1986 (above) and of the later by Western JR 1972 *Monarchy and Revolution: the English State in the 1680s* (Macmillan), though Miller J 1984 (above) is more cautious. The founding charter of the revisionist view of Stuart history, demoting parliament to a less influential and ambitious role, is Russell C 1976 Parliamentary History in Perspective 1604–29, *History*, LXI. It is supported by Sharpe K 1978 *Faction and Parliament* (Methuen), combatted in Cust R and Hughes A 1989 *Conflict in Early Stuart England* (Longman), and restated in Russell C

1990 (above). Kishlansky MA 1986 *Parliamentary Selection* (Cambridge), provides a new perspective. Elton's view of the diminishing importance of the court, 1953 *The Tudor Revolution in Government* (Cambridge University Press), has been subsequently modified by himself in 1976 Tudor Government: The Points of Contact, III The Court, *Transactions of the Royal Historical Society*, 5th series, **26** and challenged by Starkey et al. 1987 *The English Court from the Wars of the Roses to the Civil War* (Longman). The same theme is pursued by Beattie J 1967 *The English Court in the reign of George I* (Cambridge University Press). The role of the court as the cockpit where power was won and lost emerges forcefully from Gregg E 1984 *Queen Anne* (Ark), and Clark JCD 1982 *The Dynamics of Change* (Cambridge University Press). To this corresponds significant revision of the traditional view that Hanoverian monarchs had lost control of appointment of ministers – and with that of policy. The realities of royal power are emphasised by Owen J 1973 George II Reconsidered, in Whiteman A, Bromley JS and Dickson P (eds) *Statesmen, Scholars and Merchants* (Oxford University Press), and by much of the enormous output of Black J, in particular 1990 *Robert Walpole and the Nature of Politics in Early Eighteenth-Century England* (Macmillan), and 1991 *A System of Ambition? British Foreign Policy 1660–1793* (Longman).

'Absolutism' in other countries is illuminated by several recent studies of institutions and statespersons. Subtelny O 1986 *Domination of Eastern Europe* (Alan Sutton) delineates 'absolutism' in a neglected region. The Russian hybrid is tackled in Dukes P 1982 *The Making of Russian Absolutism* (Longman); Longworth P 1984 *Alexis: Tsar of all the Russians*; (Secker and Warburg) and De Madariaga I 1981 *Russia in the Age of Catherine the Great* (Weidenfeld and Nicolson). Essential for the Hapsburg Empire are Spielman JP 1977 *Leopold I of Austria* (Thames and Hudson); Evans RJW 1979 *The Making of the Hapsburg Monarchy* (Oxford University Press); Dickson PGM 1987 *Finance and Government under Maria Theresa 1740–1780* (Oxford University Press), and Beales D 1987 *Joseph II*, vol. I (Cambridge University Press). Vierhaus R 1988 *Germany in the Age of Absolutism* (Cambridge University Press), is ably complemented by one of the best accounts of Prussian 'absolutism' in any language: Behrens CBA 1985 (above). Gagliardo JG 1991 *Germany under the Old Regime* (Longman) ably summarises the latest foreign scholarship. Elliott JH 1986 *The Count Duke of Olivares, The Statesman in an Age of Decline* (Yale University), and Kamen H 1991 (2nd edn) *Spain 1469–1714* (Longman), offer useful correctives to the traditional picture, while

Thompson IAA 1982 Crown and Cortes in Castile 1590–1665, *Parliaments, Estates and Representation*, **2**, no. 1, and 1984 The End of the Cortes of Castile, *Parliaments, Estates and Representation*, **4**, no. 2, supply full-scale revisionism. Italy is well represented by Symcox G 1983 *Victor Amadeus II, Absolutism in the Savoyard State* (Thames and Hudson), and Denmark by Munck T 1979 *The Peasantry and the Early Absolute Monarchy 1660–1708*, (Landbohistorisk Selskab, Copenhagen). The traditional account of Swedish 'absolutism' found in Roberts M 1967 *Sweden as a Great Power 1611–1697* (Arnold), still awaits revision.

The Régusse clientele

LEIDETS

Jean de Leidet-Sigoyer and Pierre de Leidet-Calissane, councillors in the Parlement, Régusse's maternal uncles, and his first cousin, Pierre, Jean's son, who inherited his father's office

Louis Decormis, president in the Parlement and brother-in-law of Jean de Leidet-Sigoyer

Honoré Rascas Du Canet, councillor in the Parlement and son-in-law of Jean

Joseph de Gaillard, councillor in the Parlement, a maternal uncle

Auguste de Thomas, marquis de La Garde, president in the Parlement, a maternal cousin

CHARLES DE GRIMALDI, MARQUIS DE RÉGUSSE, PRESIDENT IN THE PARLEMENT OF AIX

Jean-François de Glandèves-Rousset, councillor in the Parlement, kin of Régusse's brother-in-law, Jean-Antoine de Glandèves, vicomte de Pourrières

Henri d'Escalis-Sabran, baron de Bras, president in the Parlement and a personal friend

Gaspard de Venel, sieur de Ventabren, councillor in the Parlement and co-chief of the Marzarinistes with Régusse

Pierre de Raffelis, sieur de Roquesante, councillor in the Parlement and a personal friend

Léon de Valbelle, sieur de Meyrargues, councillor in the Parlement and brother of Régusse's business partner, Antoine

Jean-Baptiste de Valbelle, sieur de Saint-Symphorien, councillor in the Parlement and cousin of Régusse's business partner

N.B.: Broken line indicates first loyalty to Antoine de Valbelles of Marseille; the Valbelles were also cousins of Oppède.

(*Source*: adapted from table in Kettering S 1986 *Patrons, Brokers and Clients in Seventeenth-Century France*, Oxford University Press)

The Oppède clientele

LAURENS
Henri de Laurens, councillor in the Parlement
of Aix, and his son, Pierre-Joseph, seigneur
(later marquis) de Saint Martin de Pallières,
husband of Oppède's daughter, Aimare

Antoine de Laurens, prévôt de la maréchaussée
d'Aix, brother of Henri

Jacques de Laurens, sieur de Vaugrenier, boss of
Drauignan municipal government, uncle of
Henri

Dominique de Benault de Lubières, councillor
in the Parlement of Aix and maternal uncle of
Pierre-Joseph

MAURELS
Suzanne de Laurens, sister of Henri, married to
Pierre Maurel, provincial treasurer, who had
two sons and a nephew, councillors in the
Parlement of Aix

ORAISONS
Aqua d'Oraison, wife of Melchior de Forbin de
La Roque

Her brother, André d'Oraison, marquis
d'Oraison, former Sabreur and first consul of
Aix

Their mother, Louise de Castellane, marquise
d'Oraison, godmother of Oppède's younger
brother, Louis, bishop of Toulon, and a maternal relative

MAYNIERS
Ties to the nobility of the Comtat Venaissin

SÉGUIRANS
Reynaud de Séguiran, sieur de
Bouc, first president of the Co
des Comptes, former Sabreur,
father-in-law of Laurens de
Vaugrenier and brother-in-law
André de Forbin de La Fare

**HENRI DE FORBIN-MAYN
BARON D'OPPÈDE,
FIRST PRESIDENT OF TH
PARLEMENT OF AIX**

PONTÈVES
Jean de Pontèves, third comte
Carcès and lieutenant general
Provence, distant cousin of
Oppède's wife, Marie

(*Source*: ibid)

FORBINS

Forbin de La Roque: uncle Jean-Baptiste, president in the Parlement of Aix, and his son Melchior, also a president, and Melchior's brother-in-law, Pierre de Coriolis-Villeneuve, also a president

Forbin de Janson: cousins Laurent de Forbin, marquis de Janson, and his brother, Toussaint de Janson-Forbin, bishop of Marseille

Forbin de La Barben: cousin Jacques de Forbin de La Barben, noble syndic and consul of Aix

Forbin de Lambesc: cadet branch of La Barben, cousin Paul-Albert de Forbin-Lambesc, bailli in the Order of Malta and Grand Prior of Saint Gilles near Arles

Forbin de La Fare: first cousin François-Anne de Forbin de La Fare-Saint Croix, councillor in the Cour des Comptes of Aix, and his son, André, councillor in the same court

Forbin de Solliès: cousin Louis de Forbin, marquis de Solliès, consul of Aix

CASTELLANES

Jean-Baptiste de Castellane, sieur de La Verdière and consul of Aix, Oppède's maternal uncle who made Oppède's son, Jean-Baptiste, his heir

PUGETS

Jean-Henri de Puget, baron de Saint Marc, co-chief of the Sabreurs, and his brother Jean-Baptiste, seigneur de Barbentan

Major European monarchs 1461–1833

France

Louis XI	1461–83
Charles VIII	1483–98
Louis XII	1498–1515
Francis I	1515–47
Henry II	1547–59
Francis II	1559–60
Charles IX	1560–74
Henry III	1574–89
Henry IV	1589–1610
Louis XIII	1610–43
Louis XIV	1643–1715
Louis XV	1715–74
Louis XVI	1774–92
Louis XVIII	1815–24
Charles X	1824–30

England

Richard III	1483–85
Henry VII	1485–1509
Henry VIII	1509–47
Edward VI	1547–53
Mary I	1553–58
Elizabeth I	1558–1603
James I	1603–25
Charles I	1625–49
Charles II	1660–85
James II	1685–88

William III	1688–1702
Anne	1702–14
George I	1714–27
George II	1727–60
George III	1760–1820
George IV	1820–30

Spain

Ferdinand of Aragon	1479–1516
Charles I (V of Austria)	1516–56
Philip II	1556–98
Philip III	1598–1621
Philip IV	1621–65
Charles II	1665–1700
Philip V	1700–46
Ferdinand VI	1746–59
Charles III	1759–88
Charles IV	1788–1808
Ferdinand VII	1814–33

Austria

Ferdinand II	1618–37
Ferdinand III	1637–57
Leopold I	1657–1705
Joseph I	1705–11
Charles VI	1711–40
Maria Theresa	1740–80
Joseph II	1780–90
Leopold II	1790–92

Brandenburg-Prussia

Frederick William, the Great Elector	1640–88
Frederick I	1688–1713
Frederick William I	1713–40
Frederick II, the Great	1740–86

Sweden

Charles IX	1604–11
Gustavus Adolphus	1611–1632
Christina	1632–54
Charles X	1654–60
Charles XI	1660–97
Charles XII	1697–1718
Frederick I	1720–51

| Adolphus Frederick | 1751–71 |
| Gustavus III | 1771–92 |

Denmark

Christian IV	1596–1648
Frederick III	1648–70
Christian V	1670–99
Frederick IV	1699–1730
Christian VI	1730–46
Frederick V	1746–66
Christian VII	1766–1808

Russia

Alexis	1645–76
Peter I, the Great	1682–1725
Anna	1730–40
Elizabeth	1741–62
Peter III	1762
Catherine II, the Great	1762–96

Map

Pre-revolutionary France: principal administrative, judicial and fiscal subdivisions

Index

Index